LOST
PLYMOUTH

LOST
PLYMOUTH

HIDDEN HERITAGE OF THE THREE TOWNS

Felicity Goodall

BIRLINN

First published in 2009 by
Birlinn Limited
West Newington House
10 Newington Road
Edinburgh
EH9 1QS

www.birlinn.co.uk

Reprinted 2016

ISBN: 978 1 78027 414 0

British Library Cataloguing-in-Publication Data
A catalogue record for this book is available
from the British Library

Designed and typeset by Mark Blackadder

Printed and bound by Gutenberg Press Limited, Malta

CONTENTS

ACKNOWLEDGEMENTS

First I would like to thank my family: Alan whose support and encouragement have been unfailing, and Tom and Stephen for their kindness.

The banner of local history flies with pride from the Plymouth and West Devon Record Office and I would like to thank Deborah Watson, Anne Morgan and Ian Conday for their time, enthusiasm and help. In Devonport, Lizzy Cook shared her local knowledge and showed me relics of the past. The Plymouth Naval Base Museum is a wonderful albeit under-funded resource, and I would like to thank all the volunteers but particularly Alan Bennett. Paul Davies lent me material on Plymouth's links to Polar exploration; Gerald Napier gave insight on Plymouth's defences as well as the loan of material; and Professor Mark Brayshay at Plymouth University shared his expertise on Plymouth's reconstruction. Other standard bearers for local history in The Three Towns are Brian Moseley with his excellent and comprehensive website Plymouth Data, and Steve Johnson with his website Cyberheritage, who allowed me to use the image of underground graffiti. Councillor Glen Gould helped with contacts at Plymouth City Council, while staff at the central library in Plymouth were unstintingly kind and friendly during my research. In particular I would like to thank Joyce Brown for her help in finding illustrations and photographs. Long distance help was given by Helen Harrison and staff at the State Library of New South Wales, the repository of much material on Bligh and Macarthur; Dr Carole Reeves at the Wellcome Institute for the History of Medicine helped with the outbreak of Plymouth Dock Disease; and the Women's Library helped me track down references to suffragettes in Plymouth and Devonport. Thanks are also due to Peter Lamb and Ted Luscombe at the SWEHS; Lady Juliet Townsend, descendant of Tobias Furneaux, for the portrait of her illustrious ancestor; Jan Carter for allowing me to use examples of naval needlework sewn by her uncle Harold Challis; Murray Rogers for the picture of the copper vesta case made from the wreck of HMS Foudroyant; Jack Leonard and Pam West for images of bank notes; Jo Rogers for information on the Boggia Family; David Emeney at Bristol Record Office for the image of the Brookes slave ship; Katherine Dunhill at the West Country Studies Library; and Renee Jackamann who to my great delight found the picture of Swilly House. I would also like to thank staff at two wonderful institutions, The National Archives in Kew, and The British Library.

INTRODUCTION

It takes a great deal of imagination to detect the outlines of old Plymouth within the city we know today, as most of the original street pattern is lost under the modern city centre. The loss of the old town is not thanks to the skilled pilots of the Luftwaffe, but thanks to successive generations of municipal planners making improvements. The city gates, guarded against the Royalist army in the great siege at the cost of the lives of 8,000 Plymothians, were knocked down by Victorian city fathers. Palace Court, where the young Catherine of Aragon slept when she arrived as future Queen of England, was demolished in the 1880s. Some buildings fell to the demands of road widening, to provide wider boulevards first for carriages then for the motor car; others were victims of the neglect of generations of landlords who saw no reason to repair and refit the houses of the poor; and others were simply in the way of progress.

Look down to Drakes Circus from the new Roland Levinsky building. Five hundred years ago that view would have included the houses and gardens of men who put the name of Plymouth quite literally on the map, planting more than 40 towns of the same name around the world. Sir Francis Drake strode the cobbled streets which once ran down that hill, and his name is inextricably linked with Plymouth, the Hoe, and that game of bowls which he insisted on finishing in 1588 before sailing out to deal with the Spanish Armada. In Plymouth his name is synonymous with a shopping centre celebrating the joys of Mammon, rather than a permanent museum to celebrate Drake and his cousins the Hawkins family and their part in British history. In 1897, patriotic poet Sir Henry Newbolt had no such qualms, painting Drake in the Arthurian mould, as a hero who would be reborn in Britain's hour of need.

Drake he's in his hammock till the great Armadas come.
(Capten art thou sleeping there below?)
Slung between the round shot, listening for the drum,
An' dreamin' arl the time of Plymouth Hoe.

That poem, 'Drake's Drum', was published as the final phase of construction had begun at Devonport dockyard, and combatants warmed up for the arms race which would culminate in the First World War. War has been at the heart of the history of the Three Towns. In Drake's time it was war with the Spanish, but through the eighteenth and a large part of the nineteenth century it was the French who were the enemy. Just as the heroes of the Elizabethan age had helped to create our idea of nationhood, so the great eighteenth-century naval heroes, their ships and their exploits, created Plymouth and its dock-child Devonport. Ships were built here, provisioned here, and crews were pressed into naval service here, a life which was not as glamorous as C.S. Forester and his Hornblower novels would have us believe. Samuel Johnson summed up the life of an eighteenth-century tar thus:

> No man will be a sailor who has contrivance enough to get himself into a jail; for being in a ship is being in a jail, with the chance of being drowned . . . A man in a jail has more room, better food, and commonly better company.

Despite these dreadful conditions, huge numbers of Plymouth men went to sea, and Plymouth gained a reputation as a city of women, strong women who took to the oars to make a living selling goods from 'bumboats' whenever a new ship dropped anchor. Some of their sisters were forced to take to the streets, picking up punters in the numerous pubs, which often doubled as brothels. Throughout much of the eighteenth and nineteenth centuries Plymouth and its satellites were crowded with soldiers, either quartered in barracks to defend the dockyard, or en route to foreign wars. They spent freely, brawled frequently and left unwelcome visitors in their wake: thanks to them Plymouth won its reputation as the VD capital of England, and punitive Victorian legislation herded prostitutes into the area round Union Street.

While the civic fathers in Plymouth may have preserved the old warehouses round the Barbican, Devonport is rich with relics of its past, unloved and largely unknown. Mount the steps at the foot of Cornwall Street where Horatio Nelson would have come ashore; explore the mysterious lumps and bumps of the Brickfields; pull back the ivy to reveal remnants of dockyard fortifications; and imagine the tatty remnant of Foulston's town centre replete with Regency bucks and their ladies. Devonport's column stands as a symbol of the brio once so evident there. Although the dockyard provided work to refit the swans of war, the fortunes of Devonport rose and fell accordingly.

Inevitably it was Devonport which was the main target of the Luftwaffe, and the houses of Fore Street beyond its gates which were among the casualties.

It is not only the physical evidence of centuries of history which has been lost in Plymouth. Religious conflict over the new English Prayer Book led to the destruction of the town's medieval records when the Guildhall was torched in 1549. But when the old Guildhall was pulled down in 1800, many of the remaining records vanished; we have the careful collection by Plymouth historian R.N. Worth to thank for what survives today, and it is guarded by the Plymouth and West Devon Record Office. These eclectic document boxes contain handwritten records of pubs and publicans, illiterate letters of complaint and heartfelt appeals for law and order. Also in the record office are plans for Outlands, the house which was birthplace of Robert Falcon Scott, along with hundreds of other plans as development devoured the marshes, fields and creeks which had separated Plymouth, Stonehouse and Devonport. The Three Towns now come under the civic umbrella of Plymouth, with Devonport and Stonehouse retaining their separate identities, but it was Plymouth where the story began.

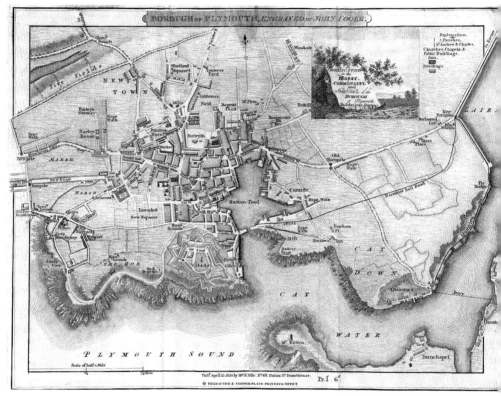

A map of Plymouth in 1820, showing the city as the building boom begins, but the outline of the old city is still visible.

CHAPTER 1

SNAPSHOTS FROM THE PAST

Little of the fabric of the medieval community that grew into the city of Plymouth has survived. As the town and later the city grew to accommodate a burgeoning population, the past was shucked off and, more often than not, buried in the rubble of new foundations. Plymouth's past has been a victim of the city's success.

Plympton was the settlement destined originally to grow into a major town, but the river became clogged with the silt from the Dartmoor tin industry, and it was the fishing port at the river mouth which benefited.

The medieval community clustered round Sutton Pool, and it was here that boats moored up after harvesting their catch of pilchards and herrings from the rich waters close by. The people of this community known as Sutton Prior traded with merchants from Normandy and grew rich on the claret trade. At that time Normandy and other prosperous areas of northern France were ruled by the English Crown, but in 1204, while the crown adorned the head of King John, the Normans and other key regions broke away from England. No longer able to trade with Breton and Norman 'cousins', merchants looked south and west for new markets. Trade routes changed, and ships were forced to sail round the Island of Ouessant, at the north-western tip of France where dangerous currents and treacherous reefs tested their crews, before ploughing through the notorious Bay of Biscay to reach friendlier destinations. Although the voyage was risky, the rewards were correspondingly great, as they returned with goods from the Mediterranean and the Atlantic. The first recorded use of the name Plymouth appears in the royal revenue accounts for 1211, known as Pipe Rolls. The record states that a shipload of bacon bound for Portsmouth and a cargo of wine destined for Nottingham were registered at Plymouth. The settlement was by this time a booming port, and its new status was recognised when the all important market charter was granted in 1254.

These medieval traders manoeuvred their vessels by oar and sail to tie up at the Quay, which lay beneath what is today Vauxhall Street, and archae-ologists believe that Southside Street marks the southern edge of that thir-teenth-century harbour. In the latter part of that century prosperity prompted ambitious plans for land reclamation, and the waterfront was moved north.

The populace lived in houses built largely of timber, but the towns' reli-gious communities resided in solid stone buildings. In thirteenth-century England one man in fifty was a cleric of some kind, and among them were

Friary Gate, long since demolished, although cobbled roadways can still be found in lanes around the Three Towns.

2

the Black Friars, whose priory is reputedly incorporated in the Plymouth Gin Distillery in Southside Street. The Black Friars, so called because they wore a black cape over their white habit, lived a simple life here. One of the principal tenets of the order founded by St Dominic in 1214 is poverty. But the Black Friars were also evangelical preachers and, like modern buskers, would have 'earned' charity by preaching, perhaps standing by the old stone cross in the marketplace. They were essentially an urban order, learned and contemplative. The first Dominican priory in England was founded in Oxford in 1221, and the community in Plymouth is believed to have existed by 1383. Although the house was probably built for 12 friars, by the time of the Dissolution only seven friars and a warden remained. Over in Marsh Barton there was a cell of Augustinian monks, where, according to the records of the Dissolution three monks lived what must have been a damp, draughty and miserable existence. Plymouth was also home to the only group of Carmelites in the Exeter Diocese. Known as the White Friars, because of their white habits which symbolised the Virgin Mary, the Carmelites had friends in high places. When the powerful Prior of Plympton, from the rival Augustinian order, protested to the Bishop of Exeter that the new community was intruding on his patch, he was backed up by the bishop. But the Carmelites appealed to the king himself and the order was allowed to remain, going about its work of quiet daily prayers for 224 years. When Henry VIII split with the Pope in Rome, the king's men arrived on horseback to seize any wealth belonging to the men in holy orders. With the demise of the Friars, the town was left with the Church of St Andrew as the focus for its spiritual needs.

The port was prone to attack from their neighbours across the Channel. A surprise Breton attack in the reign of Henry IV was disastrous. Devon gentleman and local historian, Tristram Risdon, wrote his *Survey of Devon* 200 years later in the early seventeenth century.

> In June, the sixth year of Henry the fourth, it was fired by the Bretons . . . who burnt six hundred houses, called the Bretons' Side unto this day; but the higher part of town continued safe, and is called the Old Town. A castle they have, garretted [*sic*] with turrets at every corner.

Whether or not Bretonside was so named because of the exploits of marauding Bretons, the events were commemorated annually by a street brawl between the Burton Boys and the Old Town Boys. Certainly after those

French attacks of 1403–4 the Castle was built to protect Sutton Pool, with towers at each corner and walls 13 feet high. Although chosen by the city fathers as the centrepiece of Plymouth's coat of arms, no such respect was accorded to its walls. As the population of nineteenth-century Plymouth exploded, the poor adapted the rounded remains into homes.

St Andrews Church was at the spiritual heart of fifteenth-century Plymouth, with the Guildhall at its centre. From the north travellers from Tavistock approached via Old Town Gate down the hill into the town. Frankfort Gate to the west brought farmers into the pig market and from Hoe Gate the approach brought people up to the junction with Notte Street, then called Nutt Street, roughly halfway between the church and Guildhall. The line of Finewell Street and the Prysten House are relics of the late fifteenth-century town, and Catherine Street is recorded shortly afterwards. Bilbury Street, today little more than an alley en route to the bus station, links us with the name of a fourteenth-century bridge and the street itself was extant by 1500.

Plymouth's name became synonymous with heroism and adventure during the golden years of Hawkins and Drake. Prosperity brought by these Spanish Wars in the sixteenth century led to the building of streets of fine houses, such as the surviving Merchant's House in St Andrews Street and the Elizabethan House in New Street. But these carved and gabled buildings built with such pride and swagger came to epitomise the very worst sub-standard housing of the Victorian era. As the population of the Three Towns exploded by 400 per cent between 1801 and 1851, so buildings were expanded, altered and, at the end of the century, demolished.

Where wives and children had watched from casement windows for returning seafarers, starving children shivered in rags as the wind wheezed through broken glass. Reforming city fathers led the nation in responding to legislation for new and better homes for the poor, sweeping away the tumble-down, neglected tenements. Piecemeal, old Plymouth became the hardcore for the foundations of the new Plymouth. These improvements were in their infancy when the Luftwaffe devastated the city. City planners turned this into a positive opportunity to put the city at the forefront of the movement for modern healthy living. The revolutionary Blitz and Blight plan completed what the Luftwaffe had begun, and wide boulevards designed for the automobile replaced narrow cobbled lanes constricted by ancient tenements.

Before the convenience of modern roads, Plymouth was best approached by water, and that is still the most scenic approach. As far back as the Iron Age, merchants sailed into the Sound with goodies from the

Mediterranean, docking at Mount Batten. Excavations have unearthed finds proving that this was one of the most important Iron Age ports on the south coast. The convenient harbour and the depth of Plymouth Sound made it an ideal port of embarkation from the sixteenth century onwards. From here the Pilgrim Fathers sailed to America, although not one was from Plymouth. The attractions of the harbour brought the navy and its dockyards, and in their wake the pubs and prostitutes. It made historical Plymouth a melting pot of races and religions.

Part of the Castle with its fine view across Sutton Pool.

Writing in the early seventeenth century, Tristram Risdon summed up the great geographical advantage that had accelerated Plymouth's importance when he wrote:

It is not long since Plymouth was accounted a mean fishing town, until the conveniency of the haven, which (without striking sail) admitteth into its bosom the tallest ships that be, where they ride safe, in either of the two rivers, to take the opportunity of the first wind.

In 1778 Stuart Amos Arnold published an eighteenth-century navigation manual called *The Merchant and Seaman's Guardian in the British Channel*. In it he gave detailed instructions to navigate into the port using the ancient system of seamarks – lining up landmarks by eye to chart a course through and past hazards.

In sailing into Plymouth take care of the Shovel and Tinker rocks; on the former is sixteen, on the latter seventeen feet. The mark to sail in clear of them, is to keep Plymouth old church just open to the west of the citadel wall. Sail in with this mark till you bring Withy hedge right up and down, and Drake's island N.W. or open Mount Edgecombe, when you may anchor in six and seven fathom, coarse sand.

If bound for Hamoaze, take care of the Winter Rock (on which there is a beacon) that lies between Drake's Island and the main. Go between the rock and east part of the island, and give the island a good birth [sic]. To clear the German Rock, which lies about two-thirds of a cable's length from the shore, and has a beacon on it, as soon as you are abreast of the rock, which you will know by running the stone wall on Block-house point right up and down, steer over towards Mount Edgecombe till you open the Passage point and Blockhouse point; then haul over for Stone-pool, till you have hid Drake's island behind Block-house point. And to clear Passage-rock (a beacon on it) bring Stone-house on the Old Gun-wharf crane; run that mark on till you bring a large fall-gate gate, that is on the hill above the Passage-house, and the highest

OPPOSITE. *The Elizabethan House saved by campaigners in the 1930s, a relic from Plymouth's golden age.*

An eighteenth-century view from Turnchapel with the Citadel standing guard over the city sheltering behind it.

chimnies on the Passage-house in one; then steer safely in for Hamoaze, and anchor in thirteen, fourteen, or fifteen fathom, or less water at pleasure.

These directions give a glimpse into a lost landscape, where patches of willow were significant enough to be landmarks visible from the Sound. Once moored, what might the merchant expect on arrival? A number of travel writers described seventeenth-century Plymouth, among them Celia Fiennes in her epic journey *Through England on a Side Saddle in the Time of William and Mary* in 1698. She was delighted by the appearance of the local stone, which she referred to as 'marble' which made Plympton 'look white like snow'. From there she rode down the banks of the River Plym to the town itself.

Plymouth is two parishes called the old town and the new, the houses all built of this marble and the slatt [slate] at the top look like lead and glisters in the sun; there are no great houses in the town; the streetes are good and clean, there is a great many tho' some are but narrow; they are mostly inhabited by seamen and those which have affaires on the sea, for here up to the town there is a depth of water for shipps of the first rate to ride; its great sea and dangerous

by reason of the severall points of land between which the sea runs
up a great way, and there are severall little islands alsoe, all which
beares the tydes hard one against the other; there are two keyes the
one is a broad space which leads you up into the broad streete and
is used in manner of an exchange for the merchants meeteing, for in
this street alsoe is a fine cross and alsoe a long Market House set on
stone pillars; there are several good conduits to carry the water to
the town, which conveyance the famous Sir Francis Drake (which
did encompass the world in Queen Elizabeths days and landed safe
at Plymouth) he gave this to the town; there are two churches in the
town but nothing fine; I was in the best and saw only King Charles
the First Picture at length at prayer just as its cut on the frontispiece
of the Irenicum, this picture was drawn and given the Church when
he was in his troubles for some piece of service shown him; the altar
stands in the Chancell or railed place, but it stands table wise the
length and not up against the wall; the font was of marble; there are
4 large Meetings of the Descenters in the town takeing in the
Quakers and Anabaptists.

Although Celia Fiennes is somewhat scathing of the lack of great houses and
fine churches, she gives a hint of the bustle of commerce, as merchants met
and traded at the exchange on New Quay, which had been built only two
decades earlier. As a post-Restoration writer, her assumption that Charles I
had given the portrait in Charles Church for some service may be politically
correct rather than factual. She was impressed though by the great bulk of the
Citadel defending the town from enemies approaching by sea.

The fine and only thing in Plymouth town is the Cittadell, or Castle,
which stands very high above the town, the walls and battlements
round it with all their works and platforms are in very good repaire
and looks nobly, all marble full of towers with stone balls on the
tops and gilt on the top, the entrance being by an ascent up a hill
looks very noble over 2 drawbridges, and gates, which are marble,
as is the whole well carv'd, the gate with armory and statues all gilt
and on the top 7 gold balls; the buildings within are very neate,
there is a long building alsoe which is the arsnell for the arms and
ammunition, and just by it a round building well secured which was
for the powder; round the works is the plattform for the guns which
are well mounted and very well kept.

The Citadel had been constructed in the early years of the reign of Charles II, strengthening the fortifications built during the wars with Spain.

Another travel writer, Edward Daniel Clarke described Plymouth in his book *A Tour Through the South of England, Wales and Part of Ireland made during the Summer of 1791*. His description is beginning to sound more like the city of the early twentieth century.

> It is a large old town, built upon an irregular plan; its streets are narrow, confined and crowded. Like other sea ports, it is populous, and has the usual appendages of dirt and noise. The inhabitants consist chiefly of tradesmen, as the more genteel families reside at Dock, Stonehouse and in the environs. The shipping, vessels of trade etc are brought to the very heart of the town, so that a person might, with ease, leap from their prows into the streets.

Dock, more properly known as Plymouth Dock, was renamed Devonport in 1824 following a petition to the king by the inhabitants. But the friendly rivalry which dates back to its birth is still evident, immortalised by the terraces at different ends of the city's football ground.

On his tour of the area in 1791, Edward Clarke decided to head out into the countryside, which divided the Three Towns at the time. Losing his way he asked for directions and was advised to climb Stonehouse Hill where he would get his bearings. This gave him a bird's eye view of the Three Towns prior to the Napoleonic era.

> At the bottom of the hill stood the little town of Stonehouse. On one side Plymouth, on the other Dock. Around, me extended the vast surface of the waters, with its vessels floating, as if, in the security of conquests, and displaying their pendants proudly to the wind. Mount Edgecumbe, peeping from its tufted groves, seemed the residence of some tutelary deity. A little spot, like a fairy island, appeared to float upon the waves. The evening became serene and mild. The marine band was playing in the barracks below while the soft notes of the music seemed to swell in the air, and vibrate upon the calm expanse of the sea. The evening gun like a clap of thunder, all of a sudden reminded me of the time I had spent there.

Like islands the Three Towns of the late eighteenth century were divided by creeks and marshes. Between the old town and Stonehouse lay Plymouth

Marsh stretching as far as King Street. The marsh was home to snipe shot by the locals, but it was also the haunt of robbers, and canny travellers waited for company before crossing in convoy on the New Road, which was soon renamed Union Street. Stonehouse Creek extended almost as far as the road to Saltash, and until 1783 when Stonehouse Bridge was completed a ferry took passengers across. On the northern side of Plymouth Dock the shore of the Hamoaze was still splintered by rivulets and Moons Cove, where the Dockyard slum of Morice Town would be built.

Just as Edward Clarke's evening reverie was shattered by the cannon, so the end of the eighteenth century was splintered by war with Revolutionary France. Hundreds of ships mustered in Plymouth waters. Naval ships fitting out for the great sea battles of the Age of Nelson; troop ships loading the cannon fodder to be sacrificed on foreign battlefields; merchant vessels gathering to be escorted down the English Channel in convoys protected from the French Channel Fleet. In the eclectic mix of records surviving in the archives of the Plymouth and West Devon Record Office is the secret order for just such a convoy. The envelope was marked 'On His Majesty's Service' and in it was this letter sent to Plymouth's Mayor John Langmead, from the admiral on board his ship *Salvador del Mundi* moored in the Hamoaze. It is dated 18 June 1803.

> I have approached His Majesty's sloop the Sea Gull immediately to proceed and take under convoy, the trade of Plymouth, Dartmouth, Exmouth and Teignmouth which may be bound to the Downes [Hampshire]. You will therefore be pleased to direct that the Trade of your Port may be held in readiness to join the Convoy immediately on its appearing off.

Then in a separate section attached, which is marked 'Secret', he gave these instructions:

> The Sea Gull on her appearance off each of the aforementioned Ports will make herself known by hoisting a Dutch Jack over a French Jack at the main top Gallant mast head firing two guns.

Other snapshots from Plymouth's past can be found in letters in the city archives and in newspaper reports. These incidents, frozen in time, enable us to strip away the sounds of the modern city: the rumble of tyres, screeching engines, the treble of acceleration, the uncertain whine of deceleration; high pitched beeps giving pedestrians permission to cross the road; police sirens which drown all other noise. The sounds which dominate the eighteenth-century landscape include: the traffic of hooves, the clicketty-clack of the night watchman's wooden rattle and the thump of leather-soled boots as the Watch thunder through cobbled streets.

In an incident reported to the Guildhall in May 1789 the watchmen were on their way to Castle Street to suppress yet another of the frequent fracas in what was known locally as Damnation Alley. On this occasion a marine was at the centre of the brawl, and as the Watch took him into custody, he put up violent resistance injuring watchman Samuel Rowden. Just as a photograph does not record the subsequent events, the fate of Samuel Rowden and the drunken marine are lost.

The perennial presence of the military led to many violent incidents as the city's parade grounds rang to the drill of infantry soon to deploy in the Continental wars. Over near Mill Bay Barracks, The Prospect Inn stood opposite the Guard Room, and naturally was the first stop for soldiers setting off on a pub-crawl. From there it was a short stumble to the Nelson's Victory, but the two pubs became so rowdy that Major Henry Bowen was forced to write to the mayor, from his office at The Citadel on 26 August 1805 to lay some of the blame with the publicans. He drew attention to

> Very irregular conduct of two public houses which the Lieutenant General considers from good information, to be not only nuisances to their respective neighbourhoods, but also injurious to the discipline of the garrison; soldiers being received into both, and encouraged in drunken dissipation there at all hours of the night.

Once the boom years of war have passed it is the noisy civilian drinkers who feature in complaints. This anonymous letter to the mayor also survives in the vaults of the Plymouth City Archive:

> October 13th 1819 Notwithstanding the caution given by your worship to the several landlords keeping Publique houses in the Borrough with respect to keeping good order in their houses I have to inform your worship that the landlord keeping the *Golden Lion in Pig Market* hath harbored in his house many people both male and female such as apprentices and others the whole of last night and until day light this morning to the great anoyanc of all his neighbors.

The spelling and punctuation are the author's own, and the letter is signed 'a neighbour residing near the house'. A year earlier, cabinet maker James Pearce wrote to the mayor on 18 May 1818 to complain of a 'down rite bodey [bawdy] house' which was keeping him and his family awake far into the night: 'Some nights there is no rest for the noise there is with the fiddler thomsen and all the family lives in the House you have hord the name of before.'

Unfortunately he doesn't name the street but the 'bodey house' was kept by 'Mrs Jinings', and according to Mr Pearce was the haunt of burglars. Inevitably it is these snapshots of bad neighbours and drunken carousing which survive, rather than the quiet industry of the majority who visited friends, attended concerts and walked to evensong, running the gauntlet of the rowdy minority. This letter in the archives was written on Boxing Day 1817:

> We beg leave to represent to you, the extreme disorderly state of the streets of this town, chiefly arising from the boldness and effrontery of Prostitutes and Apprentices, who do not hesitate to insult the Passengers of an evening especially in Frankfort Place.
>
> As we understand that that you have already stated that you have given directions to the constables to take up any disorderly persons in the streets, we beg further to say that there must have been a gross neglect of duty on their part, or the inhabitants could not have been annoyed to the degree they have been,
>
> We rely on your worship, and the other magistrates taking some prompt and effectual measures to remedy this evil, which is now so much a topic of complaint in the Town, as to cast a disgrace on its internal administration of justice.
>
> We beg further to add that the houses in Friary Court usually resorted to by beggars and well known to the Town serjeants have lately harboured many disorderly persons who should be sent out of the town.

By day too, old Plymouth was busy and noisy. Streets resounded with the clunk of wooden-wheeled carts and the stumbling gait of horses climbing the gradients. But if you left that cart on the street overnight the Inspector of Nuisances would take you to court, and your misdemeanour would be reported in the newspaper. Plymouth was one of the last towns to have an Inspector of Nuisances well into the latter half of the nineteenth century. Part

A line up of eminent citizens pose for the artist as fishermen pack mackerel for the London market at the Barbican in 1840.

of the Inspector's job was to check for blocked drains, overflowing cesspits and refuse. Shovels scraped the stone streets, as young lads picked up the dung, which could be dumped into the sea at Dung Quay. Even in the 1960s, 'Tuggy' Reynolds brought his horses over on the ferry from Torpoint every Monday morning to collect the waste from the Dockyard, before hauling it out into The Sound to dump at sea.

Wooden fishing boats bumped the side of the quay at Sutton Pool. *The Times* reported in 1865 that the Plymouth fleet had 60 sloops, which were using trawl nets shaped like a triangular pocket. The catch was slapped onto wooden trestles to be slit, the gutted fish flopping into waiting baskets, which fish sellers such as Susannah Perry would carry through the streets selling the catch to passers-by. Susannah was listed as a 'fishseller' in the census of 1851, which also records her as 53 years old, single and living in Kents Court sandwiched behind Willow Street. Among her near neighbours were Irish immigrants Michael Riley, a labourer from Dublin, and 18-year-old Fanny Penny, a domestic servant from Cork. There were immigrants from the Continent, including 54-year-old Italian Peter Ginvebio and his four-year-old grandson. Hatter George Manning was born in London and lived with his 15-

year-old daughter Harriet. Close by are weavers of sailcloth, flax dressers and spinners from Dorset; with a trio of female basket makers living appropriately at numbers 4 and 5 Willow Plot; then there were pipemakers and lime burners; and in Morley Lane, 72-year-old lamplighter John Bailey from Middlesex.

The commercial shopping centre, which will attract people from all over the region, is not in evidence until the late nineteenth century. Until its demolition in 1800 there were busy market shambles beneath the arches of the Old Guildhall. The short-lived local newspaper, *The South Devon Monthly Museum*, recalled the scene in an article in 1833:

> The Hall itself was erected on arches, under which, and around the building, the butter and poultry market was held, and in an enclosed court behind it were collected the corn-market and the vegetable market to the great annoyance of all passengers, there being on the market days scarcely a possibility of passing, and great was the clamour and dire the confusion that prevailed.

Before shop fronts were extended onto the pavement, goods were sold on the street or from the front room of people's homes. If you had banged on the

The old Guildhall, showing the covered market under the arches.

door of 17 Mount Street, Plymouth in 1851, you could be measured for boots cobbled by Thomas Dainty. Groceries were available from Greenwich pensioner James Ellis at 23 Frankfort Street, where you might also be served by his wife Mary or 14-year-old granddaughter Elizabeth. At 41 Frankfort Street was tailor James Bamford, or you could have bought a coat made by Robert Stone round the corner in King Street, a rather larger commercial concern as he employed two men and a boy in his business. Whether there would have been space at 1 Russell Street for Polish tailor Abraham Jacobs to fit and measure his tailoring clients is uncertain, as there were 21 people living at the same address. At 2 Russell Street, baker Jane Haddy ran a business employing two men, a boy and an errand boy as well as her daughter Mary. Her fresh loaves of bread were probably sold on the street from a basket, the baker's cry mixing with that of other hawkers who were close neighbours. These included two china sellers who had come from Stafford; a cutler in King Street; and an 85-year-old Polish travelling jeweller. He was one of the many eastern European Jews who flooded into the city, whose legacy is the eighteenth-century Ashkenazi Synagogue in Catherine Street, the oldest of its kind in Britain.

Among the street hawkers and peddlers were those who brought a variety of objects for sale from as far away as London. Although they were required to have a licence, many did not. Hawking their wares on handcarts, or from trays suspended by straps from their shoulders, their calls echoed from stone walls. Attracted by the gewgaws on offer, buyers could pick up titbits of news and gossip, which travelled across country with them. One hawker was William Deeley from London, who was hauled up before Devonport magistrates in 1825. His prosecutor was George Gidgeon, Inspector of Hawkers' Licenses, who told the court that Mr Deeley had been selling goods by auction at Devonport, contrary to the statute, and by which he had incurred a penalty of £10. The case was reported in the *Devonshire Freeholder*:

> The defendant admitted the sale, but said, as he was the manufacturer, which he could prove, he became exempt from the penal clauses of the Acts, and as a proof of which, he produced a letter from the Solicitor to the Hackney Coach Board, Mr Donne, sent in consequence of being informed against at Exeter, and in which it was stated, that he was not liable to be fined. On the part of the Crown, Gideon contended that the Act only gave permission to manufacturers to sell in cities, Boroughs, or Market Towns, and as

Devonport did not come under either of these denominations, he was liable to the fine. The Magistrates after a consultation convicted him in the full penalty of £10 and costs.

Barter was commonly used among the poor, although some coin did change hands. In November 1825 a rash of counterfeit sovereigns circulated. The *Devonshire Freeholder* warned its readers to gauge the weight of sovereigns carefully before accepting them:

> We understand that there are a great number of counterfeit sovereigns in circulations in this town. We were informed by a gentlemen who saw two, in the possession of a peace officer, that the execution of them is very superior; one was silver richly gilt, and only to be discovered by the weight: the other, he believed, was platina; with the exception of the edge which was uneven, they were nearly equal in point of execution, to the real ones. The public will do well to weigh sovereigns before taking them.

Thanks to the *Freeholder* we even know the name of one of the culprits, after his arrest in 1826. His job as armourer's mate on HMS *Ocean* combined with long periods of tedium at sea would have given him access to tools and raw materials and the opportunity to use them. A constable had been tipped off that 'Samuel Lane had been offering base coin to various persons in the market; in consequence of which, he took him in custody, and on his person he found 2 counterfeit shillings and one sixpence.'

Forged banknotes were even more common, until artists like the great Thomas Bewick were commissioned to engrave elaborate plates, which were difficult to copy. Forgery and even the 'passing' of forged notes were both capital offences until 1832. Such harsh penalties were intended to act as a deterrent, but those agitating for the reform of this penalty argued that instead the death sentence left courts unwilling to convict. In February 1826 the *Devonshire Freeholder* warned its readers to be on the lookout for yet another spate of forgeries:

> We saw a one pound note yesterday morning which had been sent back to a trader of this town marked *Forged*, being a portion of a remittance sent to London a few days since. The note was well executed, but the paper appeared of a different texture from the genuine notes.

Cargo of all sorts from ships wrecked or stranded in the Sound was sold by salvage companies, such as J. Pridham at his saleroom in Notte Street. Sales catalogues included items as varied as lengths of muslin and calico; bonnets and umbrellas; books, furniture and Japan boxes; rum, green tea, chocolate and china. In periods of peace some decommissioned naval ships were broken up, their timbers wrenched apart and sold for firewood. At 32 Whimple Street, J. Holland had a factory shop selling 'cabinet furniture made by the most experienced workmen and in the choicest woods'.

From Whimple Street it was a short step to Catherine Street, and the euphemistically named Hospital of the Poor's Portion, better known as the dreaded workhouse. Babies were born there, children grew up there, the elderly died there, those who were mentally ill were confined there, and it was the last resort for any citizen.

The building itself was constructed in 1630, and in those days had gardens and an orchard. The Poor Law had been passed in 1601, during the reign of Queen Elizabeth I, to deal with the homeless and helpless who had no visible means of support. With a constant flow of sailors in and out of the port, unemployed or disabled seamen frequently resorted to the workhouse. But the town could also dispose of such men, quite legally, by forcing them to take passage on a ship. By law they could oblige ships' masters to take on board one vagrant for every '20 tons burthen'. But as much of the shipping passing through Plymouth was of a lower tonnage, the Workhouse Guardians successfully petitioned parliament to reduce it to 15 tons.

The elected management of Plymouth's workhouse, the Guardians, were perpetually in debt, largely thanks to the increase in population. In 1841 the workhouse master was Robert Burnard, with his wife Elizabeth acting as matron towards the 245 inmates. These ranged from 90-year-old Rachel Pool, to Mary Metherill incarcerated there with her two sons of 5 years and 5 weeks. But thanks to the Hele and Lanyon Trust, 16 boys aged 8 to 13 were given some education by schoolmaster Robert Nugent.

Coughing, chattering, clutching injured limbs, the poor queued outside the nearby Plymouth Public Dispensary, built in Catherine Street in 1798. Among them would have been labourers from the town's many quarries, whose backbreaking work transformed the landscape. West Hoe is one remnant of the many outcrops of limestone, which were pick-axed and blasted, transformed into the new squares and streets of terraced houses like

OPPOSITE. *Tucked behind St Andrew's Church, the courtyard of the old Plymouth workhouse, The Hospital of the Poor's Portion, shortly before demolition in 1870.*

Durnford Street and Treville Street. In 1863 at 15 Treville Street, on a site under the modern Post Office, a young Stanley Gibbons looked up from the counter of his father's pharmacy shop as the bell rang. Two sailors dragged a sack of postage stamps into the shop and sold them to him for £5, a month's wages for the sailors. Stanley Gibbons made a profit of £495 on the deal and two years later launched the price list known by generations of stamp collectors.

In March 1872, a new sound was added to the streets of the Three Towns, as the first horse drawn tram left Derry's Clock. There was a fine view of the burgeoning Victorian city as passengers travelled along Union Street, across the Halfpenny Bridge, up Stonehouse Hill to Cumberland Gardens in Devonport. Plymouth had the first tram system in Britain, and it was also one of the last to survive when the sound of the internal combustion engine arrived to transform the streets.

Sunshine and a gentle breeze caught on camera as a brush tram rattles past the Theatre one lunchtime at the opening of the twentieth century.

CHAPTER 2

THE SENIOR SERVICE

Plymouth's prosperity and history has been shaped by the presence of thousands of military and naval personnel who have walked the city's streets. The first English fleet of warships known to have assembled in the waters off Plymouth was in 1296 during the reign of Edward I, and since then a string of heroes have set sail for war from this western port. The ill-fated Black Prince mustered his men in Plymouth in 1348 before sailing for Gascony to slaughter the French and claim half their country in the name of his father. Drake and Hawkins sauntered the streets and imbued the name of Plymouth with cachet in the golden Elizabethan age. But it was when the Dutch replaced the French and Spanish as our enemy that the strategic necessity of a port in the far west of England was first recognised and Devonport was born.

Chatham was the natural dockyard for the navy; it was close to the seat of government in London, with ample anchorage for the English fleet. But in

A view of Devonport published in 1772.

June 1667 the Dutch sailed across the North Sea, up the Thames and into the River Medway. Capturing the *Royal Charles*, pride of the navy and our largest warship, the Dutch saboteurs then torched the bulk of the English fleet before escaping back the way they had come. The construction of a naval dockyard at Plymouth far from the marauding Dutch was a direct result of this hit-and-run raid. But ironically it was the arrival of a Dutch prince, William of Orange, which accelerated those plans. William, a Protestant who was married to the English Princess Mary, landed at Brixham in 1688 at the invitation of the aristocratic architects of the Glorious Revolution. His reviled and now deposed Catholic predecessor James II, meanwhile, made an ignominious escape to exile in France. The Sun King, Louis XIV took up cudgels on behalf of the deposed James and began plotting to restore him to the throne. French naval establishments sprouted along their Atlantic seaboard and it was clear the English needed a naval base in the west to counter the threat.

Devonport was not the only site mooted for England's westernmost dockyard, Admiralty surveyors had visited Dartmouth, Bideford, Exmouth, Torbay and Oreston, but it's easy to see how the ample moorings available in the relatively safe and sheltered Hamoaze would have swayed the decision in Plymouth's favour. In fact when the Admiralty eventually plumped for Plymouth, Cattewater was their choice. Repairs and refits were managed from a hulk moored there already, ships were also repaired nearby at Turnchapel and Teat's Hill, and there were several rope walks in the vicinity. But when contracts were awarded, the architect chose instead the marshy ground and muddy bank of the Tamar at Point Froward on the eastern side of the Hamoaze. This was an age of wooden docks, but Plymouth Dock, as it soon became known, was state of the art – the first stone naval dock in the country.

Celia Fiennes visited during her *Tour Through England And Wales on a Side Saddle in the Time of William and Mary*, published in 1698. The settlement which was to become modern Devonport was still in its infancy, but the builders had been hard at work.

> The Dock yards are about 2 mile from the town, by boate you goe to
> it the nearest way; its one of the best in England, a great many good
> ships built there, and the great depth of water which comes up to it,

OPPOSITE. *Steps leading from the beach to Cornwall Street, Devonport's first street originally built for dockyard workers in about 1700.*

tho' runs for 2 mile between the land, which also shelters the shipps; there is a great deal of buildings on the Dock, a very good house for the Masters and severall lesser ones and house for their cordage and making ropes, and all sorts of things required in building or refitting ships; it looks like a little town the buildings are so many, and all of marble with fine slate on the roofs, and at a little distance it makes all the houses shew as if they were cover'd with snow and glisters in the sun which adds to their beauty.

As the dockyard grew so the first streets of terraced houses were built beyond its walls to house the civilian workforce. This rash of building work started at North Corner in about 1700 when Cornwall Street was laid out up the slope from the little beach on the shore of the Hamoaze. Other streets soon followed. Most of Devonport and Stoke was owned by the St Aubyn Estate whose tenants were given leases for a period of three lives.

A century later, travel writer Edward Daniel Clarke was equally impressed by Plymouth's upstart neighbour. In his guidebook, *A Tour Through the South of England, Wales and Part of Ireland made during the Summer of 1791*, Clarke dismissed the parent settlement at Plymouth, it was Plymouth Dock which impressed him:

> It may appear singular that I should thus pass negligently over Plymouth and proceed immediately to the description of a place, which is entirely the offspring of the other, The reason is this, the town of Plymouth, although rich and populous, does not afford the excellent accommodation to strangers, which is met with at the Dock. They are two places entirely separated and distinct from each other. The dock-yards, store houses and other offices belonging to the Royal Navy, are situated about two miles distant from Plymouth. By this means has been formed by gradual increase of inhabitants which might be stiled a new edition of Plymouth, on every respect more sumptuous and inviting than the original. We found here a handsome town, well built, paved, broad and elegant. It is larger than Plymouth, and in the peculiar beauty of its situation far exceeds it.

When Clarke was given a guided tour of the dockyard itself his enthusiasm becomes even more obvious. The naval base at Portsmouth had been an earlier stop on his itinerary, and Robert Waters, the contractor who had

Original dockyard walls are still found in parts of Devonport.

constructed the new dockyard at Plymouth Dock, was a Portsmouth man. This may have been the reason for the similarity that Clarke found between the two dockyards.

> We found everything here [Plymouth Dock] nearly upon the same plan, and conducted in the same manner as at Portsmouth, only upon an epitomised scale, and the whole is formed into so regular a system, the place itself wearing an appearance so compact and neat, that it carries with it an air of improvement; as if Portsmouth had afforded the outline in modelling the docks at Plymouth, and those defects which are observable in the former, were omitted in the latter. There is here a wet dock and a dry dock, with a bason [sic] two hundred feet square. They are hewn out of a mine of slate, and lined with Portland stone. The dry dock is formed after the model of a first rate man of war; and the wet dock will contain five first rates. In this place there are conveniences of all kinds, both for building and repairing ships; and the whole forms as compleat, though not so large an arsenal, as any in the kingdom.

Repair and refit were the principal tasks of Devonport from its infancy. This entailed literally cutting off the bottom of a hull infested with shipworm and

Early shipwrights were accommodated in hulks such as this depicted in 1829.

replacing it. Badly ventilated wooden warships were prone to the ravages of dry rot, a problem exacerbated by the use of poorly seasoned timber at times of timber shortage. During the Commonwealth period thousands of oak trees had been harvested to support a surge of shipbuilding. But landowners had failed to replant, and by 1804 there was a massive timber shortage. The story goes that Admiral Collingwood conducted a one-man replanting programme as he strode through the fields and lanes of England dropping acorns from his pockets. And no wonder. An eighteenth-century 74-gun third-rate ship of the line was 160 feet long and demanded 2,000 oak trees and ten years' labour to construct.

Devonport's first master shipwright was Elias Waffe and under his skilful hands the first warship of any size to be built there was the *Looe*, launched on 5 August 1696. The last ship to be built in the yard was the *Scylla* launched in 1968, now sunk as an artificial reef. Until the mid nineteenth century and the advent of the 'ironclads', ships were built from oak. Only timber with perfect grain was used, and shipwrights would travel in person to handpick individual trees whose limbs conformed to the shape required.

Devonport shipwrights were responsible for building Lord Nelson's favourite ship, HMS *Foudroyant*, between whose mighty oak walls he began his affair with Lady Hamilton. This 80-gun ship was commissioned in January 1788 and launched ten years later on 31 March 1798. Nelson hoisted his admiral's flag on board in June 1799, and it was from the *Foudroyant* that he directed and led the recapture of Naples and Malta from the French. The *Foudroyant*, named after a French ship captured as a prize, returned to Devonport where she served as guard ship for the naval base until 1862. Even then the ship described by Nelson as perfect was converted into a training ship for HMS *Cambridge*. In 1892, nine decades after she was commissioned, the *Foudroyant* was finally pensioned off by the navy and offered for sale. But there was a public outcry when she was bought by a German company, which intended to break her up. Although attempts were made to house a museum to the illustrious admiral within her wooden walls, she was bought by a wealthy businessman who sailed her round the coast as a tourist attraction. A hurricane force storm hit her at 6 a.m. on 16 June 1897 as she lay anchored two miles off Blackpool. Torn from her anchor, she was driven onto the shore, narrowly missing the North Pier. The crew was saved by the Blackpool lifeboat, while a local syndicate salvaged parts of her 2,000-ton hull and its copper sheathing, producing souvenir medals and walking sticks. In November that year Devonport's most famous old lady was broken up by another storm and taken to the bottom of the Irish Sea.

HMS *Foudroyant* was one of a new breed of ships built on French principles. French design had long been admired. While the French navy employed mathematical calculations in ship design from the 1680s, the English navy did not. The eclectic mix of prize ships seized from other navies and veterans

A matchbox souvenir made from copper sheathing from Devonport-built HMS Foudroyant.

which had been patched and partially rebuilt led to complaints. Captains described some ships as 'crank,' and complained they heeled over so much in windy weather that the gun ports on the leeward side could not be opened. These warships therefore had only half their potential firepower in such conditions. Meanwhile the ships of other nations were sailing rather more upright, with all their batteries open and therefore ready for action.

English naval vessels were tough and smaller than those of our Continental neighbours. Although French warships were renowned as faster, the competence of English captains and the cohesion of their crews overcame these design handicaps in the naval sea battles that led to Britannia ruling the waves.

The first blueprints for British naval design were not established until the 1750s, and even then rarely used until the end of the century. A *Treatise on Naval Architecture* published in 1800 outlined the design faults:

> The ships previously composing the British navy were so extremely long, in proportion to their breadth, at the same time so deficient in bearings forward, that, in a heavy sea, they pitched and laboured with such violence as to endanger, considering this as the slightest inconvenience they were to expect, the loss of all their masts. . . . The absence of these defects, which became too discernible in the

Keyham Steam Yard took a decade to build and was finished in 1854; here it is in 1863.

vessels of different countries, were at last, too glaringly apparent to be neglected by Britain. The practical experience derived, as already and repeatedly observed, from the superior qualifications of vessels captured from the enemy, caused an alteration of construction, and introduced, as it were, a total different system into the British practice.

Ship construction began with a process called 'lofting' in which the architects' plans were translated either from a scale model or later, as literacy became more widespread, from drawings. Carpenters worked in pairs in giant saw pits, the man above guiding the massive saw which was accurate to an eighth of an inch, while his mate below was showered in sawdust. Knuckles, elbows and bends were cut to shape to be jointed together, and water and heat were utilised to bend the wood for the final micro-adjustment. Masts were seasoned in the mast pond, and thousands of miles of rope where made in the ropery. Hemp for rope-making was shipped in from Russia in one-ton bales, along the northern sea-route which had been established in the sixteenth century. The fleet that sailed out to meet the Armada in 1588 was rigged almost entirely with Russian cordage and cable. During the Second World War, raw materials were so hard to obtain that the rope-makers had to be content with whatever could be salvaged. The ropery that still stands in Keyham Yard was first constructed in 1760, but after a suspicious fire destroyed the fabric of the building in 1812 it was rebuilt with stone floors and iron columns to support the upper storey. It was the largest fire-proof building in the world at that time, but a bomb in the Second World War reduced the length to its current 1200 feet. It stands silent today but staggering numbers of men were required to walk the rope in the intricate process involved in rope-making. A cable 24 inches round required the strength of 200 men to manufacture. Outside the walls of the dockyard there were 14 commercial ropewalks whose major client was the navy. The ropewalk in Cattedown was the last to succumb when it closed in 1966.

Our thrifty ancestors let nothing go to waste, recycling remnants of rope in a process known as 'oakum picking'. This was a tedious task given to workhouse inmates, and an old naval punishment, which was noted for flaying the skin from thousands of crewmen's fingers.

Devonport's dockyards had tasks and machinery for any job the navy might need, even a hand uncurling machine, which was used in the Royal Clarence Yard for untwisting hair to fill mattresses. As all naval provisions were stored in barrels, these were made in the cooperage. The massive

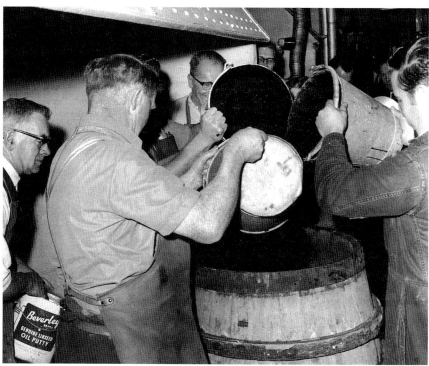

The last apprentice cooper undergoes the traditional initiation ceremony in 1963 . . .

. . . and emeges tarred.

operation required to service the needs of the navy required specialised skills, and in 1844 the Admiralty built Keyham College to train apprentices for the Devonport yards. Apprentices passed through the gates of Keyham College for a mere 127 years before it closed, and in an ignominious finale was demolished in 1985.

The dockyard was serviced by its own railway, used mainly for transporting goods and equipment, but also with passenger trains whose carriages were allocated in line with the strict hierarchy of naval life. Long leave and holiday specials were also run. As befitted a community which was in so many ways autonomous, the dockyard had a dedicated hangman's cell which is still to be seen in the old ropewalk. Even in the twenty-first century, capital punishment could still be imposed for arson, treason or killing the monarch within the walls of the dockyard. To date 147 men have swung for their crimes in that cell.

The frenzy of building, repair and refit that accompanied the wars with France was carried out largely in the open air, at the mercy of the elements. But in 1814 when the Peace of Amiens was celebrated with gusto, a dockyard roof was finally installed. Within a decade the new fangled roof was suspected to be the cause of a mysterious and terrifying plague, which affected men at the docks in Devonport. Rumour and anxiety spread through the town, and the outbreak even hit national headlines with *The Times* dubbing it Plymouth Dock Disease.

First to succumb was 45-year-old William Cowle who called in sick on 1 August after a small nail went through the sole of his leather shoe into the left foot. Wounds were an occupational hazard for craftsmen whose job was to construct the wooden vessels that were the pride of the British navy. William Cowle's wound was inflamed and painful and was treated with a poultice of oatmeal and boiled water by Dr James Bell, the resident doctor at the dockyard. By 2 August the wound had become larger, more painful and was leaking pus. Inflammation spread over the arch of his foot and eventually a piece of shoe leather that had been driven into his foot by the nail emerged, and the patient began to improve. But on 7 August William developed a temperature, headache, nausea and thirst, and Doctor Bell found that the inflammation had spread up his leg. While today's solution would be to prescribe antibiotics, there was no such option in that hot summer of 1824. Instead the patient was bled. Over two days the doctor drew 26 ounces of blood, but as his left leg swelled, William's pulse got fainter and faster. On 9 August his leg had become erysipelatous, a term describing a superficial bacterial skin infection.

Oars raised to salute Princess Victoria and the Duchess of Kent on a Royal visit in 1833; the controversial covered slipway thought to have 'caused' Plymouth Dock Disease is on the left.

As infection spread up William Cowle's leg to his thigh and then his groin, the whole limb became enlarged and 'its size excessive'. Two weeks after that insignificant industrial accident in the sawpit, the infection had spread to the abdomen, which had become tender. On 15 August blisters developed on the abdomen, and William's extremities became cold. He died that night.

Construction workers in the dockyard worked 12-hour days in summer to take advantage of the light. So John Henwood would have been tired when, at the end of his shift on 4 August, he lacerated his right hand sawing through the trunk of a fir tree. This was a not infrequent accident, and when he visited the doctor for first aid his hand was treated with bark and sulphuric acid. Two days later, 50-year-old John Henwood was too ill to visit the surgery so the doctor called round to see him at his Millbrook home. He lay in bed with a high temperature, headache and thirst and his entire hand had become inflamed. Just as William Cowle had improved early on in his illness, so John's temperature dropped and he felt better. But then the entire arm swelled up and the familiar red skin infection was spreading. His medical notes reveal that the wound on the back of his hand was opened and pus 'could be pressed out as from a sponge'. A few days later the doctor gathered 8 ounces of pus from the forearm! But John Henwood began to improve and three weeks after his injury his hand and forearm were 'nearly sound'. Mysteriously though he began to complain of pains in his *left* leg and thigh, which had become swollen, but there was no rash. By this time the 50-year-old was weak and his body had become emaciated. Six weeks after his injury, despite his physical state, the doctor made an incision into the swollen area above the knee and another on the back of the thigh. The medical notes record 'an immense quantity of well-formed pus' was discharged. On 2 October gangrene set in, and John Henwood died nine days later.

As the number of cases and the death toll mounted, speculation was heard in homes and on street corners. Rumours spoke of the unhealthy nature of the dockyard roof put on in 1814 to protect workmen and materials during construction. Speculation chattered of the use of new materials which may have introduced this mysterious malady – the principal suspect was teak. Also suspected were mineral oil and new fangled plasters, or perhaps the contagion was fostered by the sawdust which permeated air, clothing and hair.

The next victim, John Bate from Princess Street lost the tip of his left forefinger when it was 'jammed off by a plank'. He died within nine days and his was the first body to be dissected, but little conclusion was drawn. Devonport morale rose a little when William Butters, a joiner from Chapel Street, Stonehouse, survived the 'plague' to the joy of his wife and six children. He returned to work two months after tearing the nail of his right ring finger with a splinter of wood while he was planing a piece of mahogany. It may have been the leeches which were applied to his head which saved him, but they didn't have the same effect when used on the next case, a robust 32-year-old sawyer from Marlborough Street, Robert Horne. He died within two weeks.

George Nichols was another robust shipwright. As he sawed timber by the mast and boat ponds in the hot and sultry first week of September, he grazed his leg. Ten days later he too was dead. The subsequent medical report into Plymouth Dock Disease, commented: 'We see here what a sneaking and insidious disease killed this fine and athletic fellow proving that "The battle is not to the Strong".'

Once again a post-mortem was carried out, and this was to lead to the ninth case and seventh death. This time it was Dr James Bell, the dockyard surgeon who was to die. He performed the post-mortem on George Nichols on 19 September and, while sewing up the cadaver, scratched the back of his right forefinger with the needle. Later that day he crossed to Torpoint to visit a patient in torrential rain. As he attended patients at his surgery the next morning, Dr Bell 'felt a smarting in the scratch over his right forefinger'. Having seen six strong men die while under his care, it is hard to imagine what went through his mind, but at noon he took to his bed. In an attempt to purge himself of the infection, James Bell tried to make himself vomit, but as he grew increasingly feverish the physician's attempt to heal himself foundered. Two fellow doctors came to his help and bled 16 ounces of blood from his arm.

The details of treatment and the progress of Plymouth Dock Disease were gathered later that year by John Butter, member of various august medical bodies and a physician at the Plymouth Eye Infirmary. He published a 'post mortem' on the disease, which he called Irritative Fever, after the newspapers had carried 'erroneous and exaggerated statements' from which he had inferred the outbreak was 'a species of Plague', tetanus or some 'new malady'. Butter and another Plymouth doctor named Dryden interviewed widows and friends of all the dead men, as well as their workmates and the medical staff, for a book called *Remarks of Irritative Fever commonly Called the Plymouth Dock-Yard Disease* which survives in the British Library. But it is only with the light cast by modern medical knowledge that Plymouth Dock Disease can be analysed.

The outbreak was caused by the streptococcus bacterium, which infiltrates the body through a wound – in the 1824 outbreak, the occupational injuries suffered by the dockworkers. The disease it causes was known in the Middle Ages as St Anthony's Fire; today it is called erysipelas. The medieval

A seagull's eye view from the column, showing the full extent of the ropery before it was bombed in 1941.

term gives a clue to the physical manifestations of inflammation of the skin and subcutaneous tissue. It was a common killer in hospitals in the nineteenth century, but its cause was not understood until the 'discovery' of germs as causative agents. Erysipelas is on the increase in the twenty-first century – although entirely treatable with access to antibiotics. Medical authorities also believe that the nineteenth-century version of the streptococcus was more virulent than its modern form.

Inevitably there were perks associated with work at the dockyard. Reputedly many of the houses built in Devonport, had narrow staircases constructed from waste wood, which was defined as under three feet long! But soon the Admiralty realised the system was being abused and clamped down. There were other opportunities for the less scrupulous. For example, in 1791 *The Times* reported that two men were sacked from the dockyard after they were caught with lengths of rope tied round their legs and thighs and lead hidden under their shirts. As a result yardees were banned from wearing long trousers when they left the dockyard after their shift! Pilfering was common and on 28 March 1792, James Wilson, Arthur Gifford and Peter Lendergreen were sentenced to seven years' transportation to Botany Bay, for stealing stores from a ship in Dock. There was larceny on a grander scale too. In May 1790 five tons of copper stolen from the yard was discovered hidden in a house in Plymouth. Copper sheathing was used to clad ship's bottoms so that vessels could remain at sea for a year or more without coming into port for anti-fouling, and all naval vessels were copper-sheathed by 1781. Pilfering became so rife during the wars with France, that in August 1801 soldiers were put on overnight guard in the dockyard.

As the dockyard expanded so did the town. In 1733 Plymouth Dock had a population of 3,000 and by 1815 this had grown to 32,000 whereas Plymouth was a mere 22,000. From the street directory of 1784, which lists traders and gentlemen but not ordinary residents, it is clear how much the community which supplied the dockyard had grown. They were served by six grocers including Richard Hawkins who was also listed as Agent in Naval Affairs; four ironmongers included the Hooper brothers Benjamin and Joseph who supplied 'ship stores and every other article for the purser's use'; three linen-drapers and two mercers and drapers; four druggists or chemists; five doctors and five solicitors; two general merchants, a wine merchant, silversmith, upholsterer and a hat maker.

But the consequent flow of money and men had its drawbacks. Brawling soldiers and sailors, spiralling food prices and water shortages hit the civilian population.

Before the era of town planning, streets and squares developed without the infrastructure of services, which accompanies modern development. Water was fetched from springs or wells in days when open countryside separated the Three Towns. Filling the holds of warships with barrels of fresh water left the town itself in short supply. It was not until a century after the Dockyard was opened that Devonport Leat was built to serve the population round the dockyard, bringing water from Dartmoor. The leat at Stonehouse had been built at the end of the sixteenth century.

Pressure on water supplies was compounded when the military descended on the town waiting for ship transports out to the wars, or returning from them. Grocers rubbed their palms with glee as the money poured in for military provisions, but housewives wrung their hands as the water in wells and springs dried up. In October 1805, the very month and year of Nelson's victory at Trafalgar, there was a national water shortage. It wasn't until 1824 that the city fathers signed a contract with the Royal Navy to supply 400 tuns of water daily to the Victualling Yard at Lambhay, with 80 tuns per day allocated as a contingency. To supply the navy on shore and at sea, livestock tramped through heavily populated areas of Plymouth, adding dung

Devonport Leat built to bring water from Dartmoor.

37

CASTLE
DYKE
LANE

and mud to the domestic detritus covering the cobbles, in order to reach the slaughterhouse in Castle Dyke Lane.

While the quartermasters of the garrison and the pursers of the fleet could negotiate special rates while buying in bulk, the locals were not so fortunate. Prices shot up, as this letter from a naval officer on board ship in Plymouth in January 1801 reveals:

> Every necessary of life is uncommonly dear at Plymouth. Flour is 2s 4d per gallon, butcher's meat from 7d to 8d a pound, eggs 2d to 2 1/2d each, and a bag of potatoes, for which before the war, no more than 1s 6d or 2s used to be given sells for 12s and 13 s. all other articles are dear in proportion.

Prices did not improve and in April 1801 there were food riots. A mob rampaged through the butcher's market in Plymouth's Shambles grabbing whatever came to hand, then went on to raid the bakers. An army of troops were called in to help: men from the Surrey, Hampshire and Bedfordshire militias, the Rangers, Associated Foot and Cavalry and a detachment of the Light Horse from Plymouth Dock. Together they must have been a formidable force. That night the streets were patrolled by infantry and cavalry, and the mob gradually dispersed. But the next day another riot broke out in Devonport. The Riot Act was read, and the cavalry charged down Fore Street, wounding several protesters.

The civil authorities had to step in and, after negotiations with farmers and traders, *The Times* reported at the end of the week:

> The market was this day (Saturday last) full of every necessity of life at reduced prices. Butter 1 shilling a pound potatoes 1 shilling a gallon. And other things in proportion. All went off quietly, without any disposition to rioting, and the farmers went home highly pleased with the protection afforded them by the Civil and Military.

As a port of departure for troops travelling to war there were inevitable punch-ups between rival regiments. In June 1789 a squabble about a wrestling match at Stoke between a sailor and a dockyard artificer escalated. *The Times* reported on 4 June:

OPPOSITE. *Cattle were driven to the slaughterhouse up Castle Dyke Lane, once a heavily populated area.*

Boxing began the riot, and for some time the soldiers were victorious; but the sailors acquiring more strength, returned to Dock, and a most shocking battle began with bludgeons, bayonets, pokers, etc. After a dreadful conflict for some hours, many of each party were left for dead:- but by the activity of Captain Passingham, of the 38th Regiment, who took the main guard from the lines, and paraded the town under arms, taking into custody every soldier found out of the barracks, the riot was at length quelled. There were killed by the sailors one artificer and two wounded; and by the artificers, one sailor killed and five wounded. Two of the wounded are expected to die.

In August 1789, only a month after the French Revolutionaries had stormed the Bastille, King George III and his queen arrived to tour the state-of-the-art dockyard. An extra 75 constables were sworn in 'in order to keep the town quiet'. Pro-revolutionary sympathies were certainly bubbling under the surface of Georgian society, but the city fathers may just have anticipated an overexcited populace crowding the streets for a glimpse of the monarch. During the constant invasion panics of the Napoleonic era, thousands of troops crowded into the Three Towns. In August 1803, 40,000 men were due in the district, and half that number were to be stationed in the immediate vicinity of Plymouth. Grocers and publicans could anticipate a windfall from the many soldiers who were billeted in pubs. By October that year there were 13,750 men in the Plymouth Garrison, with an extra 1500 sailors and marines available at an hour's notice.

Arms and ammunition were in wide circulation and their availability brought its own tragedies, murder and suicide while under the influence of drink. In April 1791 *The Times* reported:

A private of the artillery on Sunday morning early, having the preceding night, slept with a girl of the town in Liberty Street, Plymouth, appeared a little hurt at a preference she paid another inamorato, and told her in a fit of jealousy, he would destroy himself. The girl cried, murder! And the soldier immediately applied the muzzle of a horse pistol, which was concealed under his cloaths, and which he had borrowed the preceding day, to his ear, and blew his brains out – he died instantly. He was the finest fellow in the company of artillery quartered at Dock, and a good soldier.

CHAPTER 3

VICTIMS AND VICTUALS

Wives and girlfriends waiting dockside for their men to disembark from wooden merchant and naval ships coming into Plymouth had to expect the worst. If their men had survived voyages of months, even years, the effects of life on board ship were debilitating. The men of the Royal Navy and merchant fleets were not a pretty sight.

Often men were malnourished when they were recruited or press-ganged into service, so the navy did at least offer a regular supply of food. But it was the quality and poorness of the diet, with minimal levels of vitamin C, which made them prone to disease.

Grilled rat seasoned with pepper is known to have been one of the high-lights of the eighteenth-century naval diet at sea and was said to taste as good as rabbit! In fact these rodents had probably been 'enjoyed' by generations of seamen, as plentiful black rats lived alongside the crews of wooden sailing ships, gnawing their way into stores in the hold. Their propensity to make inroads into naval stores such as biscuits and cheese, imparted a delicate flavour to the rats' flesh. But unknown to naval commanders, the rats provided something other than variety to the diet of ships' crews. Rats synthesise vitamin C in their bodies and were thus capable of providing one weapon in the fight against scurvy, a disease which was the scourge of the navy.

The first signs of scurvy were a pale and bloated complexion as gradu-ally the skin turned yellowish and then livid. Lips turned green and sailors became listless, breathless and their knees grew stiff. Their gums became itchy, swollen and bleeding, then soft, spongy, putrid and fungous, with the result that their breath stank. On the legs and body, red, blue and black spots appeared – some as large as a man's hand. As the legs swelled, ulcerous sores covered with coagulated blood appeared on the surface. Shipboard injuries were commonplace, and any existing wounds or bruises developed into putrid ulcers. As the disease advanced, pain spread through the body, often

Naval rations included a portion of tobacco which crewmen prepared themselves, as in this photograph from 1908.

in the chest, and diarrhoea developed. Some naval surgeons observed that the urine developed an oily saline scum on the surface if left in a flask. As they lay in their hammocks below deck in the damp and smelly conditions common on sailing ships, the seamen lost the use of their limbs, and the body haemorrhaged from nose, gums, intestines and lungs. In the final stages, ulcers burst and breathing became increasingly laborious. Unless it was treated this was not a disease from which a sailor would recover.

Theories for the treatment of scurvy abounded throughout the eighteenth century. Half a pint of seawater per day was one 'treatment', and for many years malt was used, but as any twenty-first-century school child knows these were useless. Once a man succumbed to scurvy, the condition also made him more prone to other health problems. In turn other diseases also worsened the effects of scurvy, and vice versa. Diarrhoea caused by poor sanitation and dysentery were both common; both destroy acidity in the gut and vitamin C cannot survive in alkaline conditions.

On 20 May 1747, HMS *Salisbury* put to sea from Plymouth with

James Lind, a naval surgeon, on board: he was about to conduct an experiment. Also on board were 12 men suffering from the dreaded scurvy. James Lind had a theory based on empirical observation that scurvy could be cured by fruit. For Lind's experiment he employed six different treatments for the sailors, the most efficacious was not surprisingly two oranges and one lemon per day, which cured one man in six days. Many ships, especially those fitted out at Plymouth, were provisioned with cider, which proved the second most effective treatment in his experiment.

When he returned to Plymouth on 16 June, Lind proposed to the Lords of the Admiralty that lemon juice be heated over a bain-marie till warm, then bottled and served to crews daily as a preventative measure. He also asserted that most berries and several fruits could be preserved by bottling, and that cabbage and green beans could be bottled with salt. But for some reason his sensible suggestions were not adopted – naval historians have speculated that Dr Lind was not well connected to the men from the ministry.

The War of Austrian Succession (1741–48), which had embroiled most of

A sailor's embroidery crafted to while away the hours at sea; this dates from before the First World War.

Europe over the issue of whether a *woman* could ascend the throne, was settled a year later. In those seven years scurvy had killed more English sailors than enemy action. James Lind published a polemic on the disastrous effects of the disease in 1753 in which he said:

> The scurvy alone, during the last war, proved a more destructive enemy, and cut off more valuable lives, than the united efforts of the French and Spanish arms. It has not only occasioned surprising ravages in ships and fleets, but almost always affects the constitutions of sailors; and where it does not rise to any visible calamity, yet it often makes a powerful addition to the malignity of other diseases.

As England waged the War of American Independence, the numbers of men in the navy reached its height and their health reached the doldrums. In 1782 there were over 100,000 men serving in the navy, of whom 23,000 were on the sick list. Then Gilbert Blane was appointed Physician of the Fleet by Admiral Rodney, and it was largely due to him that daily rations of lemon juice were issued as a prophylactic in 1795.

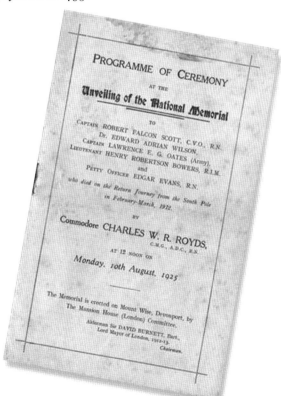

Commemorative programme for the unveiling of the Scott Memorial at Mount Wise.

John Rennie's architectural gem, the Royal William Victualling Yard.

All was well for half a century, but in the mid nineteenth century lime juice was substituted for lemon juice in the interests of economy, as limes were available from British colonial territory in the West Indies. This was a mistake. Lime juice contains only half the vitamin C of its sister citrus the lemon.

Scurvy still killed naval men, even in the twentieth century. During Captain Robert Falcon Scott's trek to the South Pole in 1912, it is believed that scurvy weakened his team, contributing to their deaths. Vitamin C itself was not 'discovered' until it was isolated in 1918.

Until the Royal William Victualling Yard opened for business in 1835, ships provisioned in Plymouth were served by a warehouse and office by Sutton Pool. The Royal William Yard covered a huge site of 16 acres. Employed within its walls were butchers, bakers and coopers (who made the barrels to store provisions while at sea). On the huge gateway into the yard from Cremyll Street there are carvings showing these trades. The slaughter-houses that provided the raw material for the much reviled salted meat only served the yard for just over two decades, after which animals were killed in the brewhouse. Beer was never in fact brewed there, because the beer ration was stopped in 1830, even before the yard was completed, but during the eighteenth century sailors were allocated a gallon of strong beer a day.

In 1755 Admiral Edward Hawke indulged in a protracted battle with the victualling department at Plymouth about the quality of beer, which was supplied because it remained palatable longer than water, although beer brewed in summer did not keep well. He wrote to the Admiralty:

> The beer which came off in the two tenders from Plymouth was very bad; so that I was obliged to direct it to be expended immediately: and if what is now coming should prove to be the same, the squadron will be greatly distressed, as good beer is the best preservative of health among new-raised men. Notwithstanding the promise of the contractors for slops, to supply better, I find what were issued to the ships at their coming out to be of the same quality with those complained of: and yet our wants oblige us to make use of them, which I beg their Lordships will please to give directions for effectually remedying hereafter.

All naval provisioning was governed, not by the health of the seamen, but by the ability to preserve food for long voyages. Salt had been the preservative of choice for centuries, but salt beef and pork still became putrid and hardened during the voyage until they were inedible. In fact sailors used to carve scrimshaw (ornaments usually carved from bone or shell) from their ration!

Bad naval health was largely attributable to the poor quality of provisions. *The Royal Navy Man's Advocate*, written by William Thompson and published in 1757, was an exposé of navy 'vittles'. Its author was victimised and driven out of the navy because of what he wrote and published:

> The seamen in the King's Ships have made buttons for their Jackets and Trowsers by the Cheese they were served with, having preferred it by reason of its tough and durable quality, to buttons made of common metal; and that Carpenters in the Navy-Service have made Truckles [wheel or pulleys] to their Ship's flagstaffs with whole Cheeses, which have stood the weather equally with any timber. . . . That their bread has been so full of large black-headed maggots and that they have so nauseated the thoughts of it, as to be obliged to shut their eyes to confine that sense from being offended before they could bring their minds into a resolution of consuming it. That their beer has stunk as abominably as the foul stagnant

water which is pumped out of many cellars in London at midnight hour; and that they were under a necessity of shutting their eyes, and stopping their breath by holding their noses before they could conquer their aversion, so as to prevail upon themselves in their extreme necessities to drink it . . . That the pork which the Fleet under the command of the late Admiral Boscawen was served with, was so rotten, that when boiled it wasted away to mere rags and crumbs, so that it could be eaten with a spoon, and that when the liquor it had been boiled in was drawn off, it flowed out of the cock of the ship's boiler like curds and whey: it was also so nauseous that it made the men sick who did eat of it; and resolving to fast rather than eat any more of it, they have thrown it privately out of their ship's port-holes to prevent being discovered by the officers of the ship.

Fortunately those who ate below decks did so largely in the dark!

The basic diet was supplemented by the infamous ship's biscuit, which became so hard that it had to be soaked. Lurking within the biscuit was extra protein in the form of weevils; a sharp tap would usually dislodge them, but would also reduce the biscuit to a pile of crumbs. Ingenious seamen developed ways of ridding themselves of weevils, by catching fish, which they laid on deck alongside the biscuits. Attracted by the prospect of this fresher sustenance, the weevils crept over to feast on the fish. These legendary ship's biscuits were six inches across and were baked at the Royal William Yard.

Great casks of water were loaded into the holds prior to a voyage, although this inevitably deteriorated during the voyage as green scum formed on the surface. Although desalination was an obvious source of water for sailing ships and the technology had been developed by Plymouth apothecary William Cookworthy among others, it was not used. The taste of rancid water was improved by the one essential ingredient of their daily life of which sailors did approve – rum. It was Admiral Edward Vernon, commander of the West Indies fleet in 1740, who concocted the recipe of half a pint of rum diluted with two pints of water. First issued on 14 August 1740, this concoction was known as grog. It was doled out at lunchtime leaving inebriated crewmen often incapable of work in the afternoons. It was the calories delivered by this alcoholic beverage which gave sailors most of the energy required for a job which was physically demanding: an eighteenth-century sailor needed 4,500 calories daily to enable him to climb the rigging, haul heavy loads and man a ship. Masts were up to 130 feet high and there was up

A portrait of a stereotypical corpulent ship's purser published in 1799.

to 20 miles of hemp rope to be climbed, stowed and manhandled on a standard ship of the line.

Casks of food and beer were opened by the purser in full view of the
men. This open government had a dual purpose: to ensure there was no
pilfering and to provide proof of the purser's probity. As purser, responsible

for provisioning the ship, a man could make a handsome profit from buying poor quality goods and pocketing the difference. Naval pursers were *expected* to supplement their pay from the profits made on provisioning their ship. For instance when William Bligh complained to the Admiralty about his inadequate pay when he was appointed purser and commander of the *Bounty*, they responded by reminding him that this perk would supplement his official wages.

Sir James Bagge, nicknamed Bottomless Bagge, built Saltram House with the proceeds creamed off while he was naval agent responsible for victualling in Plymouth. But organised embezzlement was partly the fault of the government, which was slow to pay its debts. When in 1630 Bagge totted up what he was owed for naval provisions supplied in the preceding years, it was a total of £50,000, which he had paid from his own pocket.

Corruption was rife in the Admiralty's food distribution service. Unscrupulous officials would condemn casks of perfectly good meat, on the pretence that they were unfit for consumption, squirreling away the proceeds. Cynical and corrupt suppliers palmed off food well past its sell-by date on hapless crews, and once they were far from land the men of the senior service

Saltram House in 1820. The original mansion was the property of James Bagge, who made a fortune supplying the navy.

had no option but to eat what was available. Theft and embezzlement were run of the mill, it was easy to alter a figure in a ledger from 9 to 1 by rubbing out the circle. In his second pamphlet *An Appeal to the Public* published in 1761, whistle blower William Thompson wrote:

> But one instance of the corrupt victualling of the Royal Navy, occur'd whilst I was there, and this too extraordinary to be forgot, was the late Admiral Martin's bringing into Plymouth Hospital and Sick Quarters, such an incredible number of sick men, as can best be verified by the books of the sick and dead List, if not falsified, at his return from a six weeks cruise, to intercept Mons. D'Anville, who then commanded the Brest squadron. The sickness by the report of the Admiral, and unanimous opinion of all, brother officers and common men, was owing to the badness of their provisions; if so, it will be easy for a common capacity to determine what must have become of Admiral Martin's whole squadron, if Mons. D'Anville had given him battle.

One senior officer who did take up the cudgels on behalf of his men was Admiral Edward Hawke. While patrolling the Channel in 1755 he had been forced to return to port when an epidemic swept through his crew, and in his brilliant close tactical blockade of the French port of Brest in 1759, Hawke was determined that his crews be kept healthy. To prevent scurvy he had supplies of fresh meat, cheese, butter and vegetables sent out to the fleet from Plymouth. Ten years earlier the Western and Channel Squadrons had been provisioned by sailing back to Plymouth periodically to take on stores. But Hawke's insistence on fresh food meant live bullocks were sailed out to his fleet. As the wooden sides of the ships bumped and scraped each other while alongside, the bullocks were hoisted in the air and winched across to the warships. They would have joined the goats, chickens and other livestock below deck. In fact Hawke was so concerned with the health of his crew that he wrote to the Admiralty to obtain permission to dispense with returning to land to clean the ship's hull, because of the extra strain it would place on his men.

Sailors quartered in the lowest decks of warships had to contend with the stink rising from a virtual cesspool beneath them. The bottom of the hull was filled with shingle ballast to maintain stability. But anything which fell into the ballast would not be fished out again – it was too dangerous – and the detritus which gathered rotted away unmolested. At the end of the

Distributing the meat ration in 1908, still done very publicly to prevent corruption.

eighteenth century shingle was replaced by pig iron, a healthier option.

In their quarters below decks sailors lived in an atmosphere that was airless, unheated and above all damp. Clothes and hammocks became saturated during heavy seas, and only partially dried thanks to the hygroscopic nature of salt.

During periods of fine weather, bedding could be aired on deck but ventilation below decks was recognised as a constant problem. Gilbert Blane, Physician to the Fleet wrote *Observations on the Diseases Incident to Seamen*, which was published in 1785:

I hardly ever knew a ship's company become sickly which was well regulated in point of cleanliness and dryness. It is the custom in some ships to divide the crew into squads or divisions under the inspection of respective officers, who make a weekly review of their persons and clothing, and are answerable for the cleanliness and regularity of their several allotments. This ought to be an indispensable duty in ships of two or three decks; and when it has been practised, and at the same time ventilation, cleanliness and dryness below and between decks have been attended to, I have never known seamen more unhealthy than any other men. The neglect of such attentions is a never-failing cause of sickness.

It would certainly be for the benefit of the service that a uniform should be established for the common men as well as for the officers. This would oblige them at all times to have in their possession a quantity of decent apparel, subject to the inspection of their superiors.

The greatest evil connected with clothing is the infection generated by wearing it too long without shifting.

Dead men's clothes, which were auctioned off to the rest of the crew when they died at sea, were said to be another source of infection, although this still took place into the twentieth century.

Blane also advocated a more adequate supply of medical necessities, avoidance of 'filth crowding and mixture of diseases' in naval hospitals ashore, and on hospital ships.

Ship's surgeons not only had to deal with disease, but with battle wounds, and the injuries that were a daily risk at sea. Bleeding was the main treatment for everything from syphilis and insanity to haemorrhages and fractures until the early nineteenth century. It stemmed from the Aristotelian idea that the body needed the correct balance of humours to maintain health. An excess of the primary humour, blood, was deemed responsible for much ill health. At its most extreme, bleeding was performed by cutting a vein and capturing the blood in a bowl. Cupping was another method. A heated glass cup was placed on the skin and as it cooled, a partial vacuum formed. Pulling the cup from the skin caused bleeding. Purging, or rather induced vomiting, was another practice.

In naval battles, casualties often bled to death. Dragging a man from the deck in the heat of battle, with cannonballs and splintered wood flying around, resulted in a massive loss of blood by the time the casualty arrived in the surgeon's cockpit: Nelson's fate at the Battle of Trafalgar in 1805.

It is known that by 1782 the more senior crewmen were issued with tourniquets, and by 1806 most crewmen had been taught how to stop a

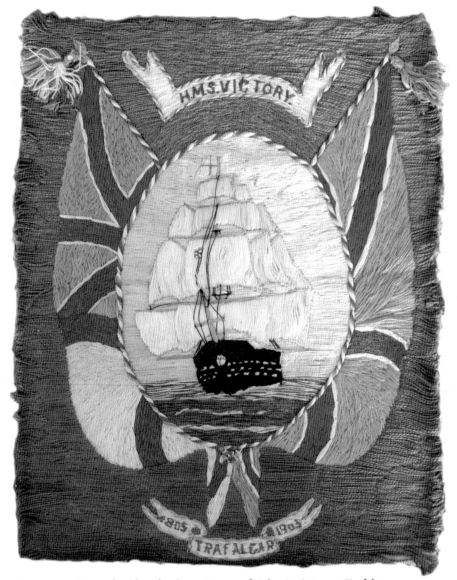

*Commemorative embroidery for the centenary of Nelson's victory at Trafalgar,
embroidered by Harold Challis.*

haemorrhage. But the surgeon's methods of treatment were hardly any more
scientific. Amputations were performed while the patient was held down and
anaesthetised by rum, which was also used as a painkiller, as was opium.

The 1860 Report of the Health of the Royal Navy reveals this sample of
deaths and injury while in home waters. A total of 4,296 cases of wounds
were reported.

Ten men were killed by injuries sustained in falling from aloft and otherwise, and one by an accidental blow from a runner hook; one by a dislocation of the bones of the neck, caused by falling backwards on a beam in a scuffle when on shore; one by a fall from a beacon on the breakwater at Plymouth, and one by a fall from a cliff. Three men were blown overboard, and killed or drowned by the accidental explosion of cartridges, while in the act of loading. One died of tetanus, consequent on extensive scalds received while repairing the lid of a steam cylinder, which accidentally closed upon him.

Nine men were drowned, five in one instance, and two in another, by the swamping of boats; thirty one by falling overboard, principally from aloft; one by falling into a dock while on shore, two while bathing, and one while attempting to desert by swimming to the shore. Two men committed suicide by jumping overboard; one died of a suicidal wound of the throat, and one hung himself. One man committed suicide by swallowing corrosive sublimate, and one while locked in a prison on shore, by swallowing a solution of the cyanide of potassium, and one death occurred by swallowing, in mistake for some other fluid, a solution of the chloride of zinc. The total number of deaths from wounds and injuries was twenty seven, of which five were marines, and twenty two blue jackets; and of the forty three drowned, one only belonged to the marines.

The report also gives a picture of some of the diseases suffered by the senior service in the Victorian age. Topping the list were abscesses and ulcers; venereal disease, in particular syphilis, was a worthy second followed closely by rheumatism. Diarrhoea was rife, although constipation was common too. Eye problems were high up the list, although the exact nature of them is not specified. Haemorrhoids, hernias, scarlet fever, measles, pleurisy and tuberculosis were all recorded, and 22 men were diagnosed with insanity. Four thousand trusses were issued to sailors to combat hernias, because of the exertion involved in constantly raising and lowering heavy casks. Voyages to foreign shores brought crews into contact with malaria and yellow Jack, a colourful name for jaundice or yellow fever. Typhus and dysentery spread all too easily in cramped conditions on board, and naval surgeons had little knowledge and few tools in their medical armoury to deal with such outbreaks. Yet in an extraordinarily far-sighted anomaly, inoculation against

The imposing buildings of the Royal Naval Hospital seen from what was once Stonehouse Creek.

smallpox was offered in 1800 only two years after Dr Edward Jenner had made his discovery.

Sick sailors were treated in old hulks, such as HMS *Canterbury*, which were moored offshore, but in 1760 the Royal Naval Hospital at Stonehouse received its first patients. Regarded as the apogee of hospital design for many years it closed on 31 March 1995, a victim of wider cuts in defence spending and diminishing naval numbers.

CHAPTER 4

A MODEL OF A MODERN MAJOR HOSPITAL

On 29 March 1797, Thomas Homewood was rowed up Stonehouse Creek to the jetty beneath the imposing buildings of the Royal Naval Hospital. This creek, which has since been in-filled, was the origin of the phrase 'up the creek without a paddle'. The 26-year-old seaman was arriving at the flagship of naval medicine. Thomas had been suffering from VD for a month, according to the notes left by his doctor, and he was to be a guinea pig in a medical experiment. The test results were published by Dr Thomas Beddoes in 1799 as *A Collection of Testimonies Respecting the Treatment of Venereal Disease by Nitrous Acid*.

Utilising toxic substances against this disease was nothing new; mercury was the treatment of choice until the use of antibiotics. But doctors at the Royal Naval Hospital had been experimenting with solutions of nitric acid. Nitric acid had been known as a chemical compound for over a thousand years, and during the Napoleonic Wars and the Crimean War, was used as a topical application to treat gangrene.

Modern health warnings advise seeking immediate medical help if this substance is swallowed today. Commonly used in the manufacture of explosives and fertilizers, it can cause severe burns on contact with the skin, gives off choking red and yellow fumes in moist air, and is a component of acid rain. Surgeons such as Stephen Hammick prescribed a dose of 1 drachm of nitric acid in a pint of water, sweetened with 4 to 6 ounces of syrup and administered the concoction through a glass tube.

The case histories of men admitted with what contemporaries described as 'this terrible disorder', reveal a level of care which began on board ship. John Fail, a 22-year-old sailor arrived 'up the creek without a paddle' on 20 July 1797. Prior to his admission to hospital he had been lying in his hammock for three months too weak to get up. Sores on his groin area improved while he was given mercury, but when it was stopped by the ship's doctor they worsened. Other symptoms including chest pains, diarrhoea, fever, a bad cough and loss of appetite were noted on his admission to hospital. After 52 days of taking nitric acid his sores were 'well', his appetite had returned and his other symptoms apart from the cough were 'suppressed'. John Fail had been suffering from VD for four months, and although his symptoms improved while he was in hospital, nevertheless he was discharged as an invalid.

Other human guinea pigs were far luckier. Drummer boy John Harvey was only 16 and told doctors he had caught gonorrhoea a month earlier while he was out recruiting! As he marched round the towns and villages of Devon his symptoms increased, particularly the inflammation and pain when he passed urine. After only 17 days in the hospital he was discharged. Some 50 cases were recorded using nitric acid as a treatment, and (apart from John Fail and another patient who died) they were all successfully treated. Trials also took place using sulphuric acid, but this was not reckoned to be so effective. Grains of potash taken as pills were also trialled, but one patient who reached a maximum dose of 70 grains of potash contained in 14 pills, complained of violent pain in his stomach, bowels and head, and the experiment was discontinued.

When the sturdy blocks of the Royal Naval Hospital in Stonehouse were opened, it was held up as the pinnacle of hospital design. For the first time

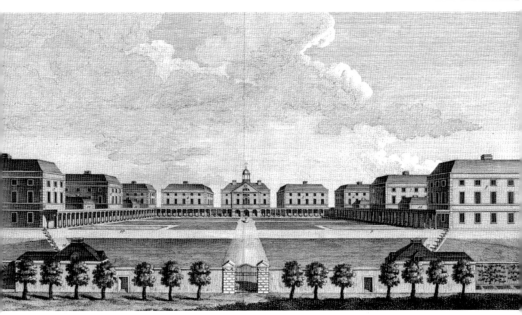

A plan of the groundbreaking hospital with two blocks removed to reveal the design in its full glory.

different diseases and complaints were treated in detached buildings, 60 wards could take a maximum of 1200 men and were grouped in a square round a central courtyard, to prevent the spread of infection. Covered walkways connected each speciality in this new 'hygienic' design, and the complex was served by one of the earliest systems of water-borne sanitation. Even the houses of the gentry had earth closets far into the nineteenth century, and many Plymouth homes were without this facility well into the twentieth century.

The result was a symmetrical group of Georgian buildings with the necessary authority and gravitas required of such an institution, surrounded by a high rubble wall to prevent sailors and marines from escaping. Once they had disembarked at the jetty, patients were fumigated at dedicated rooms in both the north and south gates.

When John Howard toured prisons in the last decades of the eighteenth century he also visited prison hospital wards and recommended, in his 1787

Although no longer the age of sail, the sewing tradition carried on in the Royal Navy. Here Edwardian naval ratings are making and mending clothes.

book *The State of Prisons in England and Wales with an Account of some Foreign Prisons*, that the exemplary design of the Stonehouse hospital should be copied. He was particularly impressed by the metal hospital beds, all too familiar in hospitals today.

> In all prisons it would be an excellent improvement to have crib beds for each person like those at the Royal Hospital at Plymouth. These may be of cast iron without sides, nearly as cheap as of oak. The beds or cradles at Plymouth are 14 inches from the floor; 3ft 1ins high at the head, and 2ft 3 ins at the feet; 6ft 2 inches long and 3ft 1 in wide in the clear. The boards on the sides (3ft 8inches long) slide in an inch groove. A medicine box hangs by two hooks at the back of each cradle, which is necessary only in infirmaries. To these cradles are hair mattresses bedding etc. If offenders have only loose straw, though a coverlet they must lie in their clothes, and of necessity be dirty and sickly objects. Therefore bedding is necessary, without this how can habits of cleanliness be produced and promoted in young creatures? or what disposition can such have for work?

Howard was not the only visitor impressed by the new hospital. French doctors who visited in 1787 were so impressed that their notes and observations became the blueprint for French hospital planning until the twentieth century.

CHAPTER 5
THE PRESS GANG

For centuries the appearance of the press gang in a Plymouth street was guaranteed to cause alarm. It was a grim reality of life in the port that, when war was declared or invasion feared, men would be snatched from their wives and children, and without further ado pressed into the service of the navy. Few would have had time or opportunity to say goodbye. Without the main breadwinner, their families were often thrown on to the parish, condemned to the workhouse.

Until the middle of the nineteenth century it was only the officers of naval ships who enjoyed any sort of continuous service in the Royal Navy. Crewman were pressed into service and paid off at the end of the voyage or cessation of hostilities. It's been estimated that only about one fifth of naval crews were volunteers. But the navy did actively recruit. One poster from 1805 tried to lure Plymouth sailors to rendezvous at the 'white flag' by dangling the carrot of prize money. It announced that

> The Flying Pallas of 36 guns at Plymouth is a new and uncommonly fine Frigate. Built on purpose. And ready for an EXPEDITION, as soon as some more good hands are on board.
>
> None need apply but SEAMEN and Stout Hands able to rouse about the Field Pieces, and carry a hundred weight of PEWTER, without stopping, at least three miles.

Blatantly a treasure hunting expedition, the poster emphasises that Captain Lord Cochrane is in charge. This was important to those who signed on: a well-liked and respected captain attracted men back to his flag time after time. And Plymouth tars who joined the *Flying Pallas* were not disappointed. She came to be known as the Golden Pallas after capturing four richly laden ships near the Azores, which were en route from the Spanish West Indies. Prize money was shared unequally among the ship's company, with captain and officers receiving the bulk, but on that voyage the entire crew came back rich men.

To make naval service a more attractive proposition, in 1696 seamen were given the opportunity to register for service. This entitled them to a yearly allowance when they were not required at sea, and when they were serving their country they were allotted an extra share of the prize money when foreign ships were captured and the vessel and cargo sold in port. For some men naval service offered an attractive escape. The navy would protect a man from his creditors if the debt was below £20; vagrants who had no means of support were at least given a hammock and food; and for criminals it was an opportunity to abscond from the law. Desperate to man the fleet, in 1795 Prime Minister Pitt the Younger brought in a substantial bounty of £70, which was offered to men if they signed up.

It was in the reign of King John that the first mention of the notorious press gang appears, and in 1545 'the most part' of the fishermen of Devon were taken to serve king and country. In times of war, merchant ships and fishing boats were often forced to remain in port because of a shortage of crewmen. During the seventeenth century the press gangs became more and more violent, and Plymouth with its seasoned population of merchant seamen and fishermen was a prime target. Press gangs were made up of naval officers and marines, and one press-gang master who patrolled Plymouth in the seventeenth century was Sir James Bagge, who built the original Saltram House.

During the eighteenth century the constant struggle with France and other Continental neighbours which culminated in the Revolutionary and Napoleonic Wars must have left the city denuded of men. There were exceptions: the tiny number of freeholders and voters in the Three Towns were exempt, and yardies at the dockyard had Protection Certificates which carried a full physical description to avoid fraud. When Henry Winstanley was in the throes of constructing the first Eddystone lighthouse, his workmen were given tokens to prove to the press gang that they could not be snatched to man the navy. Licensed pirates, or privateers as they were known, were also exempt during the French Wars, but this did not prevent them being taken by mistake. On 3 March 1801, 14 men from the ten-gun Plymouth privateer the *Lord Nelson* were taken to serve on a man-of-war, despite Admiralty protection. The owner Mr P. Symons was alerted and managed to use his influence to ensure they were returned, and the privateer sailed that evening.

Nowhere was sacred to the press gang. On 9 March 1790 there was a 'hot press', a surprise sweep of the port planned with great secrecy and conducted after dark. A gang of Royal Marines marched into the church at Plymouth Dock, clearing the gallery of every able-bodied male. Another gang of Marines invaded the theatre, nearly causing a riot. Detachments raided the gin shops, quays and fishing boats, and carried off watermen whose income was taking passengers across the numerous creeks and waterways. Although the navy was really in search of seamen, they 'also pressed landsmen of all descriptions, and the town looked as if in a state of siege'.

A fragile peace with the newly crowned Emperor Napoleon ended in 1803, and as France was once more on the warpath so was the press gang. An extra 10,000 seamen were needed. One unlucky casualty was the master of a Plymouth fishing smack, Mr Rokestrew, who encountered the gang on the night of 2 June 1803. A 'large mob' gathered, according to the Plymouth correspondent of *The Times*. What began as a scuffle escalated, as the press gang was 'obstructed and assaulted'. The unlucky fisherman was caught in the line of fire and killed, as efforts were made to disperse the mob. Although no one was arrested or tried, a coroner's jury brought in a verdict of wilful murder.

But the press was also active at sea. When war was declared, warships were forced to lie idle waiting for sufficient crewmen, so the gangs boarded merchant ships as they returned to port, seizing sailors and leaving a skeleton crew. It was an unwritten rule that ships setting *off* from port were not fair game. A fleet of trawlers, fishing near the Eddystone lighthouse on 30 March 1790, were all boarded, and two men taken from each boat. Similarly a few days later, on 10 April, six East Indiamen were waiting off the Eddystone rocks for a favourable wind, when armed men boarded them and took nearly 300 men who had no doubt been anticipating sweet reunions in port after a long voyage. They were almost certainly unaware that yet another war with France was brewing.

Popular novelist Tobias Smollett left us an account of the press gang at precisely this period in his novel *The Adventures of Roderick Random* published in 1748:

A squat tawny fellow, with a hanger by his side and a cudgel in his hand, came up to me, calling, 'Yo, ho! Brother, you must come along with me.' As I did not like his appearance, instead of answering his salutation, I quickened my pace, in hope of ridding myself of his company; upon which he whistled aloud, and immediately another sailor appeared before me, who laid hold of me by the collar, and began to drag me along. Not being of a humour to relish such treatment, I disengaged myself of the assailant, and, with one blow of my cudgel, laid him motionless on the ground; and perceiving myself surrounded in a trice, by ten or a dozen more, exerted myself with such dexterity and success, that some of my opponents were fain to attack me with drawn cutlasses; and after an obstinate engagement, in which I received a large wound on my head, and another on my left cheek, I was disarmed, taken prisoner, and carried on board a pressing tender, where, after being pinioned like a malefactor, I was thrust down into the hold among a parcel of miserable wretches, the sight of whom well nigh distracted me. As the commanding officer had not humanity enough to order my wounds to be dressed, and I could not use my own hands, I desired one of my fellow-captives, who was unfettered to take a handkerchief out of my pocket, and tie it round my head to stop the bleeding. He pulled out my handkerchief, 'tis true; but instead of applying it to the use for which I designed it, went to the grating of the hatchway, and, with astonishing composure, sold it before my face to a bum-boat woman then on board for a quart of gin, with which he treated my companions, regardless of my circumstances and intreaties [sic].

I complained bitterly of this robbery to the midshipman on deck, telling him at the same time, that, unless my hurts were dressed, I should bleed to death. But compassion was a weakness of which no man could justly accuse this person, who, squirting a mouthful of dissolved tobacco upon me through the gratings, told me, 'I was a mutinous dog, and that I might die and be damned.' Finding there was no other remedy, I appealed to patience, and laid up this usage in my memory, to be recalled at a fitter season. In the mean time, loss of blood, vexation, and want of food, contributed, with the noisome stench of the place, to throw me into a swoon; out of which I was recovered by a tweak of the nose, administered by the tar who stood centinel [sic] over us, who at the same time regaled me with a draught of flip [sic], and comforted me with the hopes of being put on board the Thunder next day, where I should be freed of my handcuffs, and cured of my wounds by the ship's surgeon.

Roderick Random does wreak revenge when he encounters an old friend on board the *Thunder*, has his wounds dressed, and is released back to shore.

Desertion was a problem. Merchant ships paid far better wages than the Royal Navy. The notorious mutiny at Spithead in 1797 was in reality a strike

The early twentieth century was the era of the new Dreadnought.

over low wages, which had been unaltered for over a century! The result was a 23 per cent pay increase.

The British navy had a huge pool of seamen from which to take its crews. The 11,000-mile coastline, plus the shores of colonial Ireland, offered a rich harvest of those who made a living from the sea. This, combined with rigorous naval discipline, made the crews of the 'wooden walls' the envy of our Continental neighbours.

Naval discipline was severe and dependent on the predilections of the captain. Under Queen Anne a serious offence tried by court martial was punished by 50 lashes. But by the time of George III this had risen to 200 or 300 lashes. Men were flogged by the boatswain's mate who trained for the occasion by flogging a barrel. For desertion a man would be flogged through the fleet, taken from ship to ship and flogged on board each one, and these deserters often died. It was not till the end of the nineteenth century that the use of the cat-o'-nine-tails was suspended, although this in effect meant its abolition. Respected Admiral Cuthbert Collingwood substituted more effective but humane punishments to show his disapprobation. These were

A treasured memento. Harold Challis made this delicate handkerchief for his wife shortly before his ship was blown up in the First World War.

dreaded by his crew far more than flogging. For example, a man might have to be available at any time to be called up on deck for extra duties.

In the same way that a ship's captain would employ known and loyal crew, so a system of patronage existed among officers. Young midshipmen would be taken on as a favour to relatives, to begin a naval career on what Collingwood called the 'precarious and unsteady ladder'. Whether captains knew the names of all their men aboard ship is uncertain; on a first-rate ship of the line with a crew of 800 men, this would be unlikely.

There was no easy way to recognise a naval man, except by his bearing, until uniforms were introduced in 1748 for the ranks of admiral, captain, commander, lieutenant and midshipman. The uniform was slow to be adopted, and supposedly was modelled on the riding habit worn by the Duchess of Bedford!

As an employer, the Admiralty was remarkably approachable. All letters of complaint from officers and crewmen were investigated. Much maligned 'round robin' letters accompany Christmas cards all over the world today, but the term originated in the navy. It was a method of signing letters of complaint to the Admiralty with all the names in a circle so that the ring-leaders could not be identified.

Although women were not admitted to the Royal Navy until the twenti-eth century, the maritime skills of some Plymouth women, prompted writer Edward Daniel Clarke, to suggest harnessing 'girl power'. In *A Tour Through the South of England, Wales and Part of Ireland During the Summer of 1791*, Clarke visited Mount Edgcumbe:

> It is usual, in this part of the world, to see women employed in the management of the ferry-boats. We were conducted on our return to the dock, by two of these nautical females. From the skill which evinced in feathering the oars, and their dexterity in managing the sails, I do not see why his majesty's navy might not be supplied, upon emergencies, with these aquatic amazons. Can any one say what the effect would be? It would at least in this experimental age, be an important attempt at improvement. Our seamen when engaged by the side of their favourite Susans, might exert them-selves with additional vigour, both from the fear of being excelled by women and haply for the preservation of those they love. At any rate it appears that many a female, who plies a bench of oars at Plymouth, would adorn our navy full as much as the ranks of our army are disgraced, by a number of effeminate figures, whom one sees daily, bepowdered and perfumed, armed cap-a-pee for the parades.

CHAPTER 6

WINDOW ON THE WORLD

Imagine the scene. Two years after a beloved son was believed to have been eaten by cannibals he arrives on the doorstep. At the beginning of May 1826 the Griffiths family in Devonport had an unexpected visitor. For two years they had mourned the loss of their son who had sailed for the South Seas on the whaling ship *Countess Morley*. When the ship returned with tales of an encounter with the ferocious natives on an island thousands of miles away, the Griffiths family accepted the inevitable. Their sailor son would not return. While the crew was ashore on one of the South Seas Islands, the young Griffiths had been kidnapped. He was attempting to rescue the ship's mate from his attackers, but as he headed for the whaler's tender, one of the islanders aimed a rock at his head. Griffiths's crewmates saw his apparently lifeless body lifted exultantly in the air by his attackers. These islanders had a reputation as cannibals, and fearing for the loss of the remainder of the crew, the ship set sail, leaving young Griffiths to his fate. But return he did, bringing him with him just one of the many tales from afar which gave Plymouth a window on the world.

The walls of alehouses and taverns must have reverberated with tales of such adventures. A reporter from the *Devonshire Freeholder* also heard the story and reported the safe return of young Griffiths in the pages of his newspaper on 6 May 1826. The unconscious Griffiths was taken in triumph to his captors' village.

> It appears however, that while preparations for eating him were going forward, he recovered, and a chief instantly announced his intention of adopting the prisoner. Griffiths was found by the tribe (by whom he was tattooed,) to be of great utility in repairing their war spears, mending their firelocks etc, and was, by them, kindly treated. He, however, desired to return to his native land, and watching his opportunity, deserted to another tribe of savages, from

One of the few black faces in Plymouth caught on camera in the mid nineteenth century.

whom he also, after a short time, made his escape; and fortunately for him, a vessel in the offing of the Island, had just dispatched a boat on shore, to which he swam off, was taken on board, and safely returned to England. He states a great many particulars of the manners and custom of the natives, the mode of worship, manner of warfare etc.

Griffiths was just one of the thousands of sailors who left their home port for all points of the compass, planting the name Plymouth around the world.

Merchant ships plied their trade with the West Indies, North and South America, Africa, India and all the ports of the vast British Empire. As a result ships' crews were multicultural and multilingual. Men who volunteered or were pressed into the Royal Navy brought back 'boys own' stories of battle and 'derring do', showing their scars as they told their tall tales. Few of these anecdotes have survived, but in the Plymouth and West Devon Record Office is the journal of James Yonge who served as a surgeon in the Royal Navy in the seventeenth century. It is illustrated with intricate maps, drawn as he arrived at each port of call. This extract was written after an encounter in 1661 off Algiers. For the ship's captain, this part of North Africa was familiar territory, as like many seamen he had been captured (probably by pirates) and sold into the slave trade.

Captain Edward Sprage had been a slave and understood the language, went ashore with another officer disguised in sailor's clothes as cockswaynes to assess their strength and the most convenient place to attack them. Ships lay prepared off the coast.

On Wednesday at noone there being a council of war and little wind, they from the shore let fly a number of cannon some of them loaded with very monstrous shell. I were there on the deck and saw the shot fly like hail about us.

Captain Sprage's boat was shot and sunk but the men saved. I went down presently to my quarters which was a platform in the after part of the hold laid over with beds to put the wounded men upon and under the scuttle. They were to come down and lay a heap of clothes for they lie soft and easy descent to bedrest. The fleet were drawn in a circle before the town, as will see in the figure and lay as near as fishers were from the Barbican, where we fought 6 hours but had not wind to manage our ships till towards evening it sprung up easterly, which blew in upon the town so we were forced to towe off, in which we incurred only the Boatswain and one man were slain. Men wounded were the Leftenant wounded deeply in the buttock with a splinter, a gentleman had the upper part of his foot torn with splinter, one Patrick, an Isle of Whyte man had both buttocks much lacerated by a shot, a boy had the calf of his leg torn by a splinter, and a Scotsman had his . . . knee torn by a bullet which . . . dressing up without amputation till the next day cost the poor man his life. All the rest recovered, some few were scaled bruised and had slight hurts.

Even 350 years later his detailed account leaps off the page. Dr Yonge then describes treating the wounded with the primitive medical techniques of his day. He was only 15 years old.

Here began my slavery for boiling small Barley water fermentations, washing towels and making lint spreading plasters and fitting the dresses was wholly on my hands, besides often emptying the Buckets they went to stool in, a nasty and mean employment but such as usually surgeons mates formerly did in the navy.

Hundreds of such stories of encounters under the bright glare of a foreign sun must have been recounted in Plymouth. Long before the era of television, sailors' yarns were painting images of sights seen.

Certainly John Sparke, who built houses in New Street, would have had mind-boggling tales of his voyage with Hawkins to the Spanish Main. He was fascinated by the smoking habit, which he encountered in Florida, and brought back the first recorded descriptions of the tomato and potato. Even if sailors had not been on Drake's epic voyage round the world, they probably knew a man who had! Few people could read, so imagine hearing accounts of such expeditions when even a journey to Exeter was an event. What a thrill to hear the tales of a salty sea dog, ensconced round a cosy fire, with the wind howling up from the Sound. This was the simplest form of entertainment and, with its huge seafaring population, Plymouth must have been well furnished with storytellers. There were tales from the fishermen who sailed for the rich cod banks of Newfoundland, spending months on that chilly eastern shore. The original Robinson Crusoe, Alexander Selkirk, arrived in Plymouth in 1720 and lived in Oreston long enough to marry a local widow, before setting sail again. Daniel Defoe had published his story, *Robinson Crusoe* in 1719, so doubtless Selkirk was able to dine out on it. He had sailed with explorer William Dampier in 1704, but when the pair fell out he was marooned for four years on the island of Juan Fernandez in the Pacific Ocean, 400 miles from the coast of Chile.

An open boat load of Huguenots found refuge from religious persecution in the Three Towns in 1685. After Louis XIV had abolished their freedom to practise their Protestant faith, the French government was somewhat surprised when thousands of them took to the sea. Many settled in Holland

OPPOSITE. *A paltry plaque marks the site of a house which belonged to great British adventurer and explorer Sir Francis Drake.*

The Oreston home of the original Robinson Crusoe, Alexander Selkirk.

but some 200,000 arrived in England. Those who settled in Plymouth joined a small community who had been baptising their children at the parish church of St Andrews since 1653. By 1733 Huguenot babies could be baptised in the new French Church, but 74 years later the descendants of those original immigrants had become so enmeshed with the local population that they had no need of a French Church. The parish registers of Holy Trinity Church similarly record baptisms of those who fled the Irish potato famine in 1845–46, while the census records them living in some of the worst slums in the Three Towns.

In 1851, the year of the second full-scale census, the cobblestones of the Barbican reverberated with the noise of Victorian city life. Among the narrow lanes crammed in between Southside Street and New Street is Stokes Lane. Number 5 no longer exists, but from this building with cracked panes and crumbling plaster, exotic, foreign voices and music poured into the street mixing with the wind and rain driving in from the harbour. In 1851 this house was home to ten Italian musicians. Thirty-six-year-old Louis Rossi is listed as the head of the household, and with his romantic Italian ways he had courted an English girl, Elizabeth, as his wife. The couple had living with them a glamorous coterie of musicians not only the ten from Italy, but a further five from Germany. Ten years later Louis and his second wife are described as grocers, by this time living at 1 Cecil Place, off Flora Street, with their two sons and a servant girl. But crammed into the same building are 13 Italian musicians, 11 German musicians, plus a couple of local carpenters.

For centuries street entertainers from Italy had migrated to other parts of the Continent, bringing with them the skills of the *commedia dell'arte*, which has given us the modern pantomime. There were even young boys with performing animals such as troupes of mice! It's known that some of these musicians were singers, while others played the hurdy-gurdy, percussion instruments like the tambourine and drums, as well as the violin. Among the lodgers at 5 Stokes Lane in 1851, were two young single Italian women also listed as musicians. What had brought them all to Plymouth? Apart from the wandering minstrels, some would have been driven out by dramatic political events at home. The nineteenth century saw a surge of nationalism all over Europe, and in the early 1820s this was evident in surges of revolution.

Seasonal migration from mountain villages in the north of Italy had become a way of life for many. French occupation of Italy in the early nineteenth century had led to a rush to grow grain even in the high mountains, leading to deforestation. The rural poor lived on chestnuts and starved when their staple food failed. An inevitable search for work further afield was established. Migration to the mulberry growing areas of Lombardy was common in May and June, the season when the trees were stripped of leaves for the silkworm. But a catastrophic failure of that mulberry crop is known to have brought at least one Italian to Plymouth. Lombardy-born Antonio Boggia arrived in Plymouth via the Italian community in London. The 1841 census lists him as a 25-year-old glass blower living in Kimberley Street. Ten years later Antonio was a looking-glass maker living at 23 Tavistock Street, and barometers made by the Boggia family still survive. The Boggia dynasty was established in Plymouth by the time Antonio died of tuberculosis at his Tavistock Street home in 1862, by which time he was employed at Devonport dockyard.

One of his great-grandsons is commemorated on the naval war memorial on the Hoe. Stanley John Boggia, shipwright 1st class, was killed during the Battle of Jutland, the major naval battle of the First World War. His ship, HMS *Defence* was a Minotaur class armoured cruiser hit by two heavy salvoes at around 6 o'clock on 31 May 1916. The ship sank in a roar of flame with the loss of 900 lives. It was one of 14 British ships lost in the battle, which was claimed as a victory by both sides.

The presence of the Boggias and other Italian artisans fulfilled a demand fuelled by the English fascination with Italy and all things Italian. This had developed during the era of the Grand Tour in the eighteenth century, when aristocratic young men and women took a gap year in Italy.

Giovanni Pelligrini was living at 29 Frankfort Street on the night of the 1851 Census, but he had been born in Tuscany, and may well have originated from the Tuscan province of Lucca, which was renowned for the craft of plaster figure making. Many of these statuette makers were seasonal migrants, making their way from the hills of Tuscany in the winter or early spring, across France and thence to England. As Giovanni is listed as a master of statuary he would have been the moulder of statuettes, with apprentices who would polish the statue when it came out of the mould, and another apprentice to paint the finished product. These craftsmen originated from an area which specialised in plaster figures of the Virgin Mary, popes and saints. But Giovanni may well have turned his tools to moulded figures of Queen Victoria and her consort Prince Albert. Hawkers carried baskets of these statues on their heads, selling to passers-by on the streets.

The prevalent English view of Italian immigrants seesawed between that of a glamorous romantic Renaissance figure and itinerant purveyors of music to the masses. By the 1850s, Italian wandering minstrels had become synonymous with what was considered a social evil – the organ grinder. This portable music box inspired incredible vitriol in the press, but would have added a flash of foreign colour to life on the city streets as the Italian organ grinder brought music to the masses.

Cartoons depicting the Victorian attitude to this nuisance were carried in newspapers, depicting for example the sanctity of the sick room disturbed by raucous music from the organ grinder on the street below. *The Times* even started up a campaign to ban what the newspaper termed, 'the orchestra of the Million'. In response to this, on 3 December 1857, *Trewman's Flying Post* carried a rather more tolerant editorial.

> Let us allow that this organ is frequently a nuisance. It may intrude upon the quiet of the sick room, or distract the student whose head is not strong enough to concentrate his ideas upon the business in hand. It may 'aggravate' the pattern women in 'sorting the things' on Monday or casting up the mornings' bills. It may injure the business

of the music master, if it intrude upon his hour; and it may suspend the domestic concert, if its overbearing strains strike up while the family piano and choir are in full swing. These are annoyance; but after all, is the infliction without its compensation? Is the Italian organ-grinder without his 'mission'? Would he exist and multiply, as he does, if he had none? The organ tribe is at least a self-supporting institution, and it must have its price or it could not go on. Is its mission unintelligible to us? Has it not carried, with more or less imperfection but with a decided progress of its own, the very pick of the finest music in the world to the humblest homes throughout the whole country? We have seen remarks upon the ruffianly oppugnance of the adult organ-grinder; but in truth, rude as they look, the men and boys from Palermo and Como carry amongst the humblest of our people no unpleasing specimen of the most kindly and gracious manners in the world. The very way in which the Italian boy receives the small copper dole, with a radiant smile of gratitude and a graceful gesture, is a lesson in *bien séance* that has perhaps been not altogether lost upon our working classes. At all events, that which is the nuisance of the few is the recreation of many. If the piano whose strains do not reach beyond the walls of the room, has to be suspended, the very same ideas are diffused throughout the attics and kitchens, the back rooms and courts of the whole neighbourhood. It would not become the 'Upper ten' to interfere; for the barrel organ is the orchestra of the Million.

The drawbacks of this particular brand of street music were so well known that the organ grinder was used as a yardstick to measure other forms of noise pollution found in the crowded streets of Victorian cities, such as cockerels and barking dogs. Contemporary newspapers also carry stories of incidents sparked by the organ grinder. For example, on 10 July 1861, *Trewman's Flying Post* carried an account of an attack on Augustin Podesta when he was on his way to a fete at Radford. He was beaten up by a young marine, William Veight, who was sentenced to 12 months in prison.

CHAPTER 7

ADVICE FROM
THE ANTIPODES

As emigrants began to take ship for distant shores, those who were literate wrote home with descriptions of the voyage and what they found there. One such was Jonathan Binns Were, who kept a diary on his trip from Plymouth to Melbourne in 1839. The diary was sent back to his brother once Jonathan arrived four months later. He sailed on 25 July on board the 447-foot *William Metcalfe* with his wife Sophia, plus his son and daughter. There were 254 people on board, of whom 196 were emigrants.

> We have also 20 sheep, 30 pigs, 2 cows, 15 dozen ducks and fowls and geese which of a morning make no inconsiderable noise and on first being roused from your morning's slumber you may suppose you were in some farmyard did not the rolling of the ship and the bursting of the waves destroy the otherwise pleasing illusion.

En route, a whaling ship, the *Grasshopper*, was spotted across the waves, and when the British ensign was glimpsed, passengers rushed to their cabins for pen and ink to send letters home.

> The letters which had been prepared for her to convey and in the haste brought on deck were found afterwards some not directed, others not sealed and others mere envelopes. I have endeavoured to give you the more minute particulars of this our first speaking that you may not only judge of our anxious desires which pervade all, but that you should also know our own hearts vibrate in sympathy with yours, when we think there may be an opportunity of communication and that it is not our fault that you are not in possession of our effusions.

For two-thirds of the voyage Jonathan was seasick, which he blamed partly on the position of their cabin in the bows. He recommended anyone following in his wake to take a stern cabin, and had this additional advice for his brother:

> Should you know any parties going on a voyage, to recommend their having all their cabin furniture fixed before starting. To have shelves and stands made to take their different articles, and not to hang their things to the sides, as the noise they make when the ship rolls (and which ships are always doing) adds much to the confusion.

Thursday was the day on which emigrants were allowed to do their washing, using seawater because the fresh water on board was so precious. Clothes were then hung in the rigging to dry. On such a long voyage through treacherous waters, the passengers lived in cramped conditions. Inevitably two babies and one of the mothers died, but three women successfully gave birth on board, although another two children were stillborn.

Jonathan Binns Were had brought with him a prefabricated flat-pack house, although when the family first landed on 15 November 1839, they put up tents as temporary homes, which struggled to keep out the weather. 'For six weeks after we came ashore the weather was most boisterous and Plymouth like, storms of thunder and lightning and such rain as those who have never been out of England can hardly conceive.'

Despite the appalling weather, Were managed to construct his kit home and the family spent the first night in their house on 1 January 1840. Jonathan warned his brother that, should he think of coming out to Australia, everything was very expensive and the new colony was full of rogues.

> They come down here by every opportunity and every ship. At the land sales, spacious tents are provided and a good substantial meal backed by the little delicacies for an excellent lunch:- pigeon pies, tongues, hams, cheese, tarts, biscuits, ale, wine, porter, ginger beer and soda water in abundance. But champagne is the order of the day, and you will see the great unwashed knocking off the tops of the bottles not waiting either for a glass or corkscrew.
>
> These lunches often cost £100 and are now become of daily occurrence and sometimes there will be two in opposition to each other. But the new arrived wealthy and unwary emigrants pay for this and thereby tend to keep the price of land so high.

CHAPTER 8

THE PLYMOUTH COMPANY
OF NEW ZEALAND

On 19 November 1840 the barque *William Bryan* joined the list of ships to sail from Plymouth planting colonies of English men and women across the globe. On board were 148 emigrants uprooting themselves from friends and family to put down roots in the southern hemisphere. The *William Bryan* was one of the first emigrant ships bound for New Zealand, and this was an enterprise hatched in Plymouth.

Both North and South Islands had been surveyed by men such as James Cook and William Bligh in the eighteenth century, but there had been no organised emigration to its shores, nor had it been officially claimed by the British Crown. The Plymouth Company of New Zealand was formed at a public meeting on 25 January 1840 to send the first emigrants out to this promising new country. An association of worthy gentlemen from Devon and Cornwall, with the Earl of Devon as Governor, had plumped for emigration as a way of offering a new life to hard-working families from the 'labouring classes' who were struggling in their native county. The company even subsidised the fare of young working-class couples – a generous offer as steerage passengers paid nearly £19 for the voyage. For struggling working-class families it was a tempting, but also daunting opportunity.

Apart from sailors' yarns what might the average Devonian have known about New Zealand? The *Plymouth and Cornish Advertiser* carried this in August 1839:

> New Zealand, between the North and South Capes is about 900 miles – the greatest breadth of the Northern Island, which is the wider of the two, is about 300 miles – diminishing to 200 and 100, and to greatly less towards the northern extremity, where at one point, distant about 150 miles from the North Cape, there is an isthmus of no more than three miles across. By the latest and it is believed the most accurate account, the area of the Northern Island

is computed at about 40,000 English square miles, while that of the Southern Island – of which Stewarts Island may be considered an appendage – is considerably one-third larger. The extent of the two islands, it is thought, must be at least 95,000 English square miles, or above sixty millions of square acres. The voyage from Britain to New Zealand, although the distance is greater than to Sydney, occupies about the same length of time, in consequence of the prevalent state of the winds; while in returning to Britain, the voyage from New Zealand is, of course, shorter than the voyage from Sydney by the distance between the two places, of 1,200 miles.

When the Company's prospectus was first published in February 1840, journalists painted images of new colonists reviving the spirit of enterprise that had flourished in the era of Drake and Raleigh. These colonisers of America had been Devon men, so putative New Zealanders would be following in the sea-boots of Sir Walter Raleigh and Sir Francis Drake. But those who took ship in the *William Bryan* on that November day in 1840 needed far more than enterprise alone. The great nineteenth-century emigrations from the old world to the new were forced by poverty, overcrowding and, for many, starvation. Yet it would have taken guts to face a six-month voyage in a cramped ship, whatever those passengers were leaving behind. The voyage of the *William Bryan* and its cargo of colonists was chronicled by Henry Weekes, the ship's doctor. In common with many ship's surgeons he kept a diary, which was later published as *The New Plymouth Settlement* in 1843. Weekes had been taken on at short notice and with the ship expected any day from London, its home port, he described how he:

> Hastily commenced the arduous task of rooting-out, in order to re-plant myself anew in another country. Reader! When I began, little did I think how painful would be the separation from a few dear friends! . . . with hurry and excitement, joined perhaps to a little obstinate pride, I managed to clear out in tolerable spirit.

The surgeon was one of the six 'principal colonists' who met daily, while the ship was loaded and provisioned, to agree the necessary infrastructure for the embryonic colony. They put their names to an agreement that they would support a clergyman, establish a dispensary and found a school. When Weekes returned home after a year in New Plymouth, none of these ambitions had been fulfilled.

Tucked beneath the walls of the Citadel, the Emigration Depot from which thousands of people left in search of a new life.

Emigrants came in from different parts of the county and were put up in the Emigration Depot at Baltic Wharf. The day they embarked was not auspicious, as Weekes recorded:

It rained in torrents and the decks were ankle deep in water. Boats and barges arrived at the ship's side with the emigrants and their luggage, some, poor things, in a most woeful plight. Each family had on average about four children, making seventy in all. There were one hundred and forty one steerage emigrants and how they could possibly be stowed away was to me a problem. Now just imagine a number of people, almost all strangers to each other, endeavouring to squeeze themselves and part of their things into little dark places called berths; grumbling all the while and expressing a wish to return; sailors swearing, pigs grunting and children crying their lungs. *Travelling* indeed makes us acquainted with strange bedfellows.

When Henry Weekes had signed on in the company offices at New Zealand House at 5 The Octagon, he was given strict instructions in a letter from Company Secretary Thomas Woollcombe:

I am especially to impress on you the positive injunctions of the Board that you preserve the most perfect order and decoram [sic] amongst the Emigrants, especially the single women whose sleeping place you will allow none of the male passengers . . . to enter on any pretence whatever.

So Henry Weekes was not only guardian of the passengers' physical health, but of their moral welfare as well. While afloat he also took the weekly church service and gave the sermon.

George Cutfield, who came from a family of naval architects based at Devonport, was the designated 'commander' of the expedition, with Alexander Mclean as captain. The ship was kept in the Sound for several days by two violent autumn gales. With an easterly wind in her sails the ship weighed anchor, as the ship's carpenter and crew sang 'Highland Laddie'. The usual stormy weather hit the barque as she negotiated the Bay of Biscay followed by a heavy swell. One man was almost lost overboard, and the constant spray sweeping over the bows threatened to soak the young single women as they negotiated the hatchway from their cabin to the deck. The captain was solicitous for the comfort of the young women as Henry Weekes recorded: 'Captain proposed to place some boards round the hatchway about 1 foot high to prevent a similar recurrence. Some ill-natured person remarked that it was only done for the purpose of seeing the girls' ankles as they stepped over.'

Apart from regular seasickness among the passengers, Henry Weekes had no serious illness among his charges, although many of the children suffered from dysentery and malnourishment. He served a daily portion of lime juice mixed with sugar and water to combat scurvy as the vessel's supply of fresh vegetables dwindled or rotted. Also on board was a small flock of hens.

Henry Weekes and the other cabin passengers played bridge to pass the hours on board, and some studied Spanish grammar and geometry. As the ship caught the benign trade winds and the weather improved, a school was set up on deck for the emigrants' children, where cabin passengers helped the schoolmaster.

The boys arc ranged along the deck with their books or slates and the girls sit round in a circle with their needle-work. We were obliged to defer this excellent institution until we got into fine weather; for excellent it is in having the twofold effect of employing both the teachers and the taught.

But all was not completely harmonious on board, as Weekes recorded:

> Many complaints made of the crowded state of the emigrants between-decks; and truly not without sufficient cause. But what I have to complain of is a dissatisfaction entirely produced by various promises made to the emigrants in Plymouth by the Company's agents, for the purpose of getting them on board without trouble – and which they knew well enough could not be fulfilled.

The surgeon does not elaborate on these breached promises made by the Company's agents before they sailed. But it's easy to imagine the clamouring concerns and fears voiced prior to setting off, to be answered by casual assurances in order to maintain calm and order among the would-be settlers.

Among the emigrants were a fiddler and flautist, who entertained the passengers by playing for evening dances on deck, which also enabled them to get some exercise. Flying fish, porpoises and dolphins were regular sights. Henry Weekes and two other male passengers even swam from the ship attached to a rope on deck, but decided not to repeat the experience when a shark was spotted the following day.

Henry records celebrating Christmas Day with a slap-up meal, although it seems unlikely that steerage passengers would have been offered such

The Octagon, site of the headquarters of the Plymouth Company of New Zealand.

delicacies: mock turtle soup, two salmon, three roast goose, boiled chicken and beef washed down with wine. Four traditional plum puddings were served followed by bread and cheese, and almonds and raisins. But as the year 1841 beckoned, and temperatures rose to over 80°F, the supplies of food and water deteriorated. As a privileged cabin passenger, Weekes certainly had access to better quality provisions than those in steerage as this diary entry on 30 December reveals: 'Water very bad, though we manage occasionally to get a better cask for the cabin.'

Four days into the New Year, the water which had been shipped on board at Plymouth six weeks earlier sounds undrinkable; of course, those on board had no option.

> Our water lately has been very bad. There are two kinds, the sulphurous which has a bluish tinge and smells strongly of sulphuretted [sic] hydrogen, and a dark coloured variety having little smell but tasting strongly of the cask. The former makes the better water of the two being exposed for some hours to the air and then boiled. One or two casks have been opened in which the water is as thick as oil, and pours like it. Whenever the water is worse than usual more sickness inevitably occurs. Good water is so very necessary during a long voyage that great attention should be paid to the casks in selecting them, and an emigrant ship should never sail without a tank, containing water for the sick at least.

Lack of decent water was not the only problem they encountered. As the *William Bryan* ran with the winds through the tropics, temperatures dropped, squalls buffeted the ship and the decks began to leak. Sailors used to foraging in strange latitudes caught albatrosses on a hook and line – evidently Coleridge's *Rime of the Ancient Mariner*, published in 1798, was not bedtime reading for anyone on board! Weekes was astonished by the 10-foot wingspan of the birds and by the length of their bodies. One measured 6 feet 4 inches from the beak to the tip of its tail.

> We have preserved their skins and the sailors make pies of their bodies. They say that by soaking them in water over night they get rid of any fishy taste they may be supposed to have. Mr McClarty, the third mate, told me they were 'very good indeed'.

A shipboard romance lightened these stormy days, and on 14 January 1841

Henry Weekes officiated at the marriage of 27-year-old blacksmith John James and 18-year-old servant girl Ann Phillips. Steerage passengers must have had a rough ride throughout the voyage as their accommodation was below the water line and therefore there were no portholes. Lanterns were particularly dangerous in the cramped conditions in steerage, and fire a constant threat for all ships at sea, and Henry Weekes described the precautions and lack of them on the *William Bryan*, with a warning to future ship's surgeons.

> The only lights they were allowed were locked lamps suspended in particular places, and attended to by the watch. But among the crew I am sorry to say that much carelessness existed in this respect. What a dreadful scene would not a fire have been with nearly two hundred men, women and children on board without a chance of escape! Our principal chance of avoiding danger was, or ought to have been, the capabilities of the long-boat; but it was in such a state that on our arrival in New Zealand it soon filled with water when hoisted over the side, notwithstanding a fortnight had been spent by the carpenter in patching, caulking and tarring her.
>
> It should be required of Masters of Emigrant Ships that no kind of open light be allowed out of the cabin, and a patent lamp should be substituted in the forecastle among the sailors for that dangerous one in common use. I strenuously recommend all Surgeons, about to take charge of emigrants, seeing the above change effected before they sail.

Despite his concerns, and the exigencies of the voyage the *William Bryan* arrived safely with no death or injury among its passengers or crew after a voyage of 140 days. But the reaction of the new colonists on arrival at their future home was unexpected.

> March 31st 1841 – Being a fine day proceeded to land the emigrants without delay. Strange as it may appear, many of them had become so attached to the ship which displeased them so much at the early part of our voyage, that we had great difficulty in inducing them to make a proper despatch.

Eventually they were lured onto land, the children were put ashore first, and where the children led their parents had to follow. But with no horses or bullocks all their worldly goods had to be dragged across the beach and up to the site chosen for the temporary settlement while the town was laid out. A surveyor from the Ordnance Survey offices in London had preceded the Plymouth settlers some three months earlier, and a stretch of land in Taranaki had been chosen as the site of New Plymouth. With fertile soil stretching in a gentle slope up from the sea, it was soon dubbed 'the Garden of New Zealand'.

In common with other emigrants of the period, Henry Weekes had brought his new home with him as a 'flat-pack' composed of panels, which took only three days to build. Settlers with fewer resources made do with tents and shelters, and used old sacks stuffed with ferns as mattresses. At first cooking was done outside, in what he called 'gipsy fashion' with a pot slung from a tripod of branches over an open fire. But soon he had constructed a kitchen. Staple crops of turnip and mustard seeds were sown and within days the green shoots were appearing above ground.

Among the passengers on the *William Bryan* was the usual complement of rats who also came ashore at the new colony and pilfered the available stores. Settlers began to clear scrub up to 20 feet high so that their plots of land could be marked out and allocated, and as the wet, cold winter set in they were close to starvation. Coastal traders were unwilling to bring in supplies because of the dangerous waters off the new settlement.

Six months later the second ship sponsored by the New Zealand Company of Plymouth arrived. The *Amelia Thompson* landed 187 passengers on 3 September 1841, to be followed by the *Oriental, Timandra, Blenheim* and *Essex* carrying a total of 585 new members of the colony.

The Plymouth Company of New Zealand was short lived. It ran into financial difficulties, not least because settlers were unwilling to buy land in the New Plymouth area because of the dangerous coastline, preferring to head for Port Nicholson. After two years it merged with the New Zealand Company of London.

CHAPTER 9

BOUNTY BLIGH AND HIS DEVONPORT NEMESIS

Conjure an image of Captain Bligh of *Bounty* fame and it will doubtless be the features of actor Trevor Howard which spring to mind. Thanks to the 1962 film, *The Mutiny on the Bounty*, where the zealous disciplinarian Bligh was played by that steely British actor, Bligh's name has become synonymous with cruelty. But he was by no means the worst, and in many ways perhaps better than his contemporaries in the treatment of his crew. Bligh's officious captaincy was contrasted on screen with the brooding, romantic Marlon Brando cast as Fletcher Christian, leader of the mutiny. While Bligh had his faults, the film tells only part of his story, and has blighted the name of the controversial captain in public imagination. Paint the scenes of Bligh's life on the canvas of his age and a different picture emerges.

As a boy William would have stood with his father watching the merchant and naval traffic in Plymouth Sound. He was the son of a city customs and revenue official, inspecting the cargoes loaded and unloaded dockside, at the Old Customs House on the Parade, so it was only natural that he would join the Royal Navy where young men could make both a career and, if they were lucky, a fortune.

His Plymouth childhood was short. Like all boys who longed for a career at sea, he was enrolled on his first ship at the age modern children are starting junior school. Records show that Bligh was registered on board HMS *Monmouth* on 1 July 1762, two months before his eighth birthday. It was common practice for the navy to take small boys on board to quite literally 'teach them the ropes' of their future career. Horatio Nelson went to sea at the age of 12. A boyhood under the harsh cramped conditions on board an English naval vessel in the second half of the eighteenth century does not tally with the contemporary view of childhood. But then childhood is a concept invented by the Victorian and Edwardian middle classes, and working-class lads were contributing to the family income at such an age.

Before a young man could enrol as a midshipman he needed to complete

The Old Customs House, where William Bligh's father worked in the eighteenth century, was derelict and ripe for demolition a century ago.

six years' service at sea. Fellow crew-members, and particularly junior officers, would have shown an avuncular interest in teaching their young shipmates the necessary skills. As a captain, Bligh himself gave regular tuition in navigation to the boys under his command.

The secrets of the octant, compasses and astrolabe were taught to these young apprentices, and from 1702 warships had a schoolmaster among their complement. But most important was that the 'young gentlemen', as they were known, learnt to climb the rigging and take the risks of life at sea. Below decks they were subject to the same appalling, cramped conditions as their fellow seamen, coupled with the inevitable swearing which was one of the chief features of naval life. This must have been where the young William learnt the colourful language which helped to blight his reputation in later life.

Of course young Bligh would not have spent the whole of his youth at sea. When ships were paid off, officers and crew had to wait for the next commission. At this date the officers were put on half pay as a retainer, but would look for work in the merchant navy to supplement their income. William probably came home to school, and may well have been a pupil at the Free Grammar School in between voyages. Once the six years was up, Bligh had to wait for a vacancy as a midshipman, but meanwhile it's known that he served on warships as an able seaman. When he was 21, Bligh sat his Passing Certificate, which qualified him as a lieutenant, and his career had begun. Soon he was on the voyage that would, quite literally, put him on the map.

This was the age of discovery, when ships of His Majesty's navy hoisted

Naval cadets and midshipmen are taught to 'shoot the sun', naval slang for navigating with a sextant.

sail and headed for the other side of the world, to record and encounter unknown peoples and coastlines. Captain Cook was at the apex of his fame and career, and it was to his ship the *Resolution* that Bligh was sent at the age of 22, and on 14 July 1776 sailed from Plymouth on an expedition which would last four years. As ship's sailing master Bligh held a responsible position, and within 18 months Cook had recognised his skills by naming Bligh's Cap, a small island in the southern Indian Ocean, after him. Although described in the ship's log by Cook as 'a high round rock' inaccessible to any living creature but 'fowls of the air', Cook's gesture must have been a fillip to Bligh's confidence. Bligh's own legacy to posterity was to chart the Sandwich Islands for the first time, as well as mapping and exploring other coasts already known but not yet recorded on Admiralty maps.

Cook's murder in the Sandwich Islands left Bligh as principal navigator for the last two years of the expedition. Seven years later he proved just how adept he was at navigation, by travelling over 3,000 miles in an open boat

A miniature of William Bligh, which his daughter took to Australia when she accompanied him on his fateful posting as Governor.

with no maps after Fletcher Christian cast him adrift. Captain James Cook must have passed on some of his own expertise and probably drilled into him the method of avoiding scurvy. Cook and later Bligh both held an enviable record for the good health of their crews over long and demanding voyages. But while Captain James Cook's reputation as a leader of men remains intact, William Bligh's is still tarnished by association with the events of the Mutiny of the *Bounty*, despite his other achievements.

Bligh's *Bounty* debacle was all tied up with the sugar trade. Breadfruit had been identified by Captain Cook on his voyages, and some bright spark at the Admiralty suggested that they would make ideal fodder for slaves working the sugar plantations in the Caribbean. Breadfruit was a staple food stuff in the South Sea Islands, whose climate was not dissimilar to that in the Caribbean. And it was a mark of the ascent of Bligh's star in the Admiralty heavens that he was chosen to obtain and nurture an orchard of the bread-fruit trees for this project. Accordingly HMS *Bounty* was modified to provide luxury accommodation for the crop. Circular holes were cut into the floor below deck so that the pots could be supported and protected through the anticipated storms. The spacious and light accommodation allotted to the South Sea produce made the crew's and officers' quarters cramped. But Bligh was on a mission, and he had a solution. On the crew was a blind fiddler who would play on deck every evening for four hours so that the sailors could stretch their legs and dance a hornpipe.

This was a prestigious mission, and among Bligh's handpicked crew was his young protégé, Fletcher Christian. It's thought today that it was the contrast of the lax life of luxury on the Island of Tahiti, plus the beauty of the island's women, which led the mutineers to revolt when they had to return to the mission on which they had been sent by the Admiralty. The use of the cat-o'-nine-tails by Bligh for relatively minor misdemeanours was the norm in the navy at the time. Tight discipline was vital on naval vessels. If Bligh had really been the sadistic monster portrayed in the film, his punishments would have been far worse. Bligh lacked imagination and empathy in his command; he believed in carrying out his orders to the letter; he lost his temper easily and had a proclivity for swearing. Uncharismatic he may have been, but unpopular among his crews he was not.

This is borne out by a far more serious and widespread mutiny which spread through the entire English fleet in 1797 – the Mutiny at Spithead and the Nore. When the mutineers presented their complaints – principally low wages and appalling food – they also demanded that certain hated officers be sent ashore. Captain Bligh was *not* among them; in fact, he intervened with

Bligh and 17 companions are cast adrift by Fletcher Christian and the crew of the Bounty. A print commemorating Bligh's efforts to bring the breadfruit trees to the West Indies.

the Admiralty on behalf of mutineers in his ship's company.

When Bligh was faced with mutiny on the *Bounty* in April 1789, the outcome was very different. Mutiny leader Fletcher Christian abandoned Bligh and 18 loyal crewmen in an open boat with four cutlasses, a sextant and enough food and water for five days. This consisted of 150 pounds of bread, 16 pieces of salted pork weighing 2 pounds apiece, 6 bottles of wine, 6 quarts of rum and 28 gallons of water. The *Bounty*'s launch was 23 feet long, 6 feet 9 inches wide and only 2 feet 9 inches deep. Despite his predicament in a small, overloaded boat, Bligh remained remarkably optimistic as he set out. Undaunted, he organised the boat's company as best he could. He continued to write the journal that he had kept throughout the breadfruit voyage and which was subsequently published in 1792 as *A Voyage to the South Sea for the Conveying of the Bread-fruit Tree to the West Indies, Including the Narrative of the Mutiny.*

> As our lodgings were very miserable and confined for want of room
> I endeavoured to remedy the latter defect by putting ourselves at

watch and watch; so that one half always sat up while the other lay down on the boat's bottom or upon a chest, with nothing to cover us but the heavens. Our limbs were dreadfully cramped for we could not stretch them out, and the nights were so cold, and we so constantly wet, that after a few hours sleep we could scarce move.

Bligh's determination and leadership skills were admirable. Calculating how far the boat needed to travel to reach a European settlement, he rationed the food accordingly. Each man was given a twenty-fifth of a pound of bread and a quarter of a pint of water three times day.

> At length the day came and showed to me a miserable set of beings, full of wants, without anything to relieve them. Some complained of great pain in their bowels, and everyone of having almost lost the use of his limbs. The little sleep we got was no ways refreshing as we were covered with sea and rain. I served a spoonful of rum at day-dawn, and the usual allowance of bread and water for breakfast, dinner, and supper.

Unknown, potentially unfriendly and possibly cannibalistic natives lurked behind the lush tropical vegetation of the islands they passed. One crewman was killed during an early attempt to replenish supplies. An additional danger was that many of these islands were also protected by reefs on which the boat could easily have been wrecked.

> The sight of these islands served only to increase the misery of our situation. We were very little better than starving with plenty in view; yet to attempt procuring any relief was attended with so much danger that prolonging of life, even in the midst of misery, was thought preferable, while there remained hopes of being able to surmount our hardships. For my own part I consider the general run of cloudy and wet weather to be a blessing of Providence. Hot weather would have caused us to have died with thirst; and probably being so constantly covered with rain or sea protected us from that dreadful calamity.

The extraordinary navigation skills, honed on his earlier voyages, enabled Bligh to sail the launch of HMS *Bounty* safely through largely uncharted waters, violent storms and torrential rain, on a voyage of 3,618 miles.

Throughout this epic journey he recorded every possible landmark, sketched islands and made notes on good harbours. On 14 June 1789 he arrived at the Dutch colony of Timor in the East Indies.

> The abilities of a painter, perhaps, could seldom have been displayed to more advantage than in the delineation of the two groups of figures which at this time presented themselves to each other. An indifferent spectator would have been at a loss which most to admire, the eyes of famine sparkling at immediate relief, or the horror of their preservers at the sight of so many spectres, whose ghastly countenances, if the cause had been unknown, would rather have excited terror than pity. Our bodies were nothing but skin and bones, our limbs were full of sores, and we were clothed in rags: in this condition, with the tears of joy and gratitude flowing down our cheeks, the people of Timor beheld us with a mixture of horror, surprise, and pity.

After ensuring that his men were given medical treatment, Bligh hitched a lift in a Dutch ship, and sailed back to England via the Cape of Good Hope. From here he wrote to Governor Phillips at Port Jackson in New South Wales giving descriptions of the mutineers and his version of events. On landing at Portsmouth he was court-martialled for the loss of his ship and honourably acquitted. His story was published soon afterwards.

> With respect to the preservation of our health during a course of 16 days of heavy and almost continual rain I would recommend to everyone in a similar situation the method we practised which is to dip their clothes in the salt-water and wring them out as often as they become filled with rain: it was the only resource we had, and I believe was of the greatest service to us, for it felt more like a change of dry clothes than could well be imagined. We had occasion to do this so often that at length all our clothes were wrung to pieces: for, except the few days we passed on the coast of New Holland, we were continually wet either with rain or sea.

This respite in New Holland, what we today call Australia, was in fact on a chain of islands inside the Great Barrier Reef. It allowed the castaways to gorge on oysters, clams and birds. Bligh would visit the Australian mainland 15 years later, in what was to be an ignominious finale to his naval career. But before that, Bligh would be court-martialled for a second time, over an incident in which he was charged with 'tyranny, unofficer-like conduct, and ungentlemanly behaviour'. Bligh's quick temper and bad language had got him into trouble once again, but the vast majority of his crew rallied to his defence. The two-day court martial in February 1805 found the charges partially proved and he was 'reprimanded and . . . admonished to be in future more correct in his language'. The lieutenant who had brought the charge was dismissed from the navy, while Captain Bligh was restored to the command of his ship, the *Warrior*. It was a mere hiccup, and two months later he was offered a prestigious job on the other side of the world.

William Bligh had met the great botanist Sir Joseph Banks early in his

Devonport-born John Macarthur, who started the Australian woollen industry by importing Merino sheep from Italy.

career, and Banks became both a friend and his patron. It was Banks who put forward Bligh's name for the vacant post of Governor of New South Wales in 1805. It was a poisoned chalice as Bligh was to discover. In young colonial Australia he would meet his nemesis, an adventurer born in Devonport in 1767, John Macarthur. Macarthur was the son of a corset maker, who made his fortune in New South Wales as a rum baron and sheep farmer.

The young colony was part emigrant and part convict, and Bligh was tasked with ending the illegal rum trade which was controlled by the local militia, called the New South Wales Corps. John Macarthur had been an early recruit to this militia, whose troops guarded convicts and acted as a police force. Leaving Devonport in 1789, his charismatic personality soon gave him plenty of clout in the colony after he arrived in 1790. Over the next 11 years Macarthur made a large fortune and acquired a powerful enemy, in the eminent personage of Sir Joseph Banks. By the time Bligh arrived, Macarthur had resigned from the Corps and had obtained a grant of 5,000 acres of land to set up in the wool trade: it is Macarthur who is credited with the intro-duction of Merino sheep from Italy. The stage was set for a confrontation between the colonist and the new governor and protégé of Sir Joseph Banks, William Bligh.

With typical adherence to the purpose of his mission, the uncharismatic Bligh soon upset the rum traders in the militia. He insisted that free-settlers like Macarthur, who had received land grants must have them verified officially by letters from London. This was a legal nicety, but Bligh was a man who did everything by the book. Freed convicts who had cleared land, started farming and built houses were told they could not do so without a formal lease. Bligh even ordered some of their houses to be demolished. With the might of the British government behind him, he started to throw his weight around, sacking officials and replacing them with men whom he had chosen. Bligh wanted to run the proverbial tight ship. But this was not a naval vessel where barked orders catalysed a highly trained crew into action and discipline could be enforced by the lash. He had been a member of His Majesty's navy since the age of eight and simply did not understand the people and pulse of New South Wales.

Former and serving members of the New South Wales Corps grew increasingly irritated as the new governor interfered in their affairs. Australia was their home, while Bligh was a mere transient. His pejorative nickname of Bounty Bligh was well known in the colony, particularly since the testi-mony of Bounty mutineers at their court martial. Soon the word 'tyrant' was being bandied around, and comparisons were drawn with the insane Roman

Emperor Caligula. When, in October 1807, Bligh wrote to London proposing that the New South Wales Corps be withdrawn, word leaked out. In December that year John Macarthur was arrested and bailed on unspecified charges linked to the escape of a convict stowaway on one of his ships. As the friction between Bligh and Macarthur continued, members of the New South Wales Corps grew increasingly rebellious. Bligh accused several officers of treason, while Macarthur claimed that the court at which he was to be tried was not legitimate. 'It is to the Officers of the New South Wales Corps that the administration of Justice is committed,' he claimed according to the court records. In a written appeal to the commanding officer of the Corps, Macarthur implored them to arrest Bligh and seize control of the colony to prevent further unrest.

On the evening of 26 January 1808, hundreds of soldiers marched through the settlement heading for Government House led by their commanding officer George Johnston. With the sound of the Corps band playing 'The British Grenadiers' ringing in his ears, Bligh reportedly hid under a bed. He was soon discovered and put under arrest.

Sydney settlers partied all night, celebrating the overthrow of the 'tyrant'. For a year the rebels ruled while William Bligh remained a prisoner in Government House, refusing to leave the colony until he was officially relieved of his position by London. He attempted to get help from the Governor of Van Diemens Land (Tasmania), without success. Nearly two years after the rebellion Bligh learnt that the British Colonial Office had condemned his overthrow as mutiny, and he set sail for England to take part in the trial.

In June 1811, George Johnston was court-martialled and cashiered for treason for his part in the rebellion at a 13-day trial in England. He returned to his farm in New South Wales. As a civilian, John Macarthur could not be tried for treason, but was exiled from New South Wales until 1817, when he was allowed to return on the proviso that he agreed to play no part in public life. Bounty Bligh was promoted to Rear Admiral of the White and Vice Admiral of the Blue, but his reputation did not recover from the events of the Rum Rebellion. He did not see service at sea again, and died in 1817.

In an interesting footnote to the story, because Bligh's wife Elizabeth was terrified of sea voyages, his daughter Mary Putland had accompanied him to the southern hemisphere. After her father's ignominious return to England, she remained in New South Wales with her husband on the land which Bligh had been granted there. As a result Bligh's journals, telescope and other personal effects are held at archives in Sydney.

CHAPTER 10

FROM PLYMOUTH
TO THE POLE

As Plymouth's polar hero Robert Falcon Scott lay dying in his tent in the Antarctic, his thoughts were with the future welfare of those left behind. As well as his sculptor wife Kathleen and young son Peter, there were the families of his fellow polar explorers, Wilson, Oates, Bowers and Evans. The words of Scott's 'message to the public' are to be seen at the foot of the monument at Mount Wise.

> Had we lived, I should have had a tale to tell of the hardihood, endurance, and courage of my companions which would have stirred the heart of every Englishman. These rough notes and our dead bodies must tell the tale.

Robert Falcon Scott carved by his sculptor wife Kathleen.

But what was omitted on the Mount Wise monument was this plea at the end of the message:

> Surely a great rich country like ours will see that those who are dependent on us are properly provided for.

Days before departure for the last push for the Pole, he had received the news that the polar project was £30,000 in debt and been forced to ask expedition members to forego a year's pay to improve finances. Ironically his death initiated a flood of donations, enough to support the families, pay off the expedition debts, set up the Scott Polar Research Institute in Cambridge and construct the National Memorial to the polar party at Mount Wise at a cost of £12,500. He would have been delighted.

His preoccupation with the fate of his dependents after his death may well have stemmed from his Plymouth roots. Scott had grown up in a family that was constantly scraping to make ends meet. When he was born in 1868, the family home, Outlands at Milehouse, had been the subject of a lawsuit in Chancery. Scott's grandfather had died leaving a will filled with bequests distributing money that no longer existed. Family ructions ensued until finally the house was settled on Scott's mother Hannah, after her father William Cumings, a Lloyd's surveyor in Plymouth, intervened. Outlands had been purchased by the explorer's grandfather, Robert Scott, on his retirement from the navy in the 1820s. At the time Outlands was a slate hung cottage, but the ex-purser built extensions to transform it into the house in which his grandson spent his childhood. Six years later Robert Scott and his brother Edward invested some of their prize money from the wars with France by buying Hoegate Street Brewery.

While the young explorer was growing up, it was his father John who was running the brewery, although by the 1881 census return he is listed as retired and is serving as a Devonport magistrate. Scott and his five siblings grew up in a household with his aged aunt Charlotte Scott and several servants. Close by was Outland Mills run by corn merchant Henry Moffatt and the 15-acre Outlands Farm run by John Jenkins. Rather grander neighbours were the Hamiltons at Swilly House. Gerard Hamilton was a retired Admiralty official whose wife Augusta, and several of their children, had been born at another nearby historic house, Widey Court.

Young Scott rode his pony to lessons at Exmouth House, the small private day school in the village of Stoke Damerel. His family was active in the church of St Mark's at Ford where Robert sang in the choir and his father

Scott's birthplace, Outlands, which was sold when the family got into financial difficulties.

was churchwarden. Despite his 'delicate' health, Plymouth's famous son was plucked from his idyllic country childhood and sent to boarding school in Hampshire where he was coached for entry to Britannia Naval College in Dartmouth. By 1883 he was a midshipman, and it was in 1886 that he joined HMS *Rover* and took part in a race that would alter the course of his life. While his ship was on duty in the Caribbean, the 18-year-old midshipman sailed to victory in a race against fellow 'middies' across the bay at St Kitts. A few days later he was invited to dinner by the commodore, where he met, and impressed, Sir Clements Markham. An ex-naval man, Markham had sailed to the Arctic in the 1850s on one of the many attempts to discover the fate of the Franklin expedition. He was looking for a young naval officer to command a future expedition to the Antarctic. After that encounter, Scott was on his list.

In 1891, Lieutenant Scott was posted to the torpedo school at Devonport, but three years later the family was hit by financial disaster. The Outlands household had been living on the proceeds of the sale of the Hoegate Brewery for several years. But John Scott had also borrowed against the capital value of Outlands, and in 1894 the penniless family left for Somerset

The grave of Fred Dailey one of the many men who went from Plymouth to the Pole during two centuries of exploration.

where John had found a job as brewery manager. Scott took a posting to HMS *Defiance* in Devonport to help his mother with the sale of Outlands. But further disaster followed, when in 1897 John Scott died leaving his wife without an income. The siblings rallied round to support their mother, with Robert giving £70 a year from his naval salary. It was his brother Archie who contributed the bulk of their mother's income. Archie's sudden untimely death of typhoid fever a year later left an even bigger gap in the family finances.

Robert Falcon Scott's star was rising. Already spotted by Markham, he applied for the job of commander of the first British expedition to the Antarctic (The National Antarctic Expedition 1901–04) only four days after it was announced in 1899, but had to wait until the summer of 1900 for his appointment.

In the years after his death, his sister commented that he had no particular affiliation for ice and snow but wanted the freedom to stretch his wings. Later, when Scott married the alluring Kathleen in 1909, she encouraged him in this ambition. But the polar pioneer may well have been initially influenced by a tale encountered in his childhood at Outlands. Although nearby Swilly House was the home of the Hamilton family when Robert Scott knew it, it was also the birthplace of another Plymouth polar pioneer, Tobias Furneaux, the first man to sail round the world in both directions.

CHAPTER 11

THE FORGOTTEN
SQUIRE OF SWILLY

On 17 January 1773, Plymouth-born Tobias Furneaux went boldly where no man had gone before – into the Antarctic Circle. Furneaux was in command of HMS *Adventure*, the ship which accompanied Captain James Cook on his second voyage. Handpicked by Cook for his navigation skills, the 37-year-old lieutenant and his boss were on a mission for king and country, in search of the fabled southern continent.

Tobias Furneaux has faded into history in the shade of the extraordinary record of Cook's three voyages of exploration. But his name lives on in the string of islands he mapped off the coast of Tasmania during that voyage to

Captain Tobias Furneaux, the first man to voyage round the world in both directions.

the southern hemisphere. There is no doubt that he would have had other Plymothians among the 80-strong complement of men on board the HMS *Adventure* when he set sail from The Sound on 10 July 1772. Only Cook knew the destination contained in his secret orders from the Admiralty. The account of that extraordinary voyage was published jointly by James Cook and Tobias Furneaux in *A Voyage to the South Pole and Round the World Performed in His Majesty's Ships The Resolution and The Adventure in 1772, 1773, 1774 and 1775*. This voyage into waters uncharted and unknown in the eighteenth century would establish the chronometer, or clock, as an essential item of maritime equipment. Before the two ships weighed anchor at 6 a.m., the precious watches were set, as Cook recorded:

> The watches were set going in the presence of the two astronomers, Captain Furneaux, the first lieutenants of the ships, and myself, and put on board. The two on board the Adventure were made by Mr Arnold, and also one of those on board the Resolution; but the other was made by Mr Kendal, upon the same principle, in every respect, as Mr Harrison's time piece. The Commander, first lieutenant, and astronomer, on board each of the ships, kept, each of them keys, of the boxes which contained the watches, and were always to be present at the winding them up, and comparing one with the other.

It was only 11 years since John Harrison had won the £20,000 longitude prize by inventing a timepiece without a pendulum, which could keep time as a ship swayed with the motion of the waves. John Arnold had taken Harrison's invention and improved on it. But it was not till 1825 that the navy routinely supplied ships with chronometers, essential for calculating longitude. A chronometer was used to keep the time of a fixed location, which serves as a reference point for determining the ship's position. Latitude is measured by the position of the sun at noon, and comparison between the two times gives the number of degrees of longitude. Armed with a bevy of watches, the two captains were embarking on an adventure to answer one of the great conundrums of their age. To quote Cook's own words:

> Whether the unexplored part of the Southern Hemisphere be only an immense mass of water, or contain another continent, as speculative geography seemed to suggest, was a question which had engaged the attention, not only of learned men, but of most of the maritime powers of Europe.

In this era of empire building, the riches of the great southern continent would add greatly to a nation's power and wealth, and Britain wanted to be that nation. The expedition was equipped at huge expense with a portable observatory, astronomical clocks, an astronomical quadrant, a reflecting telescope, an achromatic refracting telescope, two globes, sextants and an azimuth compass. As well as recording the heavens and landmass, the expedition was to chart the uncertain weather of this unexplored region. On board the ships were a wind gauge, portable barometers, thermometers and a device to measure the temperature of seawater at different depths. This was the first expedition with a complement of scientists: astronomers to chart the heavens of the southern hemisphere, botanists, zoologists and a landscape artist to record the images seen by European eyes for the first time. It was a huge honour for Tobias Furneaux to be picked by James Cook as commander of HMS *Adventure*.

Tobias Furneaux was born on the family estate at Swilly, now the site of a council estate built by Plymouth City Council in the 1920s. He had joined the navy in February 1755, but it was while serving as a second lieutenant on HMS *Dolphin* in 1767 that his reputation was made. Under the command of Samuel Wallis, his cousin, the ship was sent off to explore the southern hemisphere. Furneaux had to take command regularly as Wallis and the first lieutenant suffered bouts of illness during the long voyage across the Pacific. While in command on 25 June 1767, Furneaux discovered Tahiti and 'took possession' of the island in the name of King George III. The timely discovery of this tropical paradise enabled James Cook to visit Tahiti during his first voyage of exploration and observe the transit of Venus in 1769. One nugget of information about Tobias's personality has survived from a shipmate on board the *Dolphin*, describing him as a gentle, agreeable man who was kind to the ship's company.

On his second and greatest Pacific voyage, Furneaux was to encounter the beauty and awe of the Antarctic which has lured explorers ever since. On the morning of Thursday 10 December 1772, the *Adventure* under his command was in the lead when an 'island of ice' was spotted. They had sighted an iceberg, as James Cook described:

> Soon after the wind moderated, and we let all the reefs out of the topsails, got the spritsail-yard out, and top-gallant mast up. The weather coming hazy, I called the Adventure to signal under my stern; which was no sooner done, than the haze increased so much, with snow and sleet, that we did not see an island of ice, which we

Swilly House where Tobias Furneaux grew up, demolished after the Second World War.

were steering directly for, till less than a mile from it. I judged it to be about 50 feet high, and half a mile in circuit. It was flat at top, and its sides rose in a perpendicular direction, against which the sea broke exceedingly high. Captain Furneaux at first took this for land, and hauled off from it, until called back by signal. As the weather was foggy it was necessary to proceed with caution. We therefore reefed our topsails, and at the same time sounded, but found no ground with 150 fathoms. We kept on the Southward with the wind at North till night, which we spent in making short trips, first one way and then another, under an easy sail; thermometer this 24 hours from 36½ to 31.

At day-light in the morning of the 11th, we made sail to the Southward with the wind at West, having a fresh gale attended with sleet and snow. At noon we were in the latitude of 51° 50° South and longitude 21° 3° E, where we saw some white birds about the size of pigeons, with blackish bills and feet. I never saw any such before; and Mr Forster had no knowledge of them. I believe them to be of the peterel [sic] tribe, and natives of these icy seas. At this time we passed between two ice islands, which lay at a little distance from each other.

In the night the wind veered to NW which enabled us to steer SW. On the 12th, we still had thick hazy weather, with sleet and snow; so that we were obliged to proceed with great caution on account of the ice islands. Six of them we passed this day; some of them near two miles in circuit and 60 feet high. And yet, such was the force and height of the waves, that the sea broke quite over them. This exhibited a view which for a few minutes was pleasing to the eye; but when we reflected on the danger, the mind was filled with horror. For were a ship to get against the weather side of one of these islands when the sea runs high, she would be dashed to pieces in a moment.

You can almost hear the explorer shiver with cold and the pain of chilblains, as he wrote those words in his cabin buffeted by the mighty Southern Ocean. Polar clothing had not been developed to combat the cold of the voyage. Portholes were kept closed in these icy regions, heightening the stench from the livestock on board, most of which died. Sails and ropes were frozen, cutting the hands of the crew as they reefed and furled, adding to the misery of chilblains, chapped hands and faces. Sugar, salted meat and butter, all became frozen, and the one source of warmth was the fire in the cook's galley. The only source of fresh water by this point in the voyage was the ice which surrounded them, and heaving it on board entailed great danger.

The *Resolution* and the *Adventure* were not large ships. Built as colliers with a full body and sturdy, almost upright bows, they were chosen for strength and the capacity to store men and provisions. The larger *Resolution* was only 135 feet long and carried 112 officers and men, with a displacement of 462 tons. The dimensions of the *Adventure* are not recorded, but she displaced only 336 tons and had a figurehead of a nymph. At least there was some comfort for both crews, in the presence of another ship. When they crossed into the Antarctic Circle the weather was clearer, and Cook recorded what doubtless every man on those ships was watching pass before his eyes.

We could see several leagues round us; and yet we had only seen one island of ice since the morning. But about 4 pm as we were steering to the South, we observed the whole sea in a manner covered with ice, from the direction of South East, round by the

South to West. In this space, 38 ice islands, great and small, were seen, besides loose ice in abundance, so that we were obliged to luff [steer nearer the wind] for one piece, and bear up for another, and, as we continued to advance to the South, it increased in such a manner, that at ½ past six o'clock, being then in latitude 67° 15′ South, we could proceed no farther; the ice being entirely closed to the South, in the whole extent from East to W.S.W. without the least appearance of any opening. This immense field was composed of different kinds of ice; such as high hills; loose or broken pieces packed close together, and what, I think, Greenlandmen call field-ice. A float of this kind of ice lay to the S.E. of us, of such extent that I could see no end to it, from the mast head. It was 16 or 18 feet high at least; and appeared of a pretty equal height and surface.

This was the Antarctic summer, but nonetheless the two ships were separated in fog, followed by a violent storm, on 7 February. The seas were so enormous that waves were breaking over the ship's bows as high as the yardarm. The *Resolution* was two miles ahead. Tobias Furneaux takes up the story:

We soon after heard a gun, the report of which we imagined to be on the larboard beam; we then hauled up to SE, and kept firing a four pounder every half hour, but had no answer, nor further sight of her; then we kept the course we steered on before the fog came on. In the evening it began to blow hard, and was at intervals, more clear; but we could see nothing of her, which gave us much uneasiness. We then tacked and stood to the Westward, to cruise in the place where we last saw her, according to agreement in case of separation; but that day, came on a very heavy gale of wind and thick weather, that obliged us to bring to, and thereby prevented us reaching the intended spot. However, the wind coming more moderate, and the fog in some measure clearing away we cruized as near the place as we could get, for three days; when giving up all hopes of joining company again, we bore away for winter quarters, distant fourteen hundred leagues, through a sea entirely unknown, and reduced the allowance of water to a quart per day.

Sensibly Cook had set several rendezvous points in the event of separation, so after his fruitless search Furneaux set sail for New Zealand. Ahead of him lay Van Diemen's Land, known from the charts of Abel Tasman when he recorded it in 1642, but unvisited since then. As the *Adventure* sailed up the west coast of Tasmania, Furneaux and his second lieutenant James Burney, brother of writer Fanny Burney, surveyed the coast. On 11 March they anchored in what was named Adventure Bay and a party went ashore for supplies. As the *Adventure* sailed north towards the continent of Australia, as yet undiscovered by Europeans, Furneaux charted a group of islands which Captain Cook later named after his second-in-command. Reaching New Zealand on 8 May the crew set about repairing the ravages of ice and storm, until the *Resolution* rejoined them. But Cook was eager to press on to the Society Islands, a group of islands in the South Pacific which he had named after the Royal Society, when first he landed in 1769. On his previous voyage Cook had left various gifts, including some counterfeit English coins, with one of the chiefs. But it was thanks to Tobias Furneaux that Georgian society was to encounter the man immortalized by the poet William Cowper as the 'noble savage': a South Seas islander called Omai. He became a protégé of Sir Joseph Banks during his two-year stay in England, and was even introduced to the King. As he made clear, in his account of the voyage, James Cook did not approve when Omai was invited on board the *Adventure* on Tuesday 7 September 1773.

Before we quitted this island (Huahine) Captain Furneaux agreed to receive on board his ship a Young man named Omai, a native of Ulietea, where he had some property of which he had been dispossessed by the people of Bolabola. I at first rather wondered that Captain Furneaux would encumber himself with this man, who, in my opinion, was not a proper sample of the inhabitants of these happy islands, not having any advantage of birth or acquired rank; not being eminent in shape, figure or complexion. For their people of the first rank are much fairer, and usually better behaved, and more intelligent, than the middling class of people among whom Omai is to be ranked. I have however, since my arrival in England, been convinced of my error: . . . I much doubt whether any other of the natives would have given more general satisfaction by his behaviour among us. Omai has most certainly a very good understanding, quick parts, and honest principles; he has a natural good behaviour, which rendered him acceptable to the best company, and a proper degree of pride, which taught him to avoid the society of persons of inferior rank.

During the voyage from Tahiti, once again the ships lost sight of each other. At Queen Charlotte's Sound, the next agreed rendezvous, Furneaux who had been delayed by gales arrived later than his boss. On the shore he found a message in a bottle giving details of Cook's intentions. Furneaux pressed on and while replenishing stores and water in New Zealand again ten men were slaughtered and, according to the expedition log, eaten by the Maoris. With a depleted crew, Tobias Furneaux set off on his return journey via the notorious waters of Cape Horn and the Cape of Good Hope. It was a lonely voyage with no sightings of other ships, nor any sign of life except the occasional whale, dolphin or seal. Still hoping to discover the great southern continent, Furneaux again skirted the edge of the ice fields at a latitude of some 60°. But the fabled land mass remained a fable. The explorers finally returned on 14 July 1774, and Furneaux resumed his naval career taking command of the 28-gun HMS *Syren* during the blockade of the American coast in the War of American Independence. At the age of only 46, Tobias Furneaux, the first man to sail round the world in both directions, died at home in Swilly in 1781. He was buried in the family vault in the churchyard at Stoke Damerel.

The Furneaux family tomb and the plaque marking his achievement.

CHAPTER 12

FORTRESS PLYMOUTH

The resilience of those who lived through the Blitz is unimaginable to those of a post-war generation. Night after night people suffered broken sleep in between the dash to and from air raid shelters. Those fortunate enough to have a vehicle drove out of the city to curl up in the back of cars and vans; others queued for afternoon buses and trains so they could spend the night in village halls and fields a few miles from the city. Andersen shelters were dug in back gardens, Morrison shelters built in homes and for many there were the hundred or so public shelters, built in August and September 1939. Many of these still lie hidden beneath the surface of the modern city complete with their detritus: metal brackets sets in the wall either side of the tunnel, the timber long since scavenged in the post-war hunt for building materials, chemical toilet buckets, posters on the wall stipulating 'no smoking' and 'no dogs', in case they grew aggressive during the noisy raids. These were sociable places where the WRVS served tea, and children had supplies of paper and crayons. But even these were not guaranteed against a direct hit, as the unlucky discovered on the night of 22–23 April 1941 when the Portland Square shelter took a direct hit, killing 72 people including a mother and her 6 children.

Air raids were not of course restricted to the hours of darkness. Trips to the hairdresser at Spooners Department Store could be rudely interrupted by the screeching siren, followed by hasty disconnection from overhead electric curlers and a trip to the store's basement shelter. As whole shopping streets were obliterated, customers and staff moved to new shopping centres like the Pannier Market. Life had to carry on. When the maternity hospital at Freedom Fields was bombed on 20 March 1941, women were in labour at the height of the raid, and 23 babies and 6 nurses were killed that night. The

OVERLEAF. *After the commercial heart of the city was Blitzed in 1941, shops and shoppers moved to the Pannier Market.*

following night another terrible raid hit the city. Sub Lieutenant J. V Evans was a guest at the Westminster Hotel in the Crescent. As the raid began he tried to make his way out of the building. As he fled through one of the hotel corridors he saw two female members of staff making their own way out in the opposite direction. He did not follow them, a decision which saved his life. His letter, written to the hotel owner following the raid, is in the Plymouth and West Devon Record Office:

> I can remember the sound of bombs coming close then there was a sensation of violent pressure and blinding flame and everything seemed to be collapsing round me. I was probably stunned for a second or so because I next found myself completely buried in brick and plaster and unable to breathe. However with a bit of desperate pushing I was able to get my head and shoulders clear and breathe freely. Everything was dark and I was at first afraid I was blind, but luckily I had a small torch in the pocket of my greatcoat and managed to get it out. This showed me that I was enclosed by a lath and plaster dividing wall, apparently supporting debris above me. I was afraid that if I moved I would be buried again so I began shouting for help. A man's voice was apparently answering me but after one or two close explosions had sent down fresh showers of dirt he moved away so I had to try and do something myself. I got my legs free and found that though one leg of my trousers had been torn away and my greatcoat was in rags I was not badly injured. Then I saw a gleam of light through the laths of this supporting wall and managed to tear them away, making a hole big enough to crawl through. You can imagine my shock when I saw the debris on fire a few feet away. I scrambled down the debris and found myself in what had been a first floor corridor leading to a fire escape. There was a loose door blocking my way but I lifted this aside and found myself ten feet above a pile of debris on the ground. I dropped this short distance and managed to join a party of people making their way out at the back and I believe we got out through the garage.
>
> It seems a miracle judging from my own limited experience that there was not a more terrible casualty list. I was very much afraid that those two maids who were in the corridor near me must have been killed, they probably knew nothing about it.

Those two young women, Grace Guscott and Poppy Curwood, were both employed at the hotel, releasing men for the forces. Their bodies were never found.

Devonport was of course the prime target of the bombers. In the first 18 months of war, over 200 destroyers were repaired and refitted at the dockyard, and hundreds of women joined the yardies clocking on at the dockyard to keep the navy at sea. But at the end of their shift they could easily return home to find the street obliterated, salvaged items of furniture and pathetic piles of personal possessions clogging the thoroughfare. Even when the working day was done, food had to be queued for, washing done in mobile launderettes provided by the WRVS and any spare hours devoted to war work. There were winter woollies to knit for sailors, gardens to dig for victory, clothes to alter and mend, as Britain struggled alone as the Continental nations fell one by one under Hitler's heel. Even before the Americans joined the war in December 1941, Plymouth had been receiving parcels of clothes, blankets and hospital supplies from the USA through the Bundles for Britain scheme.

Men and women stood guard on buildings as fire watchers, watching while the Luftwaffe rained down incendiary bombs; they stepped into the uniforms of Air Raid Protection Wardens; they rescued victims from the rubble of their homes and volun-

ABOVE. *Underground the cartoons still survive which were drawn by boys using the air raid shelter at Sutton Road High School.*

OVERLEAF. *Devastation viewed from the roof of the Guildhall after the raids of 1941.*

teered as firefighters as the city burned with a glow which could be seen for miles. It was said that the intense fires of the burning city transformed night into day.

Searchlight beams raked the skies from all sides of the Sound, from Wembury Point and Mount Batten to Picklecombe and Penlee. From the rocks bordering Firestone Bay six huge searchlights scanned the skies tracking the Luftwaffe for the coastal artillery batteries at Drake's Island, Millbay, and vantage points on both sides of the navigation channel. In Central Park a battery of four anti-aircraft guns once stood on a spur looking south across the station, a prime target. Radar stations plotted friend and foe from vantage points at Wotter, inland, to Rame Head, Wembury, Staddiscombe and Western King on the seaward side. Watchers at observation points and pill-boxes scanned the coast to west and east, in case of attempted enemy landings, while the approaches by water were made hazardous by a boom across the Hamoaze blocking access to Devonport, and a minefield mid-channel to the east of Drake's Island.

Many of the teams who defended Plymouth and Devonport were reusing defences built over previous centuries. As a naval and military base, war and the fear of cross Channel invasion have come to Plymouth's door for centuries. The legacy is to be seen in the earthworks above ground and archaeological remains beneath the modern city. On 15 December 1942 a muffled explosion disturbed the commander in chief of Plymouth in his base at Admiralty House. Beneath the immaculate lawn in front of the Victorian mansion, sappers and pioneers were carving the nerve centre for the defence of the south-west. Into this vital communications hub, top secret messages from the boffins at Bletchley Park and Cheltenham were received; naval manoeuvres on and beneath the sea could be tracked; and troop movements by British and United States forces logged. Rows of WRENS perched before wall-mounted switchboards, connecting the likes of Winston Churchill and Bomber Harris with the admiral. In a glass-fronted eagle's nest accessed from the second floor, the admiral watched the progress of war in the plotting room below. Radar communications from airfields all over the south-west helped plot enemy activity on a giant wall map two storeys high. Balanced on wooden ladders before this map of Great Britain, men and women pinned and plotted German and Allied activity. To one side, wall racks held symbols to denote convoys, submarines and other shipping, another held details of forces in the air, another those on land. Cryptographers elsewhere in the nerve centre decoded messages. Personnel often worked long hours, sleeping between shifts in bunk beds below ground.

There was a sick bay, messes for all ranks, a dining hall and bathrooms; all were built to withstand a 500lb bomb. Water was stored in a 5,000-gallon tank and the whole complex was air conditioned and lit by 'daylight' bulbs. Ventilation tunnels helped to keep the air sweet, and all entrance tunnels were sharply bent to minimize the effects of bomb blast. The plotting room and surrounding buildings had been built into an existing deep dry ditch, part of the Lines dug to defend the Royal Dockyard in the eighteenth century.

On 18 May 1798 the Mayor of Plymouth published plans for the organisation of the civilian population of the city in the event of invasion. It was not the first time, nor would it be the last, that civilians would be called upon to participate in the defence of the fair port of the west. During the Civil War sieges, the population had helped the garrison by feeding and watering them, dressing their wounds and building the city walls. In 1798, when the mayor called on his fellow townsmen 'to act together with the fullest effect', the enemy was the French Revolutionary Army and invasion was anticipated. The notice would have been pinned to the door of the Guildhall and numerous other public places, as well as shouted on street corners by the Town Crier for those who could not read. It anticipated the 'plunder of this rich and fertile island' and called for 'diligence to provide against it'.

Volunteers with 'an intimate acquaintance of the district' were asked to form a Corps of Guides. Labourers and 'artificers' were asked to form the equivalent of a Pioneer Corps, presumably to build and repair defences. To service the growing number of soldiers flooding in to the area, a transport corps was needed to help move supplies and men, and volunteers who owned wagons, carts and draught horses were asked to register. Farmers were also asked to register, so that in the event of invasion their cattle could be driven 'out of the reach of the enemy' and, although it's not specified, presumably to feed the troops. Bakers and millers were asked to enrol so that they too could be called upon to feed the defending army. To run these various departments efficiently, businessmen were asked to offer their services.

Of course gentlemen of means could join the Independent Volunteer Corps with a splendid uniform of many colours. The jacket was scarlet with black velvet cuffs and the collar glittered with gold buttons. Beneath was a white waistcoat nicely setting off the blue pantaloons, which were edged with red as were the gaiters. The whole ensemble was topped with a round hat with white feather on top. In fact by 27 August 1807 *The Times* claimed that 'So ardent has been the spirit of volunteering in the garrison at Plymouth, that near 1200 rank and file have turned out for general service.'

CHAPTER 13

OBLITERATED
BARRACKS

Devonport's Brickfields Close is known to the locals as Raglan, a clue to the area's auspicious past: beneath it lie the remains of a massive Victorian barracks, built by a brilliant architect and inventor who designed the Victoria and Albert Museum and died during the early stages of construction of the Royal Albert Hall. Francis Fowke was a workaholic, whose enthusiasm for design and engineering led to his death from overwork at the age of only 42. One of his earliest achievements was Raglan Barracks in Devonport, hailed as a groundbreaking design which improved living conditions for the thousands of soldiers who passed through its imposing stone gates. The gatehouse and guardroom still stands, a lonely, unmarked memorial to a man of genius.

The concept of housing soldiers in permanent purpose-built accommodation is a relatively recent one, and the first recorded purpose-built barrack block in England is known to have stood in 1596 at Plymouth Fort. On early plans this is marked showing eight rooms, in two groups of four standing back to back, with a porch over the door and a corner fireplace in each room. The idea had crossed the Channel from the Continent where purpose-built barracks were used to house foreign armies in the Spanish Netherlands. This was prompted by antagonism from the locals and an attempt to maintain the health of troops abroad by providing them with decent living conditions. The first known use of the term 'barracks', which is derived from the French, as opposed to 'soldiers' lodgings', was used to refer to wooden-framed and weather-boarded buildings at the Tower of London in 1670. These had been put up to house Irish troops.

Traditionally armies had been billeted on the frequently unwilling local civilian population, and churches all over the country had been used by Commonwealth soldiers as stables and lodgings. But all was to change with the short reign of James II from 1685 to 1688. The Catholic King James was, rightly, uncertain of his popularity with his people and parliament, and built up a large standing army, linking the army inextricably with absolute

Scarred by graffiti, the imposing guardroom and gatehouse of Raglan Barracks.

monarchy. Following the Glorious Revolution of 1688, one of those pivotal moments in English history, when James II was deposed, parliament drew up the Mutiny Act to rein in the power of the army. Among other provisions, this made it illegal for soldiers to be billeted on civilians, and they could only be billeted in pubs and inns. It must have been a popular piece of legislation, because it had become the norm for soldiers to be given 'free quarter' throughout the seventeenth and eighteenth centuries. This was a system whereby the soldier did not pay for his board and lodging, instead handing the householder a receipt which enabled them to reclaim the costs from the Treasury. Whether by accident or illiteracy few were reimbursed.

As Plymouth Dock grew during the eighteenth century, so did the defences and the corresponding numbers of troops required for its security. Ships patrolled to seaward, but on the landward side the 'lines' were constructed isolating the dockyard town from its neighbours. The Board of Ordnance decided that the angled slopes of the glacis, or killing ground, were not enough to defend the vital naval resources. The defensive Devonport Lines already stretched 2,100 yards in an arc from Morice Town to Mount Wise, and Cornish miners were recruited to deepen the ditch in 1779. When work began on constructing a defensive wall 14 feet high, the good people of Dock went to their MP to complain that they felt boxed in and deprived of air. In the House of Commons on 5 February 1790 during the debate on

Boundary walls in York Street, Devonport, thought to be the only remnant of the cluster of barracks built there in the eighteenth century.

ordnance estimates, Captain McBride the Plymouth MP 'adverted to the extraordinary works which were going forward at Plymouth'. He likened it to the 'Wall of Jericho', which was depriving people of fresh air and cutting the residents off from the sea, and contended that it ought to be reduced to 10 feet. As a placatory measure the Duke of Richmond built Richmond Walk.

The remains of these defensive ditches and walls are still visible in Devonport Park, although the six barracks built behind the 'lines' to house the defenders are long gone.

Furthest south was George Barracks, approached from Pembroke Street facing across to Plymouth. This was a substantial stone-built edifice with bastions at the innermost corners designed to cover the field of fire. Marlborough Barracks lay furthest north looking across to Morice Town and Granby next door. These were less substantial buildings constructed with timber frames filled with 'brick nog', similar in appearance to half-timbered buildings constructed in the Tudor era. Covering the line of sight inland across to Stoke and Mill Lake was a trio with Frederick to the north and Cumberland to the south. Between the two was the most substantial, the stone-built Ligonier Barracks named after a field marshal who led a charmed life despite a long army career in which he served at nearly all the great Continental battles of his day. For eight years during a sparkling career, Jean Louis Ligonier was governor of Plymouth Garrison (1752–60) covering the period these new barracks were built. His French Huguenot family had arrived in England at the end of the seventeenth century when he was a young man. Ligonier served under the Duke of Marlborough at all the great battles of the War of the Spanish Succession and led something of a charmed existence on the battlefield, surviving 23 bullets at the Battle of Malplaquet in 1709. During the War of the Austrian Succession in the 1740s, he was knighted on the field of the Battle of Dettingen by George II, an historic occasion as that was the last time a king led his troops personally into battle. While leading a cavalry charge at the age of 67, Ligonier's horse was shot from under him, but he survived to retire to his Surrey home where he lived till the age of 90, reputedly surrounded by a harem of young women!

These mid eighteenth-century barracks were designed not only to house men but to be defended in the event of an attempt to capture the dockyard. There were three or four hundred men housed in each block according to capacity, with separate staircases for the officers and men. Upstairs soldiers slept in shared wooden bunk beds: 14 men to a room, which was 25 feet by 16 feet. Naturally officers were allocated more space and did not have to share a bed.

During the numerous invasion scares of the eighteenth century, increasing numbers of troops had to be quartered in Plymouth and inevitably discipline became a problem. The outbreak of the American Revolution in 1781 signalled the beginning of an era of revolution, and cataclysmic events across the water in France led army commanders to fear that their men would be infected with revolutionary ideas. Thomas Paine's shocking pamphlet *The Vindication of the Rights of Man*, published late in 1791, was the talk of the nation. In it Paine spoke out in support of the French Revolution, called for the monarchy to be overthrown and proposed universal male suffrage, ideas which were anathema to the ruling classes. Talk and drink were considered a potentially explosive mix in the pubs and inns where soldiers were billeted, usually in groups of three or four. So it was at this point that barrack-building for the troops began to be seen as a priority, and parliament gave George III the right to erect permanent barracks in 1792. A year later France and England were at war.

As one of the main departure points for this new round of Continental wars, Plymouth and its Dock were once again swarming with troops. Shepherd's woollen mill near Frankfort Place was converted to Frankfort

Part of the best preserved Napoleonic Barracks in the country, Maker Barracks in Cornwall.

This house in Acre Place was home to Francis Fowke during his posting to Devonport.

Barracks, a group of houses in Clowance Street, Dock were converted into Racket Court Barracks in 1794, and Mill Bay Barracks was built close to Mill Prison housing American and French prisoners of war. Maker Barracks across the water from Devil's Point is a surviving example built in the first decade of the nineteenth century.

Francis Fowke appears on the scene in Devonport in about 1850 and is listed in the census return of the following year as a lieutenant of the Corps of Royal Engineers living with his wife Louisa and two-year-old daughter at what was then known as St Jean d'Acre Place, now Acre Place.

The family had recently returned from a posting to Bermuda where Fowke had indulged in his favourite sport of sailing and shown his talent for innovation by inventing devices to improve the rigging of yachts. While on the island he had also designed a new barracks to house troops in this important colonial outpost. Barracks maintenance and construction had become part of the remit of the Royal Engineers in 1818, and during his training Fowke would have studied barrack design at a time when the health of the British army and its living conditions were a hot topic. When a man took the King's shilling it was certainly not to improve his standard of living. The military were housed in conditions which were deemed worse than their civilian counterparts condemned to the workhouse or prison. As a result, the life expectancy of soldiers stationed at home was half that of their civilian counterparts.

It was the commander in chief of the British troops in India, Major General Sir Charles Napier, who attacked military top brass with damning criticism of the squalid housing conditions endured by soldiers. It prompted a new form of barracks, importing the Indian idea of a veranda, and what Fowke designed for Devonport was an example of this 'pavilion' style, although the myth survives that Raglan Barracks had been intended for troops abroad and was only built in Devonport when it became surplus to requirements! In what today appears an obvious health precaution, the privies and cookhouse were housed in separate blocks, innovations laid down in Napier's guidelines for barrack design, and gone were the back-to-back rooms in earlier designs.

Just as modern housing was constructed on the site when the army no longer required it, so Raglan Barracks was built on the 11 acres covered by its eighteenth-century predecessors, Ligonier, Cumberland and Frederick Barracks. In its heyday the 4½-acre parade ground echoed with boots marching to the barks of a sergeant major; bristled with those theatrical moustaches so beloved of the Victorian army; and glittered as the sun twinkled on brass buttons polished to perfection. Alongside were the accommodation blocks built of yellow brick with long verandas running along the front. The barracks could accommodate two regiments of men, some 2,000 soldiers and 80 officers, en route for service in all parts of the Empire, and was lit by a thousand gas jets, an innovation designed by Fowke, which he was to use in

Raglan Barracks in its heyday, showing the vast parade ground.

his greatest memorial, The Victoria and Albert Museum.

This was the era when men from the Corps of the Royal Engineers designed and built all over the British Empire in their role as military engineers, but were responsible too for many of the great public buildings constructed in major British cities thanks to their civil role. They were the designers of hospitals and prisons, and many of the innovations to improve sanitation were carried out by them. It's estimated that half the trained professional engineering manpower in the country in the first half of the nineteenth century were Royal Engineers.

Francis Fowke's genius was soon recognised. In 1855 he was on the team which designed the British contribution to the Paris Exhibition and was soon talent-spotted by Prince Albert who commissioned him to design the Officer's Library at Aldershot Barracks and then the South Kensington Museum, which was renamed the V&A in 1899.

He also turned his talent for design to projects for the army, designing a new type of drawbridge, a collapsible pontoon bridge plus a military fire engine used by the army in the 1860s. He pre-dated both Whitworth and

Armstrong in adapting larger ammunition for the rifle commonly in use by the army at the time. On a more frivolous note he patented an improved umbrella and a design for a folding camera, which became known as the bellows camera.

While the men of the British Army were well-housed in Raglan Barracks while they waited to be shipped all over the Empire, their naval counterparts who would crew the troopships were less fortunate. While crews were paid off when their ships returned to port, there was no need for the navy to provide accommodation for their men on land. But as warships became increasingly sophisticated, the navy needed men with more specialised skills, and long-term service for naval ratings was introduced in 1853. At first these crewmen were housed in hulks when they were between ships, but this was not a healthy option. A seamen's barracks in Devonport was mooted first in 1864, but work did not begin until 15 years later when Hawkins and Boscawen barrack blocks were built close to the gates of Keyham Dockyard. They were used for some 80 years before demolition in the 1960s. Four large open dormitories ran the length of each block, each hung with 125 hammocks, and this gave a temporary home to men waiting for transfer between ships, or returning from leave.

CHAPTER 14

PRISONERS OF WAR

When our American cousins arrived in Plymouth in the third year of the Second World War they were greeted with flowers, kisses and open arms: Britain was no longer the last bastion of freedom against the armies of Germany and Japan, the mighty United States had joined the battle at last. But during the revolutionary war 150 years earlier the Americans came as prisoners not liberators.

Thanks to the campaigning Quaker prison reformer John Howard, we know something about the conditions in which prisoners of war were kept in Plymouth in the eighteenth century. On a visit to France in 1778 to check on the welfare of British prisoners of war, he heard complaints about the treatment of French POWs in England. On his return he started his inspection of prisons with those housing POWs. In his *Report on the Prisons of England* published in 1784, Howard reports that there were 392 French prisoners in Mill Prison on 3 February 1779. But he detected some favouritism toward the 298 fellow jailbirds from America. He wrote:

> The wards and courts in which they [the French] were confined, were not so spacious as those appropriated to the American

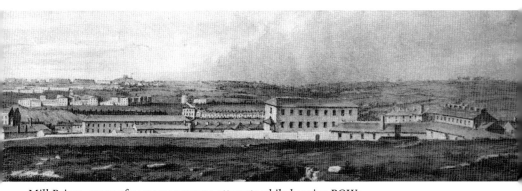

Mill Prison, scene of numerous escape attempts while housing POWs.

prisoners, nor were they so well accommodated with provisions. The hospital which had fifty patients in it was dirty and offensive.

Lying offshore was the prison ship *Cambridge*, which housed another 396 prisoners, but the following day Howard noted a further 250 were coming on board. Conditions on these disused warship hulks could well have prompted complaints, but it was the diet which Howard noted: 'The bread was heavy and the meat bad; and too little attention was paid to the sick.' This was not very different from the conditions on serving ships of the Royal Navy at the time, but the prisoners were soon allotted a hospital ship, the *Tiger*, as an infirmary.

Howard returned to Plymouth in the 1780s and his report gives a total of 10,352 prisoners of war from America, France, Spain and Holland, who had an unscheduled sojourn in gaol in Plymouth between 1777 and 1783. The majority of these, some 7,600, were French. Incredibly, of that 10,000 only 179 died.

On 28 August 1793 *The Times* reported a happy event among the ranks of the prison population in Plymouth:

A female in the clothes of a French midshipman was last week brought to bed of a fine boy in the Mill Prison at Plymouth. The sailor and her infant are well taken care of.

This unnamed French sailor was not the only woman known to have served in male disguise in the navies of the eighteenth century.

The immediate impact of these unwilling foreign guests was a heightened state of vigilance in the city. Escape attempts were not only a frightening figment of their host's imagination, but a reality. The details are scattered throughout the pages of contemporary newspapers. In November 1806 *The Times* carried this story of a thwarted Great Escape:

On Saturday night a daring escape attempt was made by the Spanish prisoners, in Mill Bay depot, Plymouth to effect their escape; twenty nine of them got into the Bog-house drain, from which they cut a subterranean passage under the prison wall, and were making their way through the hospital avenue, when they were detected by one of the turnkeys, and their escape prevented. This is the second attempt in the course of the week which has been frustrated by the vigilance of the turnkeys.

The wounded and sick cared for in the prison hospital were not averse to 'having a go', their ingenuity and stamina has to be admired. In July 1801 *The Times* reported:

> On Thursday evening a large hole was fortunately discovered at the foot of the north wall of the Mill Prison Hospital, Plymouth, by the mere accident of the stick umbrella of one of the officers of the prison giving way into apparently solid earth, as he was walking by. The masons were called, and on digging found a board propped up with the gravel of the walk upon it to deceive watch sentries; and beneath, at the foot of the walk, there was found an opening large enough for two men to get out a-breast. It was of course secured and stopped up directly, or perhaps in the course of the night, many might have escaped. Five escaped on Tuesday through the drain, but were soon secured by the vigilance of the guard.

There were stories of spies scouting out the naval dockyard and garrison defences. On one such occasion a foreign gentleman was deemed to be asking too many questions of his boatman, and made a hasty retreat to neighbouring Cornwall. On 7 September 1790 a 16-gun brig flying French colours sailed into The Sound. It was revealed that she had been mapping the coast and taking depth soundings.

Fears of invasion were real and rife throughout the Napoleonic Wars. Plymouth and its environs was an obvious point of entry, and in August 1779 a joint Spanish and French fleet of 88 ships loitered off Plymouth for four days. But the only French invasion force to land in mainland Britain was at Fishguard where it was routed by fishermen. France's bloody and earth-shattering revolution in 1789 had not been without its sympathisers in England. And there were still some who hankered after a Jacobite king on the throne of England, long after the defeat of Prince Charles James Stuart at Culloden field in 1746. These were all potential suspects when the rope-house at the dockyard was razed to the ground in a spectacular fire in 1812. *The Times* does not specify a source but the implication of this story, which appeared on 18 June, is that arson was suspected:

> The investigation of the cause of the late fire in Plymouth Dockyard still continues. A person who was in Dock, a few days previous to the fire, and left on the morning for Torpoint, and from thense [sic] took a chaise towards Falmouth is said to have been pursued.

It is well known that to combat boredom POWs carved and whittled objects from bone to sell via their gaolers. A little money could lighten the burden of prison life, providing extra food and comforts. Some POWs, allegedly the French, were even more ingenious. When a spate of forged currency began to appear in Plymouth in 1809, the blame was laid on the citizen soldiers of Napoleon's army. POWs used the materials to hand, paper made from rags for banknotes, and beaten sections of drainpipe for coins. But warning readers to be on the look out, local newspapers revealed the coins 'will not stand the test of "tinging"'. Another clue was that the fake one shilling pieces were all dated 1804 and slightly larger, paler and much lighter than the real thing. Forged Bank of England one pound notes, the press revealed, were rough, spongy and of coarse texture. There's no doubt that these French forgers were skilled. In December 1809, some French prisoners in Dartmoor turned their hand to forging notes produced by the Plymouth Dock Bank. The counterfeit signature of Mr Marshall, one of the bank's proprietors, was so convincing that when it was presented even *he* thought it was authentic!

By May 1801 Mill Prison was at capacity, and 3,000 POWs were marched 'up country' to staunch potential rebellion. At times of heightened invasion panic, they were marched off to the interior so that they could not form a fifth column. Ten years later the heavily fortified Channel Isles, close to the French coast, were threatened by invasion. This would have given the French a major toehold in the Channel and at the entrance to the Atlantic, so the British government decided to reduce the number of prisoners near the two principal naval stations and arsenals at Plymouth and Portsmouth. From their incarceration in the benign climate of the south-west, the POWs were taken by sea to Scotland. By 1809 the British had taken so many French POWs that cartels were set up in Plymouth to exchange the sick and elderly.

A paradox of war is the honour with which combatants have been treated, no longer faceless enemies but fellow men. One example of this is the funeral of Captain William Henry Allen, an American prisoner of war who died on 18 August 1812. Captain Allen had commanded the United States sloop *Argus* in a fierce battle in St Georges Channel with the British sloop *Pelican*. Captain Allen lost his left leg and died in Mill Prison Hospital three days later.

At noon on Saturday 21 August the lengthy funeral procession left Mill Prison for the burial at St Andrew's Church. The cortège was led by a guard of honour, two companies of the Royal Marines, and marched to the mournful notes of the Dead March from Handel's *Saul* played by the Royal Marines

Band. Captain Allen's coffin was covered with velvet, draped with the American ensign, topped by his sword and hat. The pallbearers were eight captains of the Royal Navy, a mark of respect to a worthy opponent. The officers and crew from the *Argus* processed through the streets in company with all Royal Naval captains in port. Officers from the Royal Marines and the British Army marched two by two, and as the procession wove through the streets of Plymouth, it was joined by what *The Times* described as 'a very numerous and respectable retinue of inhabitants'. After a service in the city's mother church, Captain Allen was buried in the south churchyard to the right of his fellow officer Midshipman Delphy from the *Argus*, who had lost both legs in the battle and been buried the previous evening.

Prisoners of war played a key role in the reconstruction of modern Plymouth. In May 1945, days after the German surrender, the chairman of Plymouth City Council's Housing Committee made a bold suggestion. Some of the thousands of German prisoners of war should be employed as labourers to build new estates for those who had been bombed out. Councillor G.P. Holmes was shouted down for his preposterous suggestion. But as the shortage of labour slowed down building work, several hundred German prisoners of war were taken on nevertheless. German and Austrian demolition gangs demolished air raid shelters recycling the rubble as hardcore on land they had levelled for bungalows in Central Park, Ernesettle, Efford, Ham, Manadon and St Budeaux.

Memorial plaque to the US prisoners of war taken in 1812.

CHAPTER 15

PALMERSTON'S PARANOIA

The principal players include asylum seekers, a mourning monarch and a playboy politician with a penchant for gunboats. The plot includes a night at the opera, a bomb-making factory in Birmingham and a Swiss restaurant. The result would be a building scheme on a scale to be rivalled only by post-war reconstruction.

On 2 December 1851, Louis Napoleon Bonaparte, former asylum seeker and nephew of that bogeyman Boney, declared himself Emperor Napoleon III. The spectre of another Emperor Napoleon on the other side of the English Channel created an invasion scare on a par with those triggered by

Officers' quarters at Fort Agaton, with decorative detail round the arches.

Gun casemate at Fort Agaton. From here artillery fire would defend the city from an attack to the north.

his more notorious namesake. And it sparked the first phase of a building scheme which has left landmarks all over Plymouth.

After France's initial flirtation with Republicanism in 1789, England had played host to many asylum seekers, among them two men who would return home and take the throne. Louis Philippe, Duke of Orleans, who had been a proponent of the revolution, fled France in 1793 disenchanted with the revolutionaries after the execution of Louis XVI. Eventually he found refuge in England where he spent the next 15 years, only returning to France after the

Battle of Waterloo. He came to the throne in 1830, revealing his empathy with the people by styling himself King of the French, rather than King of France, a subtle distinction. As this new Bourbon king was installed, so another contender for the French throne crossed the Channel to seek asylum in England. This latest refugee was Louis Napoleon Bonaparte the nephew of Boney himself, but he managed to endear himself to the British people by volunteering as a special constable during the Chartist risings.

In 1848, fed up with a government which they regarded as increasingly monarchist, the French revolted once again and reverted back to Republicanism. Napoleon's namesake was elected president of a new French Republic. Those who had met Louis Napoleon Bonaparte during his exile in England saw this as a positive event in Anglo-French relations. But there were others who remembered he had sworn to avenge the French defeat at the Battle of Waterloo. Just as invasion panic had been triggered by his uncle, so the advent of a new Napoleon set the wheels of paranoia pirouetting. Anglo-French relations seesawed between suspicion and friendship, not helped by Napoleon's declaration in December 1851 that he was henceforth to

Highly polished cannonballs stacked ready for action in the event of invasion.

be known as *Emperor* Napoleon III. It was an echo from half a century earlier.

A month afterwards, on 17 January 1852 *The Times* declared, 'We have now a dangerous and faithless neighbour'. In June the government passed new legislation to recruit volunteers for the militia, but it was the arrival of Lord Palmerston as the new Home Secretary later that year that would have a lasting impact on the coast at Plymouth. Palmerston was famous for being a bit of a playboy and for what was nicknamed 'gunboat diplomacy'. It was a simple, inexpensive method of putting the frighteners on potential enemies when they had irritated the British. A show of naval potential was made at sea, rather than sending troops overland, and it usually had the desired effect.

Long before he was in a position to influence national defences, Palmerston rather like Churchill in the 1930s, warned that the nation should be armed against the enemy on the doorstep, the enemy which had meant the slaughter of thousands of Englishmen for centuries – France. New technology in the form of the steamship had 'reduced the English Channel to a river', he warned in 1851.

> Neither England nor any other first rate power ever stood in such a condition of comparative military weakness as that in which the United Kingdom (to say nothing of our foreign possessions) is now placed. There is close to our shores a nation of 34 million people, the leading portion of which it cannot be denied, is animated with a feeling of deep hatred to England as a power . . . we ought to be on an equal footing, if not in our means of attack, at least in our means of defence; but this is not our condition.

Palmerston's pragmatic assertion was that 'Nations have no permanent friends or allies they only have permanent interests'. To protect those 'interests', Palmerston lobbied for the fortification of the main naval bases and in 1853 work began on strengthening the Devonport Lines. It would take another ten years to complete.

A year later the tiff was forgotten. France and England were bosom pals formally joined by an alliance. They may not have been reading from the same hymn sheet but they were united in opposition to another imperial power, Russia, and were fighting as allies in the Crimean War. Now that Napoleon was officially an ally, he and Queen Victoria exchanged state visits. When Napoleon allowed British troops to march across France to speed up

the motherland's response to the Indian Mutiny in 1857, the relationship began to appear cosy.

But events would intervene in the form of Italian émigré Felice Orsini. On 14 January 1858, Napoleon and his consort were in their carriage on their way to a night at the opera when Orsini threw several home-made bombs at them. Although the royal couple survived, 8 bystanders were killed and 156 wounded. As the newspapers reported the ensuing manhunt, it turned out that the plotters were Italian and French refugees who had found political asylum in England, among them Orsini himself. Other revelations followed: the bombs had been manufactured in Birmingham and smuggled via a series of couriers, some of whom were English, via a Swiss restaurant in London to the plotters in Paris. The final revelation was that even the explosives had been English-made.

Within days jingoistic French officers from four regiments stationed across the Channel announced they would happily invade Britain, and these war cries were published in the French press. Rumours flew. The *entente cordiale* was close to breaking point

In April 1858, the *Plymouth Chronicle and Cornish Advertiser* summed up the mood among its readers:

> Had Napoleon III fallen by his [the assassin's] hand, would not France, blinded with wrath for the death of her Emperor, have bitterly charged England with nourishing and sending forth the assassin. . . . Has not the outburst of feeling in the French army and people, produced by the attempt of 14th January, proved the reality of the danger we foresaw in 1855.

The paper continued in an outpouring of bile against asylum seekers:

> Let Napoleon III perish by the hand of one of these foreign desper-adoes whom we shelter, and to whom it is undeniable, we have of late been permitting a license forbidden to our own subjects, and the Anglo-French alliance would be sundered in a moment.

This Devon leader writer also expressed fear of the new imperial power seen to be threatening European peace – the Russian bear – the campaign in the Crimea which had killed so many Englishmen, was recent history.

OPPOSITE. *HMS Warrior, Britain's first ironclad, while undergoing restoration.*

Mr Disraeli has justly styled the Anglo-French alliance 'the keystone of modern civilisation'. Without it Europe would be Russianised and our own liberties placed in danger.

But it was the effects of yet another war on the English pocket, which must have struck a chord most with the provincial readers of the *Plymouth Chronicle*:

> Within five short years three wars have come upon the British Empire, two of them of a magnitude never but once before encountered in our history. A hundred millions of added debt and taxation have been thereby imposed upon this country, and probably about 30 millions on the government of India.
>
> And besides all this, within the last six months a terrible commercial crisis – the most disastrous on record – has swept over the United Kingdom, prostrating trade, ruining thousands, and throwing myriads of the working classes out of employment.

The guardhouse at Fort Austin, Forder completed about 1868.

Panic in the press was soon allayed by former asylum seeker Napoleon III and the man who was by now Prime Minister, Lord Palmerston. The Emperor apologised via the British Ambassador for the jingoism of his French officers, while Palmerston tried to bring in a bill to increase the penalty for conspiring to murder a person abroad. The idea of kow-towing to the French, even to prevent foreign refugees from plotting murder, was too much for British parliamentarians and the bill was thrown out. This was swiftly followed by Palmerston himself, who was forced to resign as Prime Minister. A new administration took over and was able to cement these peaceful overtures. The foundations would last only a few months before cracks appeared once again.

To help rebuild relations, a second state visit by Queen Victoria and Prince Albert was organised for August 1858. Part of the trip was a tour round the newly fortified port of Cherbourg and an inspection of the pride of the French navy. Instead of cementing the relationship, the mortar truly began to crumble. What alarmed the royal party, and Prince Albert in particular, was the marked superiority to the British navy. The prince had been impressed too by the new fortifications at Cherbourg. Martello towers had been thrown up along the south coast of England during the Napoleonic invasion scares, but by the middle of the century they had been allowed to decay. Bricks and mortar, the Prince asserted, were essential to the defence of Britain. Palmerston agreed and persuaded a sceptical Prime Minister William Gladstone to acquiesce. Plymouth needed a protective wall of forts to ring its dockyard and naval arsenal in the event of attack by land.

The Queen, doubtless prompted by her adored husband, wrote to her Prime Minister expressing her concern that the British navy did not match up to the superior French fleet.

Even during periods when the British had had a smaller fleet than the French, it was British seamanship, discipline and tactics which had enabled us to retain superiority. But new technology was about to change the face of shipping forever. Three French armour-plated ships which had been in use in the Crimea had been regarded with derision by some British naval commanders, who nicknamed them 'floating batteries'. But by 1859 the French had 10 new ironclad warships on the production line and 34 large frigates. By comparison the British had only 26 frigates and 6 ironclad ships in production. An arms race was in progress, and the first British 'ironclad', the *Warrior*, was not in service until 1863.

Britain had felt secure in the knowledge that the navy was her main defence in the event of attack. French progress with their new ironclad fleet

Secure behind a chain link fence, Ernesettle Battery showing the drawbridge across the deep defensive moat.

ruffled this security. The demands of the vast British Empire was stretching naval resources. Trade was protected by the navy; pirates and slave traders were pursued by the navy; unexplored oceans and coastlines were plotted on charts by the navy. In 1861, for example, there were over 60 warships stationed off China and the East Indies with another 23 off North America and the West Indies. British warships patrolled off Australia, South America and Africa. In parliament, MPs questioned the wisdom of relying on defences at sea when naval establishments were vulnerable to attack overland.

When Prince Albert died in 1861, Victoria retired to Osborne House on the Isle of Wight in mourning for her beloved Consort. Her presence on this small island off the south coast, not far from the naval base at Spithead, was a security risk in the event of French attack. Prince Albert's dismay at the French defences and navy; his support for a scheme of south coast forts; coupled with the Queen's geographical presence off that coast decided the matter.

Palmerston's Plymouth forts extended in a defensive girdle round the city. Land prices coupled with building costs left the government with little change from three million pounds. Military architecture in Europe had remained little changed since medieval times. Bastions projected from castle walls to give a better line of fire, but the Plymouth forts of the mid nineteenth century were polygonal in shape, intended to dominate the ground between with artillery fire. Plymouth's Breakwater Fort, however, was constructed from iron, with a roadway across the breakwater of Portland stone. Remnants of the inland defensive circle can still be identified, for example Knowle Battery at Ernesettle, which was completed in 1869. On the former parade ground is the new primary school.

In addition to the fortifications themselves, there was the ordnance to defend them. Nothing was allowed to stand in the way. The limestone headland at Mount Batten was excavated to improve the firing line from Fort Stamford in 1863, and revealed an Iron Age cemetery.

In November 1864, a brilliant Russian military engineer was invited to inspect the forts at Plymouth to report on their efficacy. Franz Eduard Ivanovitch Todleben had been in command of the Russian defence of Sevastopol during the Crimean War. For a year the city, which was a fortress naval base on the Black Sea, had withstood French and British bombardment. On the whole he approved, although he felt some of the glacis, or so-called 'killing grounds' were a little too steep.

It's easy to forget what an age of innovation and change the Victorian era was, so that by the time Palmerston's forts were completed they were already out of date and the range of modern artillery had increased. The British navy would soon outbuild their erstwhile rivals, but some of the forts would remain part of coastal defences. Coastal artillery existed until 1956, and Crownhill Fort was in use until the end of the Falklands War.

CHAPTER 16

THE *PLUCKY* TRAGEDY

Plymouth's fishing fleet frequently had to run the gauntlet of Royal naval gunboats and artillery fire on the way to their fishing grounds. Passengers on steam packets, ferries and pleasure boats too, were forced to duck as shots whistled over their heads. Masts and sails on the fleet of 'hookers', which fished with hook and line until the advent of trawl nets, were frequently damaged. Fishermen had called public meetings and enlisted the support of MPs, but it took the death of a Turnchapel fisherman, a national inquiry and a court martial to make their lives safer.

The thirtieth of October 1891 was a clear day, with a strong wind blowing in from the east as the Plymouth hookers sailed out to sea. The Eddystone lighthouse was clearly visible, as were the houses at Cawsand and another fleet fishing in Whitsand Bay. Some three or four miles outside the breakwater, the little two-man boats cast anchor and got their gear out. As they waited for the fish to bite, they were not even aware of the gunboat steaming out from the naval base for target practice. Henry Harcom and his brother had cast anchor in about 20 fathoms, when suddenly two or three shots hit the water a hundred yards west of their boat the *Sunbeam*. But local fishermen were accustomed to shots whizzing overhead during target practice. When John Harcom commented that one day they would be in danger, back came the riposte from Henry that if the gunboat continued to fire so close they would be in danger today. But as the subsequent naval inquiry was told, the fish lie close to the land at that time of year and fishermen had to run the gauntlet of gunboats 'to earn a shilling'. At other times of year they fished off the Eddystone, where there was no danger.

Another of the fleet of 30 fishing boats raised her sail in a bid to alert Lieutenant Freemantle, captain of the gunboat *Plucky*. Freemantle was in charge of a batch of gunners firing breech-loaders, who were almost at the end of their training.

As the *Plucky* shifted her position slightly to the west, the first shot struck the Harcom brothers boat, the *Sunbeam*, right amidships, tearing a hole through the boat, right below John Harcom's feet. Immediately she began to sink. She was going down so fast that John did not have time to pull off his sea boots. Fortunately both men could swim; they clung to spars from the wreck, frantically waving their oilskins as they struggled in the water. As two other fishing boats came to their rescue, shots were landing around them. One of the rescue boats sailed in close to the gunboat's cutter, told the crew what had happened and they hoisted a red flag. But the *Plucky* continued firing.

The second fishing boat to be hit was the *Alfonso*, which was anchored to the east of the fishing ground about three miles from the Breakwater. As they saw the *Sunbeam* go down, Francis Harris and shipmate George Hisbent hoisted their mainsail to alert the *Plucky* to their presence. A shot whistled towards them, hitting the port rigging, and both men leapt into the water, grabbing a spar for buoyancy. Within minutes, 50-year-old George had lost his grip and drowned, leaving a wife Ellen, a daughter and three young sons. Thirteen years earlier George had been in another fishing boat which was hit during target practice, but on that occasion had escaped with broken ribs.

The tragedy made national news. *The Times* leapt on to the side of the Plymouth fishermen, thundering in its leader three days after the accident:

Fishing boats moored at the Barbican in the late nineteenth century.

There is plenty of room in the sea, and practice in the immediate neighbourhood of Plymouth breakwater and of a favourite fishing ground does seem to be an unnecessary abridgement of the right of HER MAJESTY's subjects to go about their lawful business.

An inquiry was held at the Naval Barracks at Keyham, at which the crew of the *Plucky* said they had spotted the masts of fishing boats but believed the line of fire was clear. A naval commander who had been out on steam trials on the same day, but was not aware of the accident, described how deceptive the visibility was. He had stationed a lookout but was unaware of a small boat riding at anchor until she suddenly appeared in his line of sight.

The Lieutenant in command of the *Plucky*, was court-martialled for negligence, despite being the son of a vice admiral.

All views were represented on the government committee of inquiry which convened in February 1892, and came down to take evidence in Plymouth in April. The eight-man committee prefaced their report by reinforcing that the need for national security required that:

> Opportunities should be afforded to the Royal Navy for carrying on target practice from ships in the neighbourhood of the great naval arsenal, and that artillery practice seawards should be carried on 'under service conditions' from important forts and batteries on the coast.
>
> The committee find that the cases in which injury to life or damage to ships, boats, and fishing gear has been occasioned during target practice bear a very small proportion indeed to the number of rounds fired.

It went on to say that people out at sea, may have supposed themselves in more danger than they actually were, by misjudging the effect or direction of a shot striking the water, although they also admitted that fishermen's operations 'sometimes have been interfered with'. Inevitably the needs of the British forces had to take priority, as the committee made clear.

> Very serious inconvenience is often occasioned to bodies of men engaged in firing from forts, by boats and small vessels, becalmed or at anchor, remaining in the line of fire for long periods of time, notwithstanding the remonstrances of the military authorities. The men employed in target practice have generally to be brought to the

forts from barracks at a distance, and they become worn out and disheartened by long delay, while rapidity of fire, which is an important element of their practice, is rendered impossible. The circumstance that many of the largest and best equipped forts are in the immediate neighbourhood of great seaports and important fishing centres, such as Plymouth, increases the difficulty, because in such localities the craft are numerous and the opportunities of finding a clear range proportionately few.

So the fishermen's safety was considered a sacrifice on the altar of war. An attempt to reach an agreement limiting target practice within defined hours failed. But the committee did make recommendations to improve safety and restrict firing as a result. Maps of the fishing grounds and their seasons were to be given to the military, and tugs would be used to prevent boats anchoring near target areas. Notices of the times and dates of target practice would be posted in public places, and a special signal given before firing commenced. Faster gunboats would be used so that they could travel beyond the inshore fishing grounds for target practice, and the amount of practice would be reduced. And in a move for better public relations special forms were to be made available so that fishermen could register complaints.

The widowed Mrs Hisbent was awarded £600 compensation by the Admiralty.

CHAPTER 17

THE KEY TO THE WEST

During four long years the people of Plymouth patrolled the walls and ramparts of the town, listening and watching for the thunder of cavalry hooves. Besieged on all sides, the town's Puritan inhabitants reputedly came close to starvation, until a shoal of pilchards was spotted ruffling the waters of Sutton Harbour. Royalist forces had even cut the water supply running through Drake's Leat in an attempt to force a surrender. But the men and women of Plymouth had taken an oath to resist the troops of the king, even if their city was razed to the ground. Their stubborn resistance to an army that was twice the size of the entire population was the key to the Civil War in the West of England.

For decades after the events of 1642–46, bells rang out to commemorate the Battle of Freedom Fields, a key defence of the city in the face of treachery. Today only the archaeologists know the position of the ramparts built to defend Plymouth and the remains of the town wall built at public expense. Even the city gates which stood along these defensive walls are lost, demolished in the face of progress.

The battles of the English Civil War were the last to be fought on English soil, and while no war is glorious to the modern mind, this was a war like no other. Like the Balkans conflict of the 1990s, it pitted neighbour against neighbour. But unlike the Balkans, the English Civil War also put members of the same family on opposing sides. Far easier to slaughter an enemy who speaks a different language, and whose customs and background are alien. It must have been almost impossible to remain neutral in the Civil War, for this was about the abuse of public money and fundamental beliefs.

Plymouth's intensely Protestant stance had largely come about because of its importance as a port of embarkation. When Charles I despatched various naval expeditions from Plymouth to harass the French and Spanish, the ships and survivors limped back to The Sound. Remnants of the army and navy were forced to rely on the charity and good nature of the locals who had been ordered to look after them, largely out of their own pockets. Among the returning army were the sick and wounded, and as Plymothians know only too well over centuries as a garrison town, the violent.

King Charles was not renowned for paying his debts, in fact he was noted for profligacy and constantly fell out with parliament when it refused to grant the cash he required. The King took advantage of the town's good nature, and the flame of resentment was lit. Fuel was added to feed these flames when Charles prevented two noted Puritans from speaking at the invitation of the local corporation.

In the summer of 1642, national events came to a head, and the English Civil War began with a skirmish outside Worcester. As towns and districts began to declare themselves for either King or Parliament, neighbouring Cornwall massed thousands of men in the name of Charles.

Plymouth's largely Puritan town council decided to act. When Sir Jacob Astley, commander of the Royalist garrison on St Nicholas Island, was summoned to the royal standard in the north, the city declared for the Roundheads. An army of citizens grabbed the resources of the garrison, plus Sir Jacob Astley's wall hangings and curtains, which were reputedly

The Sound, venue for war games, pleasure seekers and fishermen.

remodelled as waistcoats for soldiers! On 11 October 1642, the council raised a tax from the townspeople, to pay for fortifications for the anticipated siege, and by 29 November, the Cornish Royalist army was at Buckland and the first siege had begun. After three fruitless weeks the Royalists trooped back over the Tamar, giving the people of Plymouth a breather.

The defences, which had started as hastily constructed earth banks, were built up over Christmas and into the new year of 1643. Local legend has it that they were dug not by teams of labourers but by the women and children of the city. Certainly there would have been no place for slackers in this bastion of opposition. The defenders received a numerical and psychological boost on 15 January, when 800 foot soldiers and six troops of horse arrived under the command of the Earl of Stamford. A week later the Royalists were besieging the city again, this time digging trenches and other earthworks near Widey House, a country house to the north of the city.

As the Cornish Royalists dug in for yet another siege they tried to prevent food coming into Plymouth from the surrounding countryside. But most of Plymouth's provisions were slipped into the city via Sutton Pool, as the Channel was controlled by Parliament's navy. Royalist guns pounded away from vantage points such as Mount Edgcumbe but without much success.

When Roundhead reinforcements from North Devon arrived and attacked the Royalist army at Modbury, simultaneously the Plymouth garrison mounted a charge from their fortified town. The second siege was over and the Royalists retreated to Cornwall. Skirmishes continued, but the fate of Plymouth changed when the Parliamentary army in the west suffered a massive defeat. Plymouth was utterly isolated. Instead of caving in and surrendering under this pressure, the town council decided to reinforce the city's defences. Starting at what remained of the medieval town wall, a stone wall of limestone and shale a metre thick was built to encircle the city. Archaeological evidence unearthed when Friary Goods Yard was excavated in 1989 revealed the solid lower levels of this wall, which took less than a year to build. With a ditch in front to provide additional height, the wall had regular forts at strategic points. Ordnance survey maps from the nineteenth century reveal the remains of these walls still in place.

While the citizens of Plymouth worked on their defences during the spring and summer of 1643, the Royalists were crushing opposition all around them. Dartmouth, another bastion of Parliament, was stubbornly holding out under siege, unwittingly giving Plymouth the time needed to complete the city wall. Finally the army that was supposed to crush the insolent citizens of

Part of Fort Resolution, a lonely relic of the long siege of the Civil War.

Plymouth arrived, under the leadership of Prince Maurice, brother of the legendary, dashing cavalry leader Prince Rupert.

As they assessed the port's defences, Royalist commanders decided that the most vulnerable point was an earthworks fort at Mount Stamford, which was helping to protect the vital shipping lane. What followed was a brutal battle and the Royalist cavalry was victorious. Still the walls of Plymouth itself were not breached. As the 10,000-strong Royalist army lay to the north of Plymouth, they received information from a couple of traitors who escaped from the city.

In the pre-dawn gloom of Sunday 3 December 1643, 400 Royalist infantrymen waded across Lipson Creek. Perhaps they hoped that on a Sunday the religious Puritan defenders of Plymouth would be less vigilant, and taking time off to go to church. The Plymouth traitors showed the troops a gap in the outer defences and with the element of surprise on their side they attacked the guard at Laira Point. As the Roundheads counter-attacked, the Cavaliers appeared on the high ground to the north of the city. But the Parliamentary soldiers stood their ground on Lipson Hill. As the morning wore on, despite the odds against them, the Plymouth garrison routed the Royalists in what became known as the Battle of Freedom Fields, which is commemorated on a monument in Freedom Park, the site of the battle. Retreating cavaliers and foot soldiers floundered in the mud as the rising tide cut off their retreat across the creek. Some drowned; many were killed or captured. It was a victory for the city to be proud of.

But there was little respite. Despite his losses Prince Maurice, based at Widey House out at Egg Buckland, gave orders to pound the city with cannon fire by day, while constructing trenches and earthworks close to the Roundhead's outer defences by night. Soon they had built an earth fort slap bang between two of the opposition's outer defences, effectively breaching the line. On the shortest day of the year, the Roundhead cavalry galloped out accompanied by foot soldiers. Twice they were repulsed, but on the third attempt they captured the new earthworks, in the process killing 100 cavaliers. Among the prisoners was Prince Maurice's personal trumpeter. This time the Royalist leaders were forced to withdraw with an army which was becoming mutinous. On Christmas Day 1643, the tired defenders of Plymouth watched as the enemy retreated to Plympton, taking with them the district's cattle. But, so the story goes, the providence of the sea intervened as a glittering shoal of pilchards arrived, scooped up in baskets by the delighted and hungry people.

Buoyed up by this unexpected Christmas present, the besieged began again to repair and restore the outer defences, until eventually a continuous three-mile line of outer earthworks stood against future attack. Prince Maurice had marched the bulk of his troops off to Dorset, and a skeleton Royalist force deterred by the growing fortifications continued to skirmish with the Roundheads throughout the spring and summer of 1644.

In July a huge Roundhead army, under the command of the Earl of Essex, marched through the West Country to tackle the remaining Royalists in Cornwall. Plymouth seemed, for the moment, secure and 2,500 men from the garrison joined them. But it was an ill-judged expedition, which was soundly defeated, many of the former defenders of Plymouth surrendered, while the surviving cavalry galloped back with the news. Once again the town prepared for siege.

Mount Batten Tower is a survivor of the defences built in preparation for this, the fourth siege. Its name is believed to stem from Captain William Batten who took 300 sailors over to Hoo Stert, where they built a tower in September 1644. It was in the nick of time, as the Royalist army was soon back, this time with the King himself at its head. By this time the tired people of Plymouth must have believed the end was nigh. Across the Tamar were the Cornish Royalists; at the outer defences was the King. Rebellious Plymouth again launched into a determined defence, and the walls were held. With 15,000 men at his command the King reasoned that the Plymouth Garrison would be overawed by the huge force massed against them. From his base at Widey House, Charles I demanded a surrender. But proud Plymouth declared the King would have to launch a full-scale assault on the city; there would be no surrender. Throughout history, besieging armies have found it notoriously difficult to capture a city. Usually the inhabitants were starved into submission, but with the Parliamentary navy to provision the city, Plymouth was confident enough to stand firm. Aware of the enormous casualties likely to be inflicted on his army, the King withdrew in the early hours of 14 September 1644.

Plymothians were able to draw breath, but were not able to relax. A small Royalist army led by Sir Richard Grenville had been left behind to blockade supplies from the surrounding countryside. Grenville had huge influence in neighbouring Cornwall, and had begun the Civil War on the side of Parliament, but defected with vital plans of battle in March 1644. Plymouth was now ringed by forts from the Blockhouse at Devils Point, to fortifications at Stonehouse, Pennycomequick, Lipson, Mount Gould, Prince Rock, Cattedown, Mount Batten and St Nicholas Island. Grenville took up position on Beacon Hill where his men built a fort and gradually amassed more troops including four new Cornish regiments. On 9 January 1645 the Royalist army launched itself at Plymouth once again. With munitions still coming in via the navy, Plymouth countered with a hail of fire launched at the advancing troops. Casualties were terrible, and in their wake the Roundhead cavalry charged once again from the city's gates, securing Plymouth for another month.

Grenville then decided to establish a position back on Mount Stamford, but Roundhead troops ferried across from the city to their own outpost at Mount Batten launched a counter attack. This infantry attack was reinforced by a bombardment from the navy in the Sound, and Grenville's troops were forced to retreat. Sir Richard Grenville was a ruthless and able commander, and no doubt was about to come up with some new strategy to take Plymouth, when he was ordered to march to Somerset where his men were needed. It was the turning point, and the fifth and last Civil War siege of Plymouth was over.

The skeleton Royalist force left behind continued the blockade, but the tide was turning against the King's cause. Of course Plymothians had no foresight of the outcome of the war, so work continued to strengthen fortress Plymouth. Palisades strengthened the outer defences and stabling was built nearby for the horses of the cavalry. Raids into the countryside round the city left the Royalist forces short of provisions, and gradually that autumn the defenders went on the offensive capturing and destroying Royalist strongholds. As the New Model Army advanced from the east, panicked cavaliers escaping to the Royalist stronghold of Cornwall began to flood into the county. But the key Royalist city of Exeter had to be taken before Plymouth could be relieved. Finally in January 1646, the Roundhead army marched west for Plymouth, and on 12 January the remaining Royalists ran.

A vastly depleted population settled down to the Commonwealth era. During successive sieges the death rate had soared from an average of less than 300 a year to 3,000 over three years. Churchgoers in the city had been campaigning to be allowed a new church, a right granted by the King in the run up to the war. By 1643, Charles Church looked very much as it does today, with stonework completed as far as the roofline, but the preacher was a Presbyterian.

The sting in the tail came with the Restoration of Charles II. There was no Truth and Reconciliation Commission, the Town Council and the pulpits were purged, and the new Royalist regime took revenge on its enemies by imprisoning them on St Nicholas Island.

CHAPTER 18

SINNERS AND CINDERS

It is a powerful irony that in its heyday as a seafaring port Plymouth was renowned as a city of women when history has seen them treated so harshly. So many men were at sea that travellers commented on the preponderance of women in the population: it was the women who brought up large families in slum dwellings; it was the women who struggled to feed and clothe their offspring; and it was the women who were forced to take up prostitution in the absence of any other income. Men who went to sea were not paid their wages in advance of the voyage, but were paid off on their return. There was some logic in this method, after all it ensured that wages were not drunk or stolen during a voyage of many months or even years. It also helped to ensure that men would not jump ship at some glamorous foreign port, leaving a vessel understaffed for the remainder of the voyage. But it also left any family in the home port without an income, although in the mid eighteenth century, Admiral Anson did allow naval seamen to apportion part of their wages in advance to their families. Unlike civilians, soldiers and marines were not even legally *obliged* to provide for their wives and offspring, and the government was unwilling to alter this in case it might affect enlistment. (This was changed in 1877.) As a port with dual importance to the navy and the army, this had a dreadful impact on the lives of women in the Three Towns.

In 1864 the British Parliament passed the first of three laws that demonised the women of Plymouth and Devonport: the Contagious Diseases Acts. Like the notorious 'Sus' law of the 1980s, police could arrest any woman *suspected* of being a prostitute, and subject her to an intimate examination by a male surgeon. Any woman found on the streets after dark, and in winter that could be at 4 o'clock in the afternoon, was a potential suspect. The doctors were looking for symptoms of venereal disease, and this crackdown on the oldest profession in the world was an attempt to improve the health of the men of Her Majesty's armed forces.

It was after the Crimean War that the VD epidemic raging in the British

Army was highlighted. It is a war remembered today for the infamous Charge of the Light Brigade and the ministrations of Florence Nightingale and Mary Seacole. As well as these early enlightened attempts at decent hospital care, the war also highlighted the poor physical health of the army. So great was public concern that parliament set up an inquiry whose results shocked the nation. The 1862 Report of the Committee to inquire into the Prevalence of Venereal Disease in the Army and Navy did not mince words: one third of all cases admitted into hospital were suffering from VD, equivalent to the loss of two battalions of men a year. The greatest number of cases were in naval ports, and the incidence of VD was even worse among the Marines. The Committee reported that statistics for VD,

> Take no account of its too frequent consequences – scrofula, paralysis, rheumatism and consumption; of the constitutions enfeebled and shattered, nor of the children affected by the syphilitic taint. Nor do these figures show the many early discharges from the army due to venereal disease. Many fine young men who join the marine divisions, are on this account, discharged with shattered constitutions before they can render any service whatever to repay the cost of training.

There's the rub; it was costing money, money wasted on training 'fine young men'. Policing the growing British Empire was an expensive business, with troops garrisoned across the world from Delhi to Durban. Britain's role of 'top nation' inevitably brought 'local difficulties' such as the Indian Mutiny, and an army at the peak of fitness made the job far easier. But the great and good of the Select Committee were in absolutely no doubt where to lay the blame for this epidemic of VD. It was the fault of

these women who keep up the disease and recklessly spread it.

The prostitutes of Plymouth, Portsmouth and Chatham, the three principal naval towns were highlighted as the root of the problem. The report continued indignantly: 'The condition of the beer houses in our naval stations and about the camps is reported as particularly disgraceful. These places are, in fact, little more than brothels in disguise.'

The prevalence of prostitution in Britain was reported as far higher than any of her Continental neighbours, and had reached 'gigantic proportions'. Police witnesses told the committee that there were 900 prostitutes under the age of 15 in Plymouth in 1861. Many plied their trade in some 50 beer houses and 20 coffee houses which were in regular use as brothels in the town.

The state of our naval and military stations at home as regards prostitution (is) so appalling that they (the police) feel it their duty to press the Government as to the necessity of at once grappling with the mess of vice, filth and disease which surrounds the soldiers' barracks and the seamen's home, which not only crowds our hospitals with sick, weakens the roll of our effectives, and swells the list of our invalids, but which surely however slowly saps the vigour of our soldiers and our seamen, sows the seeds of degradation and degeneracy, and causes an amount of suffering difficult to over-estimate.

Today servicemen and women are subject to routine medicals, as their Victorian counterparts had been until 1857, when they were stopped because of their unpopularity with the men. One obvious solution to the problem might have been to reinstate routine medicals and examine and treat soldiers and sailors for VD, but this was not seen as a possibility: 'The Committee concur with most of these professional witnesses who have given evidence before them, that it would not be fair to punish a soldier or seaman for contracting the disease.'

One low-cost solution suggested was to provide greater facilities for 'washing in private' on board ship or in barracks: 'It would also be well to encourage bathing amongst the men and to point out to them, through their medical officers, the use of washing as a preventative measure against this and other forms of disease.'

Men in barracks and on board ship were also to be encouraged to occupy their time to keep them away from the 'haunts of vice'. There should be 'Liberal provision for all healthy, innocent and manly occupations and amusements which can relieve the tedium of life in barracks and on board ship.'

Finally the report questioned 'Whether it be wise to quarter in towns notorious for the prevalence of venereal disease, regiments returning from foreign service, while the men are flush with money.'

But of course Plymouth was a main port of entry for returning troops from all parts of the Empire anxious to spend their wages.

Witnesses called to give evidence to the Committee revealed that there were three different classes of prostitutes in the Three Towns. At the top of the pecking order were what the police called 'lady girls', who were well-dressed, lived in good houses and were frequented by gentlemen. Most prostitutes fell into the middle category, and were frequented by soldiers and sailors and the working population. The third was termed the 'tramp class', as Plymouth-based Inspector Silas Annis told the committee. 'They inhabit the lowest kind of brothel, hang about the fields at night, and get hold of men going home, and intoxicated soldiers and sailors.'

These women were described by the inspector as 'very dangerous'. Inspector Annis had served in the police force for 17 years and was with the Metropolitan Police detachment based at the Dockyard, but his jurisdiction covered an area within 15 miles of the yard. Under the auspices of the Contagious Diseases Acts of 1864, 1866 and 1869, he led a team of nine constables and one sergeant who patrolled the streets, in plain clothes, to arrest suspected prostitutes. Brothels were also visited on information given by soldiers, sailors and malicious neighbours who were able to blacken reputations. As VD was present in epidemic proportions in Victorian England, the symptoms were not in any case a guarantee that a woman was involved in prostitution. As a tract published by campaigners against the acts said: 'These spy-policemen not infrequently through mistake, busy interference, or malice, present to virtuous women the submission paper, which by their threats of consequences in case of refusal to comply, they force their affrighted victims to vice.'

The 'water police' as the dockyard police were nicknamed, do not come out of the affair well. They were heavy-handed in their treatment of the women, barging into their rooms without knocking, forcing the women to dress in front of them and refusing them the opportunity to make childcare arrangements before they were locked-up.

If a woman refused to submit to arrest, she was taken before a local magistrate. Those who acquiesced, were taken to one of two examination rooms, the Inspector actually lived above one of these rooms at 2 The Octagon.

The often unwilling subject was taken to a waiting room before her examination by the surgeon, although a nurse was always present, according to the police. Inspector Annis told the committee that 'A patient is placed on a reclining chair, her dress arranged by the nurse with all regard to decency. The doctor examines the external parts, and if no sign of contagious disease is visible, uses the speculum in some cases to examine the vaginal passage and mouth of the womb.' If the woman was 'found healthy' she was told to attend again in a fortnight. Although doctors were beginning to understand venereal disease, they looked for a mucus discharge, a symptom which was not evident in advanced cases. Those who were deemed diseased were taken to the Lock Ward of the Royal Albert Hospital. This model Victorian institution served a dual purpose as an edifice to imprison prostitutes and as a hospital for the deserving poor. It had been built by public subscription to offer the needy an alternative to the infirmary at the dreaded workhouse, and Florence Nightingale had been consulted on its design. It was the first hospital in England to be certified under the Contagious Diseases Acts and was subsidised by the Admiralty, making it dependent on the admission of women to the Lock Wards. But to start with, the women were housed in a former artillery store and magazine nearby: a grim prospect.

When the Lock Wards were first opened, a journalist from the *Illustrated London News* praised the glorious views from its windows across the harbour to Brunel's bridge to Cornwall. Five years later the window-panes were replaced with opaque glass and bars were put on the windows.

It is a sobering and moving sight to read the 1871 census return for Morice Ward. Listed are the names of 77 women imprisoned in the Lock Ward of the Royal Albert Hospital, because they have VD. The youngest is

The Royal Albert Hospital, a place of healing for most, a prison for some.

16-year-old Hetty Hancock who was born across the water in Cornwall. The Matron would have been optimistic that because of Hetty's youth she could turn her from a life of vice. Kate Fitzpatrick is also 16 and one of four women from Jersey. Troops had been stationed in the heavily fortified Channel Islands throughout the nineteenth century, because of their strategic location at the gateway to the Atlantic. Kate's surname may denote a father recruited from Ireland where significant numbers of British soldiers originated. Only one of the patients is married: Amelia Gleeson, who was born in Jersey 30 years ago and may be one of the many women forced to walk the streets because her husband is serving abroad, or paid off when his ship returned home. Eighteen-year-old Maude Ryder was also born in Jersey. Forces families have always followed as regiments and battalions decamp to another posting, which may explain why her 21-year-old sister was born in Plymouth. Only 21-year-old Mary Westaway was born abroad. It's likely that her father was serving in the army when she was born in Madras, and Mary may well have lived through the tumult of the Indian Mutiny in 1857.

Although most patients originated in Devon or Cornwall, from towns such as Kingsbridge, Dartmouth, Ivybridge, Dawlish, Bodmin and Truro, there are two women born in London. One of these is Elizabeth Harding who is a widow at only 22. Perhaps she followed her husband to the Marine Barracks in Devonport, or was a naval wife who turned to prostitution when her husband died. At 47 years old, Jane Smith is a good 15 years older than any of the other women. Born in Plymouth, she is described as a widow. It was the poor and destitute who turned to prostitution when there was no other means of earning a living.

As well as the 'fallen' women on the 1871 census, there are two babies recorded in the Lock Ward: Elizabeth C. Burrington and Fanny Bulson. Eight-month-old Fanny and her 20-year-old mother Elizabeth were both born in Tamerton, and may well have travelled to the anonymity of the city to escape the disapprobation of a small rural community. Elizabeth Burrington was only five months old, but was in the Lock Ward with her 25-year-old mother, also called Elizabeth, and her aunt Mary Burrington who was 32. The Burrington sisters were daughters of sometime butcher and cattle drover Thomas. Ten years later Mary was still single and living with her daughter Eliza and her parents in a court in Batter Street. Baby Elizabeth Burrington may have had an uncertain start to life, but 20 years later she was looking after her 73-year-old widowed grandfather Thomas at How Street in Sutton, until her marriage in the summer of that year. Her mother died in the summer of 1884; she had never married.

Tower at Washbourne Close, Devonport, last remnant of the Royal Albert Hospital.

A contemporary snapshot of the Lock Ward survives in the British Library, thanks to the pen of Caroline Nicholson. A member of the Congregationalist Church and retired schoolteacher, she was the author of an anonymous propaganda pamphlet entitled, *From What I Saw At The Royal Albert Hospital Devonport, on the Morning of May 12th 1873*. Miss Nicholson was an active member of the National Association for the Repeal of the Contagious Diseases Acts, on a national and local level. She wrote a series of pamphlets for the national organisation about the evils of life under the acts in Devonport. Her description of the Lock Ward is not sensationalist, but indignant.

> The tour was conducted by the matron. The first ward which we entered is a lofty and pleasant room; there were plants in the windows, which, the matron informed me, were watered by the inmates. 'You are fond of flowers aren't you girls?' said she. A few of the 'girls', each standing by her bed, responded 'Yes' in a tone which I thought constrained but which seemed to satisfy the kind-hearted matron, who continually gave me the impression that she believed her 'girls' were all glad to be there, and would all eventually be reclaimed *if only they could be in hospital often enough* to be brought under her influence. She assured me that the oftener a woman came into hospital, the more probable was it that she would reform. That so to say, the oftener a woman goes back to the soldiers and sailors for whose benefit she has been healed in the hospital, and is by them rendered again a fit subject for medical treatment, the less hardened she is likely to be.

From this ward of hardened fallen women, the tour continued to a second ward, in which those who had been scooped up from the streets for the first time, were segregated.

> Nearly all were extremely young. Several had babies. One saw all at a glance these were girls who had no mothers, or worse than none; who had lived in such places of service as they could get; who had read silly novels, and had been bewildered by the flattery of so-called 'lovers'; and who had found themselves within a few months, deserted by their seducers, mothers but not wives, and last –worst degradation of all – registered as 'prostitutes' under the Acts. Formerly these 'first cases' were not admissible unless the baby had died or disappeared; they were sent to the workhouse. But in time it occurred to some benevolent mind, that it would be much better for the girl-mothers – (doubtless, also for the soldiers and sailors!) if a ward in the Hospital could be set apart for the noble work, first of healing – bodies; next, of forming their manners; last, of sending

them forth systematically to 'consort' with the 'celibate army', for whose use they are prepared.

Miss Nicholson also described the hospital chapel, where the 'civilian' patients were segregated from the fallen women by a red curtain which divided the room. Lock Ward patients were dressed in blue serge dresses, with appropriately modest caps and red neckerchiefs. 'During the service I did not like to look at the women, but I saw that there were many very young amongst them; a few very fair to look upon, several dressed with much care; some had sweet voices too.' Her account seethes with genteel outrage, particularly as she sat through a sermon on the theme of hypocrisy. 'When we remember that the Chaplain who denounces the sin of fornication, is *paid* by those who say that it is impossible to maintain a celibate army *without* fornication, the preaching is worse than mockery.'

Not all the women endured their stay quietly; there was a riot in 1876 when the authorities stuck rigidly to the rule of one letter a week, depriving one inmate of a 'mourning note'. No other Lock Wards in garrison towns restricted letters, but the medical officer at the Royal Albert argued that it prevented contact with men outside and therefore prevented disturbances.

Word soon travelled when a woman had been examined, or admitted to the Lock Wards. Landladies reacted by throwing them and their meagre belongings onto the street, condemning them to continue a life funded by the 'wages of sin'. The Three Towns were essentially forces' towns, and in 1871 one in three men over the age of 20 were either in the forces or employed by the Admiralty. There were few job opportunities for young, single women apart from low-paid work in domestic service, dressmaking and millinery. Despite Plymouth's growing role as a regional shopping centre, shop workers at this period were young men. Poverty-stricken married women could resort to money from the 'parish', essentially handouts which enabled them to stay out of the workhouse, but young single women were not entitled to this outdoor relief, as it was known. Little wonder then, that seamstresses and milliners among others resorted to occasional prostitution as a way of supplementing a meagre income. These laundry women, tailors and milliners would have earned six to eight shillings a week for 14-hour days, which was half the pay of a male labourer. A prostitute could earn the same amount in a day if a ship had just arrived in port. Prostitutes were able to dress better, had a room of their own and had none of the restrictions of a life of drudgery 'below stairs' as a domestic servant working 18-hour days.

The fatherless daughters of forces fathers were considered particularly

The Orphan Asylum, set up to keep fatherless daughters of military and naval men from a life on the streets.

at risk of becoming 'fallen women', and the Royal British Female Orphan Asylum in Devonport was one of the charitable institutions set up to help. In a letter to the Admiralty in June 1869 asking for an annual grant, the honorary secretary, Lorenzo Metham, outlined the ideals of the charity:

> That the female orphans of men who have faithfully served their country, and more especially of those who have lost their lives in the public service, have a moral claim to be supported and maintained by their country. That being destitute, ignorant and unprotected, it is from them as a class, that the ranks of prostitutes are largely recruited in our seaport towns, and consequent disease produced among our soldiers and sailors.

In the light of the public concern about the health of the forces and the Contagious Diseases Acts, this was a forceful argument to the Admiralty. Then he played the guilt card:

> It is therefore expedient, as well as just that they should be removed from the neighbourhood of the haunts of vice by which they are

surrounded; that such a provision would remove the disgrace which, at present, attaches to the Country for having so long neglected its duty towards its brave defenders, and would be an inducement to men of a better class to enter Her Majesty's Service.

A comparatively small sum would be required to provide for all cases of female orphanage, such as are created by the casualties of actual service, arising from fire, shipwreck, actions with pirates etc, and for which relief is often immediately and urgently needed.

The Admiralty was not persuaded, and did not award a grant until 1872.

With the advent of the Contagious Diseases Acts, police raided beer shops in notorious areas such as Lambhay Hill and Castle Street, and prostitutes used by soldiers and sailors were forced to live in The Octagon area, effectively creating a red light district. As a result 'respectable' ladies would walk only on the south side of Union Street, as prostitutes used the north pavement.

It was not until 1870 that any organised opposition to the acts was established. On New Year's Day, The Ladies Protest against the wrongs of the acts was printed in the *Daily News*. It was signed by 124 women including Florence Nightingale, as well as feminists such as Harriet Martineau, and was an early call against the infringement of civil liberties. Lurid tales of the forced internal examination of young women were told at public meetings. Speakers held up the vaginal speculum and described the horrific damage inflicted by doctors with this instrument. In Plymouth as elsewhere, the acts' opponents stemmed from the non-conformist and in particular Quaker community. It was not an easy cause to champion. Chemist Alfred Balkwill, bookseller Mr Sellick and Richard Bishop a draper were all prominent campaigners. William Littleton, a naval outfitter in Devonport, as well as local registrar of marriages, lost business thanks to his ardent activities for repeal. John Marshall a former labourer at Millbay Docks, was the paid organiser of the repeal association, and he and his wife ran the local office and rescue home on Union Street. In 1870 they organised and held 20 meetings agitating for repeal of the acts, and that November John Marshall was sentenced to two months hard labour for interfering with the activities of the 'water police', as Inspector Annis and his men were known. Plymouth members also helped in an underground railway, much like that operated by

OVERLEAF. *Union Street, which became the centre of the red light district thanks to the Contagious Diseases Acts.*

the French Resistance in the Second World War, which smuggled women out of the area. But these rescued girls had little option but the drudgery of domestic service to keep them, literally, off the streets.

Repealers claimed that far from helping to snuff out prostitution, the acts created a workforce of prostitutes, kept disease free, in the words of their campaign literature, 'to be fitted again for the lusts of man'.

As prostitutes became restricted to certain areas, all men knew where to obtain their services, which it was argued increased immorality among soldiers, sailors and civilians. Women who resorted to temporary prostitution in times of crisis would be publicly stigmatised by a stretch in the Lock Wards and pushed into long term prostitution because they were unable to find other employment.

In 1878 the appeal campaigners published a penny tract called *State Legalization of Vice*, one of the propaganda weapons of the campaign.

> The object of these laws is to provide for men the means whereby they can lead a bad life without incurring its physical consequences.
>
> No indignity offered to a man can equal these enforced surgical examinations of women by men. A far less affront offered to a man would be immediately resented.
>
> A plausible plea is put on behalf of the innocent wives and children of depraved men. We ask who are the persons that carry diseases to these innocent victims: Not women, but men.

The Contagious Diseases Acts were repealed by parliament in 1886.

CHAPTER 19

NANCY AND THE SUFFRAGETTES

The slow-burning fuse of the women's suffrage campaign in Plymouth was lit on 11 June 1869, when the constituency sent a petition to parliament. This was only three years after Liberal MP John Stuart Mills had first petitioned the House of Commons, and half a century before Nancy Astor became the first woman to take her seat in the House of Commons as MP for Sutton, Plymouth. Nancy's historic victory in the by-election caused by her husband Waldorf Astor's elevation to the House of Lords was not the result of militant suffragist activity in the Three Towns, although the movement certainly had its moments in Plymouth. Nancy was a firm proponent of temperance. She had escaped from a first marriage to an alcoholic and knew first-hand the harm which drink could do. Her entry to parliament coincided with an attempt to relax the licensing laws, which had been introduced in 1914, and in her maiden speech she produced this snapshot witnessed in the Plymouth slums:

> I was coming back from what they call the poorer parts of town, and I stopped outside a public house where I saw a child of about five years old waiting for its mother. Presently she reeled out. The child went forward to her, but it soon retreated, and the oaths of that poor woman and the shrieks of that child as it fled from her – that is not an easy thing to forget, and that is what goes on when you have increased drunkenness among women.

Despite her Conservative party ticket, Nancy Astor was seeing the proposed licensing laws from a women's point of view, rather than lining up with the traditional business allies of Conservatism. Nancy had not been a suffragette, but the woman who became the first sitting female Member of Parliament had proved the point of those who had. Representing the views of women was exactly what the campaigners for women's suffrage had marched for, gone on hunger strike for and even died for.

Suffragette activities in Plymouth kicked off on 19 November 1908 at the Royal Hotel. That afternoon the militant arm of the suffrage movement the Women's Social and Political Union held the first of their regular At Homes, where ladies could come and take tea between 4 and 6 p.m. and meet the local organisers. The WSPU newspaper, *Votes for Women* was handed out on the streets outside theatres in the evenings by volunteers. Its pages offer a record of some of the first activities held in Plymouth. This piece written by Annie Kenney, the ex-textile worker who was the West of England organiser, was printed in the issue of 26 November 1908:

> On Thursday evening a very large audience gathered in the Market Place to listen to Miss Mary Philips and Miss E Howey; there were some interruptions, chiefly by small boys, but the crowd on the whole was sympathetic and interested. A large number of copies of Votes for Women have been sold in the street, and this has helped to rouse public interest here.

The campaign in the Three Towns hotted up with a Drawing Room Meeting held by Miss Morden and Miss Howey in Albert Street, the Hoe, and public meetings outside the Dockyard gates at Keyham and Devonport as workers came off shift. The highlight of the first week was a public meeting at the Guildhall where national leaders Annie Kenney and Mrs Pethwick-Lawrence were booked. A team of local volunteers spent three days driving round the Three Towns in a decorated wagonette to advertise the event. Annie Kenney told the packed audience that she was convinced that the present government was going to give women the vote. Quoted in *Votes for Women* she said:

> If we don't get the vote we shall be more militant than ever before. We younger women are not going to grow grey in asking for the vote; we are going to go grey in working for constructive reform as voters. We are going to grow grey alongside the young men of this country, doing everything to build up a better, happier, and purer country than we are living in at the present time.

At that meeting on 27 November the militants decided to open a shop in the city and raised more than £36 towards its expenses, but record of its location has not survived as records of the Women's Social and Political Union were confiscated by police. The address given for WSPU correspondence was 11 Albert Street, the Hoe and that could be a possible candidate.

The shop, which had a dual function as the branch office or 'committee room', would have been a colourful addition to the shopping scene, with a window decorated with the purple, white and green colours of the suffragette movement. It was a way to recruit and raise money. Among the merchandise on offer were WSPU playing cards, the militant newspaper *The Suffragette*, packets of tea, tea sets and stationery. Buttons, bows, Boadicea brooches, hat pins and purses were offered to tempt those who were sympathetic to the cause but were not inclined perhaps to go to the lengths of violence or a prison sentence.

By January 1909 the suffragettes had extended their campaign, holding 'At Homes' in Mannamead, Saltash and Devonport as well as Plymouth. But that year, frustrated by the lack of progress within the movement, the militants stepped up their campaign, launching a series of high profile attacks on politicians. Letterboxes were firebombed and windows smashed. When in January 1913 a bill to extend the vote to women was thrown out of parliament, the suffragettes became more desperate. With First Lord of The Admiralty Winston Churchill in Plymouth to inspect the Fleet, they saw their chance. On 3 April 1913 no one apparently spotted women with pots of paint and brushes daubing graffiti on buildings on the Hoe: 'To Save the State From Shipwreck Give women the Vote' and 'No security until you give women votes, no matter how big the navy'. Churchill's visit coincided with Mrs Pankhurst's appearance in court in London, and the Plymouth activists painted a reference to the practice of force-feeding women while on hunger strike in prison. One of the shelters on the Hoe was graffiti-ed with 'To Churchill: no rest for the government while they torture women'. When the inscriptions were discovered, workmen were called out straightaway and the propaganda was scrubbed off with turpentine, soap and water. But the suffragettes had not finished and later the same day telephone wires were cut in Lipson. The year 1913 saw the height of the militancy, which was to be subsumed for the greater good of the nation with the outbreak of the First World War. Two further incidents in Plymouth give some idea of the bravery and militancy of the local suffragettes. The first was a bomb planted to blow up that symbol of Plymouth pride, Smeaton's Lighthouse on the Hoe. But it was an amateur attempt. A can filled with what *The Times* described as 'black powder' was left at the foot of the tower. Although the paraffin-soaked wick

had been lit, the sea breeze had extinguished the flame. An arson attack on 15 December 1913 was more successful, setting fire to a wood yard at Richmond Walk in Devonport. The blaze spread to Hancocks fairground next door and

Richmond Walk, scene of a successful arson attack by suffragettes.

the caravans and roundabouts were destroyed. The suffragettes 'claimed responsibility' by leaving a copy of *The Suffragette* newspaper and a postcard calling for Votes For Women.

CHAPTER 20

THE ALPHA AND
THE OMEGA

In October 1562 John Hawkins set off from Plymouth on the voyage that established the slave trade. His fleet of three ships – *Jonas*, *Swallow* and *Salomon* – would establish the triangular trading route from England to West Africa, across the ocean to the Spanish Main, returning home north towards Florida, on to Newfoundland, then across the Atlantic with the Gulf Stream. It was a voyage which took just under a year, and was steeped in controversy, not because Hawkins bought and sold African men and women to work on plantations in the Caribbean. No such scruples existed until more than 200 years later. Indeed Hawkins was so proud of his achievement that he incorporated a bound African into his family crest. What caused the controversy in the mid sixteenth century was that Hawkins had strayed into the trading territory of England's great rivals, Portugal and Spain, without a licence. In the legal and diplomatic wrangling that resulted, particularly with Spain, Hawkins was backed up by his Queen who wrote personal letters to both the Spanish Ambassador and King Philip. Hawkins's voyage had turned a profit despite mishaps, and this could only enrich the Crown. Things got ever better for the merchant adventurer. When he set out on his second slaving expedition on 18 October 1564 he had the official backing of the Queen.

This second voyage was just as dangerous as the first, but we know far more about it thanks to the account written by one of his officers, John Sparke, who in later life served two terms as mayor of Plymouth. Hawkins was sailing through waters packed with pirates; past islands infected with tropical disease; and had to curry favour with the cannibalistic Caribs, the original inhabitants of the islands which still bear their name, to replenish his water supplies. Hawkins was a captain who considered the health of his crew of prime importance, unlike many of his contemporaries. Favouring smaller crews, his ships were not as cramped, and consequently healthier. He also avoided replenishing supplies at ports known to harbour tropical diseases, thus protecting his men and resulting in a low casualty rate on his voyages.

How he treated his human cargoes is not known, but his general reputation was as an honourable and kind man. One example of his kindness was during this second voyage. The French had established a tentative toehold in Florida, but when Hawkins dropped anchor in July 1565, the garrison was mutinous and starving. Relations with the locals were not good, and only the garrison commander René de Laudonniere was determined to stay put. John Hawkins offered the French a lift home, and when Laudonniere refused, the Plymouth sea captain made an astonishing, humane offer. He left the French with one of his ships and sufficient supplies to keep them going until relief arrived. In exchange he was given what was in effect an IOU, which he is known not to have redeemed. In order to top up his depleted stores for the voyage home, Hawkins had to go via the plentiful Newfoundland cod banks. Set this altruistic action in the light of the great land grab across the Atlantic indulged in by European adventurers in the sixteenth century, and it is even more remarkable. The French outpost which he provisioned was staking a claim to Florida, in the same way that Walter Raleigh staked a claim to Virginia in 1584.

It is for his ignominious role in bringing England into the slave trade for which John Hawkins is remembered. Of course the pearls, sugar and leather hides which he brought home in exchange helped to build the wealth of Tudor Plymouth, as did the piracy which he and his cousin Francis Drake indulged in. But he played a major part in ship design, reducing the top-heavy superstructures which the ships of old King Henry's navy had featured and building up the English navy in the decade before the Armada. By the age of 30, Hawkins was well-travelled as a merchant and privateer through the family shipping business. He had seen the effects of huge Atlantic seas on the top-heavy ships beloved of the Henrician navy. While the navy remained a purely defensive force, patrolling English shores against possible invasion by the Continental Catholics, this mattered little. But as Elizabeth's sea dogs grabbed gold from Spanish ships on their way back from the West Indies in state-licensed piracy, the chances of war with Spain correspondingly grew. Naval ships needed to be updated. In his role at the Navy Board, Hawkins was the probable designer of the first of this new breed of ship, believed to be the *Foresight* launched in 1570. Hawkins's cousin Drake was a fan of the alterations which made these Elizabethan galleons less top-heavy. A subsequent model, the *Revenge* launched in 1575, was chosen by Drake as his flagship against the Armada fleet because he believed her to be the most perfect galleon. In his role as treasurer of the Navy Board, Hawkins identified and purged the fraud and sharp practice

which flourished at the time, saving the Queen substantial sums of money. He was not only a practical and experienced sailor, but the Hawkins family shipyard was the largest in Plymouth.

Hawkins and Drake are often referred to as swashbucklers, a term coined in the sixteenth century meaning swaggering bully-boy adventurers. The two men grew up together. Drake probably spent part of his childhood with the Hawkins family at their home in Kinterbury Street, but Drake grew up the quicksilver, impulsive hero, while Hawkins was steadier and more methodical. As a seaman Drake attracted enormous numbers to crew his ships, but Hawkins was the captain who was likely to bring a man back alive. Drake is the name most commonly linked with Plymouth; it is Drake whose statue tops the Hoe; but it was John Hawkins, and his father and brother, who gave Plymouth riches and status in the sixteenth century by establishing it as an ocean port and naval base provisioned by the surrounding countryside. It was the Hawkins family who enabled the building of the old Plymouth whose vestiges still stand round Sutton Pool.

If Plymouth has been ashamed by the legacy which accompanies the establishment of the slave trade by Hawkins, the city can be proud that it was also the origin of one of the most potent propaganda images in history: the black and white drawing of the interior of the slave ship *Brookes*. This revealed in shocking detail the cruelty of the 'middle passage', when slaves were transported from Africa to the sugar plantations of America and the West Indies, satisfying a demand for labour established when the Sugar Islands were first colonised by Europeans. This image was first published by the Plymouth abolitionists in 1788, and caused such revulsion that 7,000 posters carrying the image were printed to highlight the cause the following year.

No record of the artist survives, and two centuries later it is difficult to plot the exact course of events, and exactly how the image came to emanate from Plymouth, but it's not too fanciful to suppose that the town's naval network acted as a conduit.

It is on record that in 1788 the British government sent one Captain Parry to Liverpool on a mission. He was to board ships in port known to be involved in the African trade. Armed with a tape measure, Captain Parry stepped aboard the first ship he came across, the choice was entirely random and it was the *Brookes*. There is no record that Captain Noble, the *Brookes*'s

OPPOSITE. *A quiet day in Kinterbury Street before slum clearance; the Hawkins family lived here.*

captain, acquiesced on this fact-finding mission, and in view of what Parry found and recorded it seems unlikely. The measurements he took were presented to the Select Committee taking evidence on the slave trade in 1790. But, how strange that those same dimensions had been published two years earlier by the Plymouth Committee of Abolitionists Against Slavery, in tandem with the iconic image. Was this just coincidence or was Captain Parry a whistle-blower with Plymouth connections? Perhaps he was so shocked by his visit that he shared his findings with a brother officer, relative or sweetheart; perhaps John Clarkson, brother of the prominent abolitionist Thomas Clarkson, who had joined the Royal Navy in 1777. It seems unlikely that an abolitionist could have gained access to the self-same ship. This is the evidence as it is recorded in the papers of the Select Committee.

Length of the Lower deck, gratings and bulkheads included. . . .	100 feet	
Breadth of beam on lower deck inside . . .	25 ft	4 ins
Depth of hold from ceiling to ceiling	10 ft	
Height between decks from deck to deck	5 ft	8 ins
Length of the men's room on the lower deck	46 ft	
Breadth of the men's room on the lower deck	25 ft	4 ins
Length of the platforms in the men's room	46 ft	
Length of the platforms in the men's room on each side	6 ft	
Length of the boy's room	13 ft	9 ins
Breadth of the boy's room	25 ft	
Breadth of platform in boy's room	6 ft	

Let it now be supposed that those are the real dimensions of the ship Brookes, and farther, that every man slave is to be allowed six feet by one foot four inches for room; every woman five feet ten by one foot four, every boy five feet by one foot two, and every girl four feet six by one foot, it will follow that the annexed plan of a slave vessel, will be precisely the description of the ship Brookes, and of the exact number of persons neither more nor less that could be stowed in the different rooms.

Dr Thomas Trotter was a naval surgeon who in 1783 sailed with the *Brookes* as ship's doctor. He was almost certainly 'resting' from naval service on half pay, and therefore at liberty to take work on a merchant ship. In his evidence to the select committee in 1790, Dr Trotter said 600 people were 'stowed' in the ship on his voyage of 1783. This was already in breach of earlier Regulating Acts, which stipulated that a ship of that size could carry a maximum of 354 slaves.

> If four hundred and fifty one slaves are put into the different rooms of the Brookes, the floors are not only covered with bodies, but those bodies actually touch each other, what must have been their situation, when six hundred were stowed in them at the time alluded to by Dr Trotter, who belonged to this ship, and six hundred and nine by the confession of the slave merchants in a subsequent voyage.

Apart from their roles as recorded in the select committee report, we will probably never know whether Dr Trotter and Captain Parry were whistle-blowers who alerted abolitionists to the cramped conditions.

Among the other witnesses to the Select Committee was William Dove a Plymouth sailor, one of many seamen who had taken ship in 'the trade'. He had sailed from Liverpool in the *Lily* under the command of Captain Saltcraig. In 1769 he was on the coast of Africa as the ship sailed from Sierra Leone down to 'Piccipini Sisters' buying slaves. The report summarised his evidence.

> Respecting the mode of getting slaves, he observed an instance of a girl that was kidnapped being brought on board by one Ben Johnson, a black trader, who had scarcely left the ship in his canoe with the price of her, when another canoe with two black men came in a hurry to the ship, and inquired concerning the girl. Having been allowed to see her, they hurried down to their canoe and hastily paddled off. Overtaking Ben Johnson, they brought him back to the ship, got him on the quarter deck, and calling him a 'teefee' which implies thief, to the captain, offered him to sale. Ben Johnson remonstrated, asking the captain if he would buy him grand trading man; to which the captain answered, if they would sell him he would buy him, be he what he would, which he accordingly did, and put him into irons immediately with another man. Was led to think from that instance, that slaves were kidnapped, and as well as from having seen children brought separately on board, and men and women without fresh wounds, or marks of old ones on them.

The iconic anti-slavery image first produced by Plymouth abolitionists. This is a later version, produced in Bristol.

These comments about wounds were a reference to the practice of selling members of tribes defeated in war, into slavery.

> They had on board between 30 and 40 children, boys and girls, some on their mothers breasts, four or five born during the passage. The slaves in his ship were in general very well treated, as well as any ship on the coast, two or three instances of great cruelty excepted.

The Committee was also interested in the notorious cruelty of slave ship captains, which the Plymouth sailor also gave evidence on

> Captain Saltcraig coming on board one evening somewhat intoxicated, scolded the officers for not manning the sides to receive him,

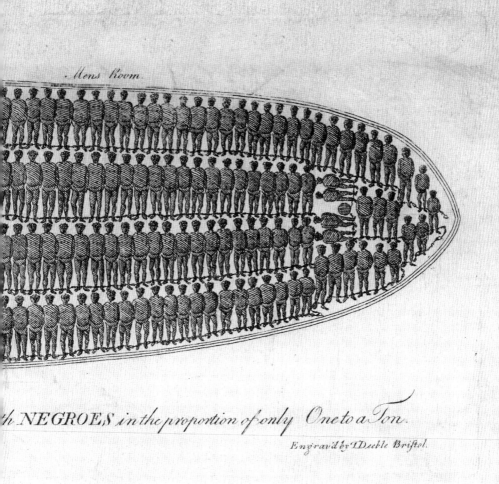

Mens Room.

h NEGROES *in the proportion of only* One to a Ton.

Engravd by I Deeble Bristol.

then with a rope's end beat many white people on deck; he then stretched a rope across, and ordering a negro, a stout fellow, out of iron, made him stand on one side of the rope, while he stood on the other, and setting his foot to the black man's, squared as if to box him, saying that he would learn him how to fight, and signified to the black fellow to make a blow at him again, which, though at first he knew not how to do, at last he did, and gave the captain a terrible blow; the captain turned about, went to the cabin, brought up a horse-whip, and beat him most unmercifully, first with the lash, then with a full sweep with the but [sic] end, till the black man evacuated both by urine and excrement, insomuch that the ship's company thought he could not survive it.

The men slaves were fettered all the Middle Passage till in

sight of Desida, a West India Island, except a few sick slaves who were let to walk the deck, and taking great care to recover them. This confinement may be necessary from their great superiority of numbers. Has known men fettered together quarrel in the night.

William Dove also told the committee that half the crew on his only slaving voyage were landsmen rather than professional sailors, who were often reluctant to join slave ships because their captains were so notorious for their cruelty to slaves and crewmen alike. In a footnote, the report adds:

If it should be asked how it happens that seamen enter for slave-vessels, when such general ill usage there can hardly fail of being known, the reply must be taken from the evidence 'that whereas some of them enter voluntarily, the greater part of them are trepanned, for that it is the business of certain landlords to make them intoxicated, and get them into debt, after which their only alternative is a Guineaman or a gaol.'

Abolitionist activist and MP Thomas Clarkson went to extraordinary efforts to find eyewitness evidence to present to parliament. There was one eyewitness he lacked: a man who had actually witnessed the kidnap of slaves from their African homes up the rivers Bonny and Calabar. Slave dealers claimed that slaves were bought at fairs on the riverbanks. But other eyewitnesses had seen canoes heading up river with weapons, rather than merchandise. One of Clarkson's friends had met an eyewitness, but did not know his name or where he could be found. The only information Clarkson had to go on was that the sailor was on his way to a 'ship in ordinary' in some port. But he was not deterred, as he recounted in his book, *Abolition of the African Slave Trade by the British Parliament* published in 1830.

I felt myself set on fire, as it were, by this intelligence, deficient as it was; and I seemed to determine instantly that I would if it were possible find him out. For if our suspicions were true, that the natives frequently were kidnapped in these expeditions, it would be of great importance to the cause of the abolition to have them confirmed; for as many slaves came annually from both these two rivers, as from the coast of Africa besides.

With this slender piece of information, the intrepid abolitionist boarded every 'ship in ordinary' at Woolwich, Chatham, Sheerness and Portsmouth, 260 in all. Plymouth was his last port of call. It was on the 57th ship, the frigate *Melampus*, that his search ended. Thomas Clarkson had found his precious witness.

The man he was searching for was Isaac Parker who turned out to be a dream witness. First he told the committee how he had sailed to the River Gambia from Liverpool in the ship *Black Joke*. The Captain was fairly humane by the standards of the day, but Parker told this shocking story.

One exception to Captain Pollard's good treatment was, a child of nine months which refused to eat, for which the captain took it up in his hand, and flogged it with a cat [cat of nine tails], saying at the same time," damn you, I'll make you eat, or I'll kill you." The same child having swelled feet, the captain ordered them to be put into water, though the ship's cook told him it was too hot. This brought off the skin and nails. He then ordered sweet oil and cloths, which Isaac Parker himself applied to the feet; and as the child at mess time again refused to eat, the captain again took it up and flogged it, and tied a log of mango wood 18 or 20 inches long, and of 12 or 13lb weight round its neck as a punishment. He repeated the flogging for four days together at mess time; the last time after flogging he let it drop out of his hand, with the same expressions as before, and accordingly in about three quarters of an hour, the child died. He then called its mother to heave it overboard, and beat her for refusing. He however, forced her to take it up, and go to the ship's side, where holding her head on one side to avoid the sight, she dropped the child overboard after which she cried for many hours.

Captured slaves often chose to starve to death rather than face the alternative, but this baby was probably still breastfed. Isaac Parker made a second slaving voyage as part of the crew of the *Lathan* under the command of Captain Colly. The systemic ill-treatment of the crew (only 5 of the 13 seamen survived) led Parker to jump ship while he was on a slave-buying expedition.

Dick Ebro, a king's son, who new [*sic*] of the ill treatment given the crew by Captain Colly, concealed him for three days in a room till the ship was gone. He then came out and employed himself in fishing, cleaning their arms &c, and remained there for five months. When there, Dick Ebro asking him to go to war with him, he complied, and accordingly having fitted out and armed the canoes, they went up the river, lying under the bushes in the day when they came near a village; and at night flying up to the village, and taking hold of every one they could see. These they handcuffed, brought down to the canoes, and so proceeded up the river, till they got to the amount of 45, with whom they returned to Newtown, where sending to the captains of the shipping, they divided them among the ships.

Here then was the eyewitness account which Thomas Clarkson had come to Plymouth to find.

CHAPTER 21

A SWEET STINK

When John Hawkins sailed home on the third leg of his infamous slaving voyage of 1562, his return cargo included animal hides, pearls, ginger and sugar. Sugar production was the *raison d'être* of the slave trade. This exotic and precious commodity was practically unknown in this country until the reign of Henry VIII, and the sweet product of the sugar cane would become more valuable to British trade than any other. It would take the country to distant wars; play a leading role in national politics in London; and bring the whiff of corruption to local politics. In the nineteenth century half the customs dues gathered in Plymouth were from sugar imports, and the city ranked fourth in the league table of English cities turning unrefined sugar into the white crystals still familiar today.

A single 120-foot tall chimney of Plymouth's last sugar refinery tottered iconically over the city centre until the Luftwaffe raids of the Second World War. Another chimney had been deemed unsafe and demolished in the 1930s. In the reconstruction of the city centre workmen were sent to tackle the demolition of the remaining refinery buildings in 1953. The granite and lime-stone factory had been built in the solid Victorian manner, which typified industrial architecture of the time, and the *Plymouth Independent* gloried in the difficult task faced by the workmen on that hot August day:

> German bombs destroyed the biggest buildings. Now workmen attack the surviving masonry. Their's is no easy task, for early Victorian factories were built to endure for centuries.

German bombs may have destroyed the main fabric of the refinery, but it was foreign competition which killed sugar refining in Plymouth. The factory which had been built with such optimism in Mill Lane could not cope with competition from the French discovery that sugar could be refined from sugar beet, and finally closed at the end of the nineteenth century.

The former sugar refinery in Old Market.

It was the man whose name is now associated with matches, James Bryant, who started the sugar refinery in 1838, and his initials were carved into the stone lintel above the refinery door. It stood in an area which had played a huge part in the city's history already, as part of the old Frankfort Barracks, and on that ground the inhabitants of the city had withstood the siege of Plymouth in the Civil War for four long years. Reputedly the huge site also included the garden of the man who put Plymouth on the map,

Sir Francis Drake. Bryant was another entrepreneur and initially set up the town's first starch works, but in 1838 sugar refining offered a more lucrative way to make money and James Bryant and his partner Burnell went into the sugar business.

Bryant and Burnell were not the pioneers of sugar refining in Plymouth. Excavations at Coxside have revealed the foundations of a seventeenth-century sugar-house, and archaeologists have evaluated another site at Plympton. There was also a cane crushing plant in the city in the eighteenth century. But the Mill Lane refinery was for decades a major employer, so important in the minds of the people of Plymouth that allegedly it was used as a political weapon in the parliamentary election of 1880. By this period the business was in the doldrums, but on the eve of his election to parliament, Edward Bates a wealthy industrialist from the north, bought the failing mill. There was an outcry as opponents alleged that Bates was attempting to buy votes with this philanthropic action. As the sitting Conservative member, Bates claimed that he had been acting purely for the city's commercial well-being. His Liberal opponent contested this. Bates's intervention had enabled the factory to save 70 jobs, but following an inquiry he was exonerated, although unseated on a technicality.

Two years before this election scandal the *Western Morning News* carried an article about the refinery. According to the newspaper, in the year 1877–78 a staggering £22,000 worth of unrefined sugar and another £53,000 worth of refined sugar was coming into the port. Much of this would have passed through the Mill Street refinery, although it stood some distance from the quay, as the *Western Morning News* pointed out:

> Thus the managers have always had before them one considerable item in the annual cost of the establishment – that of carriage. For this they have their own cattle, and their own drays, wagon and carts, and forming quite a wing of itself is the stables or rather suite of stables. This cartage and maintenance of horses also represents a large sum of money spent by the company, while the public carriers also come in for their share of the business.

Streets round Mill Lane, were choked with traffic when the factory was at its most productive. But the lungs of the inhabitants of the narrow streets and courts would have been choked with the smell. Above their heads two chimneys belched out smoke into the airless centre of old Plymouth. In 1878 the British and Irish Sugar Refinery Company's Plymouth works employed 100 men, ploughing an annual £5,000 into the local economy and supporting an equivalent number of families. The manager and chief boiler lived in what are described as sugar refinery houses, which were part of the site. The 1861 census returns reveal that the works manager was 38-year-old George Prideaux, who lived at the plant with his wife Martha and four daughters under the age of five. His household naturally included a housemaid, cook, head nurse and an under-nurse. The lodge-keeper was Richard Baker, who had been born in Halifax, Nova Scotia; perhaps his father was a fisherman in the Newfoundland Trade. Another cottage was home to 22-year-old confectioner Charles Wilson. The all-important job of head boiler was held by 46-year-old John Benson, who also lived on site with his wife Catherine and their five children. Benson is described as born in Hanover, Germany, the country of origin of many master sugar bakers who came to work in England.

The art of sugar refining had spread across Europe from Venice, and the techniques were carried by German and Dutch sugar makers who were regarded as the masters. In 1764 those trade secrets were revealed in a book published by a Frenchman Duhamel de Monceau. What was refined was raw brown sugar, which had been milled from crushed sugar cane in the West Indies. Thanks to journalist James Greenwood, we have a description of a sugar works of the Victorian era, which he described in his book *The Wilds of London* published in 1876.

You could taste its clammy sweetness on the lips just as the salt of the sea may be so discovered while the ocean is yet a mile away. It was a sort of handy outer warehouse, that to which we were first introduced – a low-roofed, dismal place with grated windows, and here and there a foggy little gas-jet burning blear-eyed against the wall. The walls were black – not painted black. As far as one might judge they were bare brick, but 'basted' unceasingly by the luscious steam that enveloped the place, they had become coated with a thick preserve of sugar and grime. The floor was black, and all corrugated and hard, like a public thoroughfare after a shower and then a frost. The roof was black, and pendent from the great supporting posts and balks of timber were sooty, glistening icicles and exudings like those of the gum-tree.

In these grim surroundings, men laboured over the production of 'white gold' turning it into the product sold in grocer's shops. Although some white refined sugar was imported direct, most came into the country in its raw state: dense, strong smelling and the colour of mahogany. It was cooked up in a boiling house, in giant flat-bottomed clarifying pans four feet wide, supported by masonry. To prevent the liquid sugar boiling over, extra rings could be added to the pan to build up the depth – it was a dangerous industry, and there were frequent and catastrophic fires. James Greenwood described the pan as a 'gigantic globular structure in bright copper'.

> The vessel was all covered in, and looked as compact as an orange, the shape of which fruit it resembles but in the side of it there was a small disc of glass, and looking through it one could get a glimpse of the bubbling straw-coloured mass within.

Once the sugar was heated up, it was clarified with fresh bullock's blood – euphemistically called 'spice'. A pan holding four tons of sugar required two gallons of blood. As in jam-making the scum was taken off the top, until the liquid sugar was clear, when it was strained through a blanket into a box set in the floor. From there it was ladled into a boiling pan, and the liquid would start to swell. The seething mass was controlled by stirring and adding butter. After 45 minutes at the boil, head sugar boiler John Benson would test it. He had immense clout and authority because of his ability to determine whether the liquid had boiled enough, and would therefore produce a sugar which was sufficiently white. He judged its readiness, by dipping an iron testing rod into the pan, then drawing a thread of sugar between finger and thumb to determine its breaking point.

> The iron rod the guardian of the pan called a 'key,' if I rightly remember, and his sole occupation appeared to consist in dipping it in at a little hole in the vessel's side, and withdrawing it again, along with a little blob of melted sugar, which he took between his finger and thumb, and drew out and examined by the light of the gas.

Because of the immense heat generated in the refinery, Benson and his labourers worked half naked. Victorian journalist James Greenwood was shocked by his visit.

> The heat was sickening and oppressive, and an unctuous steam, thick and foggy, filled the cellar from end to end. Presently, however, when one's eyes grew somewhat accustomed to the gloom, a spectacle of a novel and startling character was presented.

Seeming, as it were, to grow out of the dense haze, busy figures appeared. Black and white figures running about, and flitting and skipping in the most extraordinary manner. Watching the figures, however, they were presently discovered to be men in a condition of at least semi-nudity. On one side of the cellar were two gigantic pans of sugar, melted and hot and smoking, and out of these the labourers, naked but for a covering for their legs and some sort of apron, and their bodies bathed in sweat, and their fair hair reeking and hanging lank about their wan faces, scooped up the liquor into the pails, that would contain half a hundredweight, and hurried across the cellar to deposit it in vast revolving basins set in motion at lightning speed by machinery, and where the brown sugar was bleached and dried, to be presently shovelled out and added to the great heap that reached high nearly as the ceiling.

The process was completed by pouring the sugar into cone-shaped sugar moulds, which have been found at archaeological digs. These clay cones had a hole in the narrow end and stood on pots for four to six days while the dark syrup drained off. This was either reused in another batch or used to make rum. These clay cones are some of the few relics to survive from the sugar industry and vary in height from 11 to 22 inches high. They were 5 to 10 inches in diameter and held between 5 and 35 pounds. They were taken to the drying floor, which Greenwood also witnessed.

It was an extensive floor, a hundred feet by seventy probably, and covering the whole of it were packed loaf-sugar moulds as closely as the cells of a beehive are arranged. The moulds were stuck point downwards into earthen jars that at once upheld them and served as receptacles for their drainings. I do not understand the process that was then operating, but what was to be seen was a dozen men of the semi-naked sort like those below crawling like frogs over the surface of the sugar moulds, getting foot and hand hold on the edges, some with a sort of engine hose squirting a transparent liquor into the moulds, and others stirring the thick stuff constantly in the latter with their hands. 'I should imagine that you were not much addicted to the consumption of sugar,' I remarked to our guide. 'I can never taste it; it has no taste, no more has nothing for me,' he answered and one could easily understand how that happened.

Next the cones were topped off with a layer of wet clay, and as the water from the clay seeped into the sugar mixture below it pushed out the liquor leaving the crystals. This was called decking or claying. After a week or so the sugar was inspected and if necessary clayed again, and a loaf of sugar would be knocked out of the mould. This had to be heated until dry before they were left to cool slowly. The result was not the snowy white sugar we know today but rather more yellow, a colour which was disguised by a blue paper wrapper.

From its infancy the sugar trade had been protected by a string of protectionist legislation imposed by the British parliament. This began with the Navigation Act of 1651, which restricted all trade from Asia, Africa and America to English ships and crews. It was a wise move in a lucrative business, which put the trade of the world at the feet of English sea captains and merchants, and laid the foundations for English dominance of the oceans. When Charles II was restored to the throne in 1660, the Navigation Act was beefed up by the stipulation that certain luxury goods, among them sugar, were to be shipped only to English or colonial ports – at this time Scotland and Ireland were considered to be colonies! The Navigation Act remained on the statute book until 1849, when free trade became the vogue in Britain.

It is thanks partly to the sugar trade that a significant part of Canada is French-speaking: in the peace treaty at the conclusion of the Seven Years War in 1756, Britain happily decided to hang on to the fruits of that war in the West Indies, relinquishing part of Canada to the French.

Sugar was also the root cause of a war which is long forgotten. On Thursday 22 January 1795, Richard Brinsley Sheridan, better known today as a playwright, rose to his feet in the House of Commons where he represented the constituents of Stafford. His speech was not prompted by the concerns of his constituents; it was sparked by the growing number of bodies which were washing up on the shores of Plymouth Sound. They were the corpses of British soldiers; soldiers from troop transports waiting to go to war in the West Indies; soldiers whose job was to ensure English control of the sugar islands of the Caribbean. These sugar islands were an essential territorial bargaining chip in any future fracas with the French.

According to *The Times* report in January 1795, Sheridan called for:

A vigorous enquiry into all the abuses and neglects which have arisen under the present administration; if such an enquiry were instituted it would appear that on board those transports various lives had been sacrificed by the scandalous cruelty and criminal neglect of ministers.

Sheridan contended that the men would be entirely unfit for service when they reached the West Indies, and should be disembarked and fresh troops sent in their stead. Nine regiments were weather-bound in Plymouth Sound, and had been languishing on board ship for six months. The autumn gales which blasted the country in 1794 had prevented them leaving port, and a gale of 6 October had destroyed 100 ships across the nation. As the troops succumbed to disease in the cramped conditions below decks, their bodies were thrown overboard. By the time the wind changed in their favour, the ships were threatened by French naval vessels lurking in the Channel. The war these men were destined for had begun with an expedition under Admiral Jervis who had sailed a year earlier in November 1793 for the French West Indies. Initially the campaign had been a success, as Jervis took Guadeloupe, St Lucia, Marie Galante and the Saints, and established an English presence on Haiti. The French were unable to send reinforcements across the Atlantic because of Britain's command of the seas, which was reinforced by Lord Howe's naval victory off the Brittany coast on the glorious first of June.

Meanwhile the revolutionaries in Paris had declared the equality of black and white, and all over the West Indies slaves were stirring. In Haiti the black followers of Toussaint l'Ouverture threw out both the French and the English; they outnumbered the 40,000 white settlers by more than ten to one.

By 1796 British forces in the West Indies had lost 40,000 men to yellow fever, with the same number unfit for service. Even by the casualty rates of the day this was a startling figure. By comparison the Duke of Wellington lost fewer than 40,000 men in the entire Peninsular War.

CHAPTER 22

LOST PLAYGROUNDS

On a fine sunny day in the early years of the young Queen Victoria, a bizarre ensemble could be spotted moving through the streets of Plymouth. Seated inside a small open carriage was an elderly man who had transformed parts of his adopted city into a grand echo of the classical cities of the Greek and Roman empires. And in appropriate homage to them, retired architect John Foulston had disguised his gig as a Roman chariot. Quite what the good people of Devonport and Plymouth thought of his eccentric behaviour is not recorded, but doubtless streams of ragged children would have run in the wake of the chariot as it clip-clopped over the streets.

Niagara Cottage designed by John Foulston.

His 'chariot' would have been harnessed outside his home, the aptly named Athenian Cottage on Townsend Hill. This was a cottage orné, a style beloved of the likes of the Duchess of Bedford who had commissioned one for her country estate at Endsleigh, near Tavistock. Artificially rustic and slightly dilapidated in appearance, it was a fashionable style in the era of the Romantic poets such as Wordsworth. A description of John Foulston's Athenian Cottage survives in the 1821 guidebook *Panorama of Plymouth*, written by S. Rowe:

A most pleasing specimen of ornamental cottage architecture – the low thatched roof and rustic colonnade entwined with parasitical plants, and all in unison with the tasteful decoration of the interior.

Those parasitical plants included convolvulus or bindweed, regarded by modern gardeners as a weed, but through the eyes of advocates of this style of architecture as a picturesque embellishment of Mother Nature.

It would be impossible today to recreate Foulston's route from Athenian Cottage, to the neoclassical civic grandeur which he designed in the early years of the nineteenth century, although remnants of the architecture which put Plymouth at the forefront of early nineteenth-century town planning still survive.

Prominent still is Devonport's Doric column, lost in the maze of buildings thrown up around it, but originally designed to be viewed along Union Street, a single finger raised in defiance to the old established town of Plymouth. Young proud newly-named Devonport was no longer merely an adjunct, the Plymouth Dock, but a rival. The column was the simplest edifice in the eclectic banquet of buildings in the Ker Street area. Like contestants in a beauty contest, architectural styles from all over the ancient world vied to attract attention. The exotic Egyptian, Oriental, Greek Doric, Greek Ionic and Roman Corinthian – there was nothing quite like it in the world to match this mixture of styles grouped on one site.

He was responsible for Union Street and its once grand central point, The Octagon. But it was not just these symbols of civic pride which Foulston designed. He drew up plans for many of the minor streets that were put up in the building boom of the 1820s. Obviously he was not the architect of all the stuccoed neoclassical houses from this period, but he set the trend that builders were only too happy to follow.

Neoclassicism had come into vogue as young eighteenth-century gentlemen, and some ladies, made the Grand Tour, a sort of eighteenth-century gap

The civic heart of Devonport built with such pride in the 1820s.

year. Just as backpackers took to the hippy trail in the twentieth century returning with joss sticks and kaftans, so eighteenth-century young bloods brought back accounts and pictures from the Continent. The excavation of Herculaneum and Pompeii, begun in 1738 and 1748 respectively, revealed artefacts from the two Roman towns which had been engulfed when Mount Vesuvius erupted in AD 79. Detailed drawings were sent back to England by Sir William Hamilton, British envoy to the King of Naples, revealing the

The quirky Oddfellows Hall.

decorations and domestic paraphernalia which had surrounded the benighted inhabitants. Those who travelled to the Bay of Naples itself could see plaster casts of the bodies caught in death. The cultures of Greece and Rome became associated with morality, rationality and integrity. By the last decade of the century the wars with France had extended to the eastern Mediterranean, and while Napoleon's troops were digging foundations for a fort in Egypt the Rosetta Stone was discovered. Under the Treaty of Alexandra in 1801, it came to the British Museum where it has been on display ever since. This became fashionable to emulate the Egyptian.

Neoclassicism is an architectural style which survives in the great build-ings of many cities, for example, the British Museum and the National Gallery. But Plymouth once had buildings which had no rival in the south-west peninsula. Foulston's greatest neoclassical structure was the palace of pleasure built during the Regency of the Prince of Pleasure. Conceived by leading citizen and doctor Edmund Lockyer, the competition to design this entertainment centre was announced in January 1810. Lockyer came up with the idea that Plymouth should invest some of the bountiful prize money streaming into the city as a result of the French wars. He was in an ideal posi-tion to know the extent of this bounty, as among his portfolio of interests he was a prize agent who conducted the sales of ships and their fittings captured from foreign powers. Foulston won the competition, putting his own money into the scheme by buying a £100 share in the name of his wife Eliza. On 10 September 1811, Edmund Lockyer, by now mayor of Plymouth, laid the foun-dation stone of a vast temple of temptations, which fronted onto Georges Place.

Devonport Town Hall just before bulldozers moved in to demolish the twentieth-century flats either side.

195

Two views of Plymouth's elegant Regency city centre.

Stretching 268 feet across, the building was fronted by 30-foot high columns supporting a portico. On the west was the Theatre Royal, and on the east a ballroom and hotel. Built in four wings round a central courtyard there was ample parking for the carriages and horses bringing visitors – 70 horses could be stabled, and there were seven coach houses in which to garage vehicles.

Fire was a constant threat in such an enormous public building, so Foulston designed what he hoped was 'the only fireproof theatre in the country'. Only three years earlier in 1808, the theatres in Drury Lane and Covent Garden had been ravaged by fire. Foulston was ahead of his time when he conceived a thick masonry wall to divide the theatre's auditorium from the adjoining hotel and circulation areas. Whether this would have contained a blaze is uncertain; the Theatre Royal was not destined to be obliterated by fire, but by the demolition ball.

His other principal fire precaution was an internal skeleton of cast and wrought iron. This supported a roof which spanned 60 feet. Floors, the gallery and partitions, and two tiers of boxes were also constructed round an iron framework. When the theatre opened it could hold 1,192, equivalent to the capacity of the present Theatre Royal.

Equally capacious was the hotel, with suites of rooms which catered for

Staff at the Royal Hotel in 1924.

20 to 30 families. Banquets could be held in a large dining room, while more intimate parties ate in 13 smaller rooms. The craze for drinking tea and coffee was equally catered for, with separate rooms dedicated to each beverage. Bachelors could battle at billiards, while a cast of servants scurried up and down stairs from the huge kitchens and icehouse, quite literally, below stairs.

This house of grandeur lasted only until the Depression of the 1930s when the theatre was converted into a cinema. A house of God which faced the eastern wing of the hotel, St Catherine's Chapel, with a theatrical triple-decker pulpit, was a victim of post-war reconstruction. Several of John Foulston's buildings which were also destined to help put Plymouth on the map as an entertainment centre and resort were never built. He might well have been intrigued with elements of the design of Drake Circus shopping centre completed in 2007. A building of similar description was among his other grand designs for the city – the Armada shopping arcade was to contain two floors of shops flanking a paved pedestrian area, lit from above through high domes of glass.

Another grand Foulston scheme was for neoclassical saltwater baths on the rocks below the Hoe to cater for the water nymphs of Plymouth, although this was never realised.

The concept of washing and bathing is engrained in modern conscious-ness, but to our ancestors it was not considered necessary or even desirable. The legendary baths so loved by the Romans at Aquae Sulis became fashion-able in the Regency period as a means of restoring health rather than cleans-ing the body. But the famous epigram 'cleanliness is (indeed) next to godli-ness' was coined by John Wesley in the 1720s, although he was referring to clothing rather than the body beneath. Bath soap was a luxury imported from Paris, and most people washed only their hands and faces, if at all, and did not wash their bodies from year to year. But in 1724 Dr George Cheyne published *An Essay of Health and Long Life* in which he advocated cold baths as a panacea for a host of diseases. As he rather charmingly described

> frequent washing of the body in water, cleanses the mouths of the perspiratory Ducts from that Glutinous Foulness that is continually falling upon them, from their own condensed dewy atmosphere, whereby the perspiration would be soon obstructed, and the party languish.

Dr Cheyne drew an analogy with total immersion at baptism, but he gave strict instructions on the way to achieve this.

I cannot approve the precipitant way of jumping in, or throwing the Head foremost into a Cold Bath; it gives too violent a shock to nature, and risques too much the bursting of some of the smaller vessels. The Natural Way is, holding by the Rope, to walk down the steps as fast as one can and when got to the bottom, bending their hams (as women do when they Curt'sy low) to shorten their length, so as to bring their heads a good way under water, and popping up again to take Breath; and thus alternately for two or three times, and out again, rubbing and currying well before they are dress'd.

He compared the effect of currying or brushing the skin, with curry-combing a horse making them 'sleek and gay, lively and active', and suggested that those who could not afford a bath in their home should find a river or 'living pond' to wash their bodies.

Soon Dr Cheyne's book was followed by the Wesleyan bestseller, *Primitive Physick*, an eighteenth-century handbook of ailments and remedies, including ways in which the poor could improve their health. It was in this bestseller that John Wesley popularised his phrase and claimed that cold baths cured everything from leprosy to epilepsy, and cancer to coughs. In 1752 Dr Richard Russell took bathing a step further. He proposed seawater as a cure-all and even advocated drinking large quantities. Fourteen years later the fashionable folk of Plymouth had their own baths on the edge of Mill Bay,

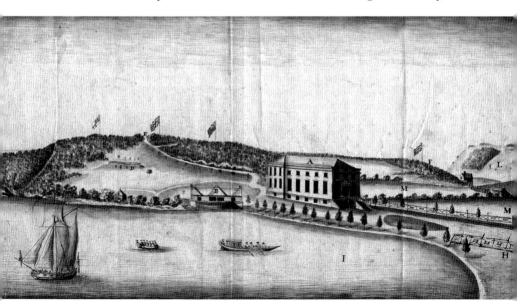

A 1766 drawing of the new baths and long room bordering Mill Bay.

in a new building shown on a plan of 1766 with formal landscaping linking it to the Long Room.

Mill Bay was also the site chosen for the Royal Union Baths, another scheme built under the auspices of Edmund Lockyer and opened on 1 May 1830. Very much in the neoclassical style, the complex included two swimming pools. The *South Devon Monthly Museum*, a short-lived local newspaper, described the neoclassical complex in 1834:

> The establishment contains eight hot baths, with commodious dressing rooms attached to them; these can be supplied with fresh or salt water, which is heated by passing a current of steam through the water after it has been discharged into the bath, or it may be heated beforehand by allowing the steam to pass through a large cistern filled with water for the purpose.
>
> There are two large swimming baths, seventy feet long, by thirty broad, having twelve neat dressing rooms attached; the one intended for the use of ladies is provided with ropes and other tackling, probably intended to assist them in the study of natation.
>
> Shower and Douche baths are always available, provided with hot and cold water; by means of the Douche a stream of water may be projected on any part of the body and continued for any length of time.
>
> For those who, swan-like, would bathe in perfect loneliness, there are provided two private cold baths, twelve feet by six.

Only two decades later the baths were swept away by the engine of progress, quite literally, with the building of Mill Bay station and the docks. But in 1898 a veritable palace of varieties was built as part of the redevelopment of Millbay Docks.

The ebullient façade of the New Palace Theatre in Union Street reflects the pride with which it was built. A pair of Spanish soldiers stand high above the street, commemorating the routing of the Armada by Sir Francis Drake. To one side, a miniature of the fanciful Eddystone lighthouse built by showman Winstanley offers a view over the city to anyone equal to the challenge. Built at the height of the music hall era, the huge auditorium was decorated in the lavish style so beloved of the Naughty Nineties. Theatregoers paid at a booth in the panelled entrance hall before ascending an Italian marble staircase to the 'saloon', which was decorated with plaster friezes of water nymphs, dolphins and cherubs.

The New Palace Theatre on Union Street, begging to be rescued.

But the smell of greasepaint and the gasps of admiration from the audience are long gone. It might be a Grade II Listed Building, but it is unloved and unwanted. Its career has been dogged by disaster. Only three months after it opened, fire swept through the building. According to a diary in the city record office, the fire was caused by 'live squibs and other weapons of stage warfare which were used in the production The Battle of Trafalgar'. Despite the efforts of fire fighters from Plymouth, Stonehouse and Devonport, soon the building 'was alight from floor to roof'. The fireproof curtain, which could have prevented the destruction of the auditorium, could not be reached. The lavish interior was wrecked. The building did reopen, but with a less ornamental interior, seven months later. Today the scene of performances by big names such as Charlie Chaplin, Houdini and Jenny Lind, is on the register of 'buildings at risk'.

The New Palace Theatre was not the first home of music hall in the Three Towns. In June 1872 Yeo's Castle Music Hall advertised shows accompanied by pianist Mr A. St John. Admission was free for men, but women were not allowed. This den of iniquity stood opposite St James Hall in Union Street. The first music hall had opened in Lambeth on 17 May 1852, but critics were soon flexing their muscles. Initially the music hall was billed as a way of taking music to the masses, dragging them from the evils of the pub to refresh their souls with exposure to the strains of an orchestra and human voice raised in song. A periodical of the time, *The Tomahawk* carried An Opinion of Music Halls in its issue dated 14 September 1867.

> The Music-Hall, as it at present stands, is mischievous to the art which it pretends to uphold. Operatic selections, it is true, are still to be heard, but they are, as a rule so badly sung and vulgarly accompanied, that it were better for the cause of art that they should be omitted, and, in many cases, they appear to have died away – unheeded and unregretted – from the programme. Nothing is listened to no-a-days [*sic*] but the so-called 'comic songs', and, in sober [*sic*] earnestness, we must express our astonishment that human beings, endowed with the ordinary gift of reason, should be found to go night after night in order to witness such humiliating exhibitions. It is quite impossible to name anything equal to the stupidity of these comic songs, unless, indeed it be their vulgarity. A man appears on the platform, dressed in outlandish clothes, and ornamented with whiskers of ferocious length and hideous hue, and proceeds to sing, verse after verse, of pointless twaddle, interspersed with a blatant 'chorus', in which the audience is requested to join. The audience obligingly consents, and each member of it contributes to the general harmony, a verse of the tune which he happens to know best. It not infrequently occurs that one of these

humorous [*sic*] efforts is received with perfect silence, and under such circumstances, it might not unreasonably be supposed that the artist would refrain, from motives of delicacy, from making his reappearance before an audience to whom his talents do not appear to have afforded unqualified satisfaction. We are all, however, liable to be deceived, and no matter how slender the amount of the success achieved, the gentleman who occupies the chair will announce, in stentorian accents, that 'Mr So-and-So will oblige again' – which he accordingly proceeds to do, in whiskers more alarming, and vestments, if possible, more hideous than on the previous occasion. This species of musical treadmill is continued until the exhausted singer has sung four songs, when (if he sternly refuses to sing any more) he is set free, and allowed to exercise, over other Music Halls the improving influence of his talent.

He continued to rant in *The Tomahawk* the following week, this time at the expense of ladies who had taken to the stage. Marie Lloyd was a performer of this popular genre of 'serio-comic' songs.

She appears on the platform and, with saucy bearing and shrill voice, howls forth the same ditty about 'cards in the Guards,' or some 'swell in Pall Mall', or perhaps, she will tell you about a domestic romance in which omnibus conductors, or policemen, or costermongers, form the important features. Wanting, alike, in point, grace, or humour, these songs can have no purpose save to indulge the degraded taste of the majority of those who nightly fill the Music Halls; amongst such of audience as have been attracted in the idea that they would hear a rational performance, there can be but one feeling – pity.

We would gladly refrain from attacking women, but in that case, we cannot be silent, for we are satisfied that these songs are not only very stupid but extremely mischievous in their results, and those who sing them must not claim at our hands any consideration on account of that sex, which they have outraged by such unseemly and unwomanly performances. Grace in a woman, like hope in the human breast, should linger when all else is gone, and it is because these 'serio-comic ladies' have no vestige of feminine refinement that we condemn them hopelessly and unreservedly.

It will be seen that we have not touched upon the more serious question of the evil influence exercised by the majority of Music Halls as they are now conducted, and we have purposely refrained from doing so. If the morality of a Briton is to be attacked, the best course is to make, in the first place an appeal to his common sense.

In Victorian consciousness Music Halls were inextricably linked to the corruption of morals, and seen as a pick-up point for prostitutes where young men were seen as vulnerable targets as they lounged at theatre bars.

Plymouth may have been far from the capital but its theatres still managed to attract some of the spectacles so typical of Victorian theatre. On 16 October 1871 the Royal Amphitheatre and Circus Company came to town with a show which included 50 horses! But the sensation of the evening was a troupe of French female gymnasts whose performance was reviewed by The Flaneur (the stroller), in Plymouth's own satirical newspaper, *The Thunderbolt.*

Their feats are simply incredible, one of them for instance climbs a *loose* rope, up and down, uninterruptedly for the space of twenty five minutes. We are told that this interesting young lady, not yet out of her teens is to challenge any six sailors in port to rival her achievements – that is she will display more endurance of bone and muscle than all six combined.

A reward of five pounds was offered to tempt any sailors who fancied taking up the challenge, but the talented Mademoiselle Blanche beat all comers. This was not the only opportunity for public participation on the stage in Plymouth. When a new Greek drama based on Sir Walter Scott's novel, *Kenilworth,* came to town, the production needed 'extras', so they advertised for '48 respectable young women, not less than 4 feet 10 inches in height' to join the 52 already recruited to pose on stage in suits of silver armour.

As a military and naval town, battle re-enactments were popular, and when the Theatre Royal staged *The Relief of Lucknow* in 1871, the cast included 42 Highlanders commanded by Major McPhearson, including pipers whose kilts caused great hilarity.

As well as the theatre, there was a bowling alley hidden behind a tobacconists 'within earshot of Derry's clock'. Thanks to *The Thunderbolt* we have a sketch of this long lost bowling saloon.

OPPOSITE. *Entertaining fare at the Theatre Royal two centuries ago.*

Theatre-Royal, Plymouth.

On MONDAY, January 30, 1804,

Will be perform'd the ASTONISHING EXHIBITIONS of the

Phantasmagoria,

OR WONDERFUL DISPLAY OF

OPTICAL ILLUSIONS.

In addition to the FOLLOWING those of

LORD NELSON, The WITCH of ENDOR, &c.

A FIGURE of one of the PRISONERS of WAR in FRANCE.

A GHOST of superior Excellence

FAME bearing *"Long Live the King."*

A DANCING DEVIL.

Mr. QUICK and Mrs. GIBBS, *who move their Eyes, and have all the Appearance of Life.*

A TURK's HEAD, *with moving Eyes and Mouth.*

DEATH and TIME—The DEVIL and the AFFRIGHTED FARMER.

A View in Plymouth of a Lady and Gentleman

A SAILOR BOY—DEATH and the DOCTOR.

SKELLETONS *of various Sizes and Shapes*

The MAID of BUTTEMERE, who was seduced by the noted HATFIELD, &c. &c.

In the COURSE of the ENTERTAINMENT

A variety of new and popular SONGS,

(From the Operas of The Cabinet, Family Quarrels, The Pirates, and No Song No Supper)

By Mrs. SMITH.

Three new DANCES

By Miss HOOPER,

And several new Comic SONGS,

By a GENTLEMAN of Plymouth and Mr. SMITH.

BOXES, 3s.——PIT, 2s.——GALLERY 1s.

** Doors to be open at Half past Six, and begin at Half past Seven o'Clock.

HAYDON, Printer, &c. No. 75, Market-Place, Plymouth

A sober, sedate and orderly shop, whose outward and visible signs
are a choice variety of meerschaums, odorously scented boxes of
Manillas, and other miscellaneous accompaniments of the science,
pursuit, pleasure, call it what you will – that Sir Walter Raleigh
introduced into England . . .

We call for our weed of the dapper little urchin, one of those
precocious specimens of humanity whose age it would puzzle a
census enumerator to detect, and having 'lighted up' with a flamer
glance around. There are young fellows and fellows of middle age;
in short, an example of almost every variety of fellow. Some are in
ordinary costume, and others are divested of coat and waistcoat,
and appear as if fresh from some very exciting sport. These come
from out a ground glass door that appears to conceal an inner
'sanctum sanctorum'. Into this we enter. There is a bar at one end,
and chairs placed so that youth, sated with the game, may sit and
take its modest bitter (with no inane barmaid to ogle). Down the
room are two parallel alleys, divided by a partition. At the head of
each partition are placed the chalk and blackboard by which the
game is scored, while at the further end two urchins are on the *qui
vive* for the heavy balls that come rattling down, and threaten to
knock the urchins off their legs. In the twinkling of an eye, however,
the urchins jump off a perch erected for their protection, pick up the
balls, and roll them up the rails for the next player. This game is
bowls, and is the nightly amusement of scores of our youths. We try
one game with an highly scorbutic youth and two or three others.
We hurl the ball in a feeble manner, which plays round the pieces
set up without knocking a single one over. We repeat this promising
performance with variations several times. If we were inclined to
be cynical we may suggest that some form of amusement more
distantly related to penal servitude or hard labour would be more
agreeable to them, but we will not view the game in that, and will
simply say that a manly game like this is infinitely preferable to
gaping vacuously at a frizzled bar divinity.

St James Hall on the north side of Union Street, was built in 1866 and ran
talent contests, which followed the performance of J. Moss 'the great comic
vocalist, author, composer' who entertained audiences with his 'mirth-
moving, merry, musical, morsels for melancholy moments mimical of men
and manners'. In September 1896 an early form of cinema called the theatro-

graph was shown there, and it was converted to the Savoy Picture House in 1920, later destroyed in the Blitz.

Free entertainment was always available on the Hoe, a public space for mass entertainment and the lungs of the narrow streets of the old city. That space was extended out over the sea when the pier was opened on 29 May 1884. Refreshment rooms, a reading room and post office were all housed on the 420-foot-long structure, and in 1891 a concert pavilion was opened. Although the pier was destroyed by the raids of the Second World War, the official receiver had been called in even before war was declared.

The Hoe was above all a promenade, and in September 1871, *The Thunderbolt*, sketched a portrait of the area as darkness fell on a typical Wednesday evening.

I am standing by the ornamental lamppost at the higher end of Lockyer Street, waiting patiently or otherwise, for a friend. It would be more correct to say that I watch the people pass. . . . Damsels of 'degrees' and damsels of no degree at all, alone, in couples in batches with young men and also without; young men of the genus 'counter jumper' in similar quantities and similarly situated; swells that are and swells that would be; soldiers, sailors, officers with their wives and sweethearts; in fact almost every path in life is represented. They are for the most part bound for the Hoe. Here come some ten or a dozen trawler boys exercising their delicate and highly trained voices, which they endeavour to render still more soul-inspiring by a judicious use of two or three tin whistles. Their destination is the covered seat below the Camera. Here they sing, laugh, groan, fight, and being also staunch followers of Darwin shew how natural the bray of an ass, the bark of a 'dorg', or the crow of a cock is to them. Should these gentlemen happen to espy any of their 'lady' friends, they immediately, with the greatest politeness, chase them up and down the Hoe, which delicate attention they still further enhance with an unlimited number of refined yells, to let the 'ladies' know how much their presence is appreciated. It is customary for the ladies to reply with a corresponding number of yells, which they accordingly do. This is their idea of 'courting'.

Now come some half a dozen urchins, mounted on fleet cart horses and broken down hacks; they drive them frantically up the street 'to grass' on the Hoe. They appear to ignore the fact that they are fearfully and wonderfully made. In the absence of Mr Kessell

Defiant wartime dancers on Plymouth Hoe.

'on duty' his wife carefully scrutinises each charger and urchin as they pass one by one through the gate.

In 1941 the BBC broadcast to the Empire from the bombed city, and across the ether millions heard a poem by writer Clemence Dane, which captured the spirit of the wartime city. Clemence Dane was the nom de plume of Winifred Ashton, friend of Noel Coward and Nancy Astor, and Academy award winner. She summed up the capacity for Plymothians to find enjoyment under the worst circumstances. The wartime concerts and dances on the Hoe had been started by Lady Astor to strengthen morale and raise two fingers at the mighty Luftwaffe, which was wreaking such havoc on the city and its people.

I've just been down to Plymouth. Did you know
That lovely place before the trouble started?
Well, you'd be broken hearted
If you could see it now, I tell you that.
The mess the 'planes have made!
Acres laid flat!
It's cruel – day and night, raid after raid
And how the people stick it out, God knows!
I wouldn't know.

But there they are, and, stubborn, there they stay.
They work all day
Between the bombs. At night – this moved me most –
An hour before the sun goes down
They flock, the ruined people of the town
To listen to the band
(Light music, nothing grand),
And dance, or watch the dancing, on the Hoe.

Who dance ? Oh – sailors – girls from a canteen –
Men at a warden's post –
A smiling couple from a salvaged home –
Or others who've lost everything. They come
For company, to change their thoughts, to rest:
And shabby clothes don't matter on the Hoe.

The waters darken, purple dyes the West,
The hill tops lose their green,
The stars begin to glow.
Black-out! As home they go
The planes are heard afar.

This was the second summer of the war;
Yet every night, sedately,
Most innocent and stately,
The boys and girls were dancing,
Were dancing on the Hoe.
The boys and girls of Plymouth
Were dancing on the Hoe.

The proximity of Plymouth to the sea has been fully exploited by generations of residents. In the early nineteenth century, the *Sir Francis Drake* steam packet took visitors out to the Eddystone Lighthouse. A journalist from *The Devonshire Freeholder* accompanied one trip in 1826, and although the prose is not quite Jane Austen, one can imagine Fanny Price and her naval brother enjoying such a trip.

Seldom have we had an opportunity of witnessing a more brilliant assemblage of rank, fashion, beauty, and elegance, than was displayed on board this justly favourite vessel on Tuesday last, when she made her second excursion, for this season, round the Eddystone – it was literally a bumper overflowing with every thing that was agreeable. Yet, though the number of visitors on Tuesday last was more than treble that of the first excursion, we could not but remark how singularly select it was. Among those present we noticed many individuals of the very highest distinction. Though the weather was not altogether as favourable as upon the former occasion, it was sufficiently fine to make the excursion agreeable – when, about half way to the Eddystone a dense fog suddenly coming on cast a momentary gloom over the whole party; but this dispersed almost as soon as it commenced, and the Sun, shining out in his brightest splendour, exhibited a more favourable view of the Eddystone than we ever before remembered to have seen; it was at that moment of high water, when every rock was covered, and this stupendous Pharos rose, gilded by the rays of a western sun, in solitary majesty from the bosom, as it were of the mighty deep, the waves slowly curling around its basis, as if wooing it to the submarine embraces of Amphitrite. The amateur band from Devonport saluted the inhabitants of the lighthouse, in passing with some of their liveliest airs, which they returned with repeated waves of their hats, an example followed by a number of the gentlemen on board, accompanied by a partial cheering, which we could have wished to have seen more general.

CHAPTER 23

GRAND DESIGNS

Was it a boat? Was it a submarine? Or a hybrid of the two? The wreck of the sloop *Maria* and the fate of her one-man crew are a monument to the eighteenth-century spirit of enquiry, discovery and passion for experiment and science. She lies to the north of Drake's Island some 19 fathoms down; her fate forgotten; the dreams of her creator drowned. Yet in the summer of 1774 their fate was the talk of the town.

The silt and sand of Plymouth Sound is littered with wrecks: HMS *Henrietta* and HMS *Centurion* lost in 1689; merchant vessels *Thetis, Erin*, and *Coromandel* all lost on the Breakwater. But the most extraordinary is that of the sloop *Maria*. She was not wrecked in a conventional tragedy, with passengers and crew clinging to the rigging as the storm and seas played with their fate. In fact the *Maria* had been stripped of her rigging before she went down to the seabed in the summer of 1774 with all hands.

The man behind Plymouth's Sound most extraordinary shipwreck was an illiterate chancer called Day. His surname is all that has survived in the accounts of his experiment. Mr Day had worked as a labourer in shipyards on the east coast at Yarmouth, where, according to contemporary accounts, he was remembered as an 'ingenious man'. Day was a cross between Houdini and Heath Robinson, a man who saw a way of appealing to the Georgian passion for gambling in a stunt which masqueraded as a quasi-scientific experiment.

He would sink to the bottom of Plymouth Sound in the carcass of a ship adapted to enable him to remain underwater. What was he trying to prove? The account of this experiment survives in the British Library, written by N.D. Falck, the man who would try to salvage the wreck. *A Philosophical Dissertation on the Diving Vessel Projected by Mr Day and Sunk in Plymouth Sound*, published in 1775 tells us:

The purport of the experiment was to prove the practicability of a single man's being able to sink a ship, to remain with her under water for a considerable time, and to rise at pleasure.

Day found a backer for his extraordinary plan, Mr Charles Blake, who saw it 'as an affair by which money might be won'. Presumably he and his friends would indulge in a spot of gambling, wagering on how long Mr Day could remain underwater and whether he would survive! The amount they won and lost and the odds which were offered have not survived. Gambling was rife in the eighteenth century, and gentlemen and ladies delighted in taking odds on such extraordinary exploits.

Blake bought a second-hand sloop for £340, which would be adapted according to Day's specifications. In the era before architect's drawings it was common practice for shipwrights to construct a scale model as a blueprint for construction. Mr Day must have been a skilful carpenter to undertake the fiddly construction work this required. These wooden models were made using a variety of techniques. Some were carved from a single block of wood; others using thin slices of wood layered in a method known as bread and butter construction – the 'bread' were the thin strips and the 'butter' was the glue; some were formed with a series of shaped bulkheads; and others by thin planks laid on a frame in exactly the same way as a ship is constructed.

His model was sent to a Plymouth shipwright Mr Hunn, who was to carry out alterations. The pragmatic Mr Hunn immediately foresaw the difficulties. He was to convert the 31-feet by 16-feet ship into an underwater 'home', holding enough air for a man to survive for 24 hours. The hull had to be tightly caulked so that the water could not seep inside, plus it had to be strong enough to withstand the pressure exerted while it lay in 22 fathoms of water. One can just imagine the quizzical slant of his eyebrows as the enormity of the scheme became apparent. The sloop *Maria* was an old ship, but in fairly good condition so she was 'graved, corked, sheathed, and generally put into good repair.'

Day planned to survive in an air chamber about the size of a bedroom, 12 feet by 9 feet, and 8 feet deep. This was built amidships, a little towards the bow. His accommodation was built inside a skeleton of beams across the floor, with strong posts every couple of feet along the sides, and four at the ends. All the beams were bolted together.

To support the chamber on all sides against the pressure of the water, it contained two rows of stout stanchions, four in each row fore and aft, about three feet every way asunder, which were tenanted into the floor and deck beams of the chamber.

The frame was covered with two-inch-thick planks, and the seams between each plank were again corked, sheathed and pitched. The whole room was lined with flannel. Access was via a small hatch, which could only be opened by knocking the hatch open from the inside with a handspike. Inside were a hammock, a watch, a small wax candle, a bottle of water and a few biscuits.

Externally the ship had been stripped of her rigging and masts, and on deck were three buoys, which would allow the stunt man to communicate with the outside world: a white buoy to signal that Mr Day was 'very well'; the red to denote that he was 'indifferent'; and finally the black buoy to show that he was 'very ill'. All three were fastened to the deck with plugs, which could be knocked out via a mechanism from the inner sanctum.

Ballast was and still is an essential ingredient for stability in a vessel. But the *Maria*'s ballast had to enable her to *sink*, and on disconnection to enable her to rise to the surface again. The complicated details of Day's method were outlined by Falck.

From the chamber through the bilge of the vessel were four leaden pipes, about six feet asunder, two on each side, and about two feet from the keel; through these pipes went iron bolts from the outside of the vessel into the air chamber: externally under the bilge of the vessel, each bolt had a strong shoulder, through which was a large ring that held the ballast; and inside the chamber the bolt had a screw, to which was fitted a nut with a lever, which on being unscrewed, the bolt, with the ballast appending thereto, was to slip through the pipe, by which the vessel was to be disengaged from her external ballast, and at liberty to rise; and to prevent the water filling the chamber, plugs were ready to drive into the pipes as the bolts slipped through.

In the eighteenth century ballast was stone or gravel, and in later periods lead. Day's ballast consisted of twenty rough rocks weighing a ton each. Attached to each was an iron ring which connected them to the bolt with rope, so that they projected below the bottom of the ship. In addition Day used water, which was to stream in through two sluices in the bottom of the bows. Her internal ballast, which would enable the ship to travel to her chosen resting place, was 10 tons of limestone. Falck, who later tried to salvage the sloop, understood what the showman intended.

To sink her, so that the external ballast should first take her to the bottom, so that the vessel should partly be suspended without her keel touching the ground, in order to render her more capable of making her way up to the surface at the disengaging of her ballast. He (Day) was however so confident of his success, that he would not admit the necessity of any precautions with respect to fixing any thing to the vessel by which she might be weighed in case of failure of the experiment, which might easily have been done.

The experiment was to be carried out with great secrecy. And on 22 June 1774 the *Maria* was duly towed out to a spot chosen near Drake's Island.

At two o'clock the plugs on the forecastle were pulled out to let in the water to take her down, but the *Maria* would not sink. Rock from neighbouring quarries was sent for and brought out into the Sound. All secrecy must have been abandoned at this point as boards were ripped up from the *Maria*'s quarterdeck and an extra 20 tons of rock was tipped into hull. To the excitement of the onlookers, the sloop began to sink.

A French illustration of Plymouth from the interior; one of a series of engravings of English ports made in 1788.

Day, who had won a reputation for arrogance and obstinacy, began to strip off his clothes, to the amazement of his patron and those watching. Declaring it would be hot in his room below decks he made his farewells and 'retired into the chamber with the greatest composure'.

As the carcass of the *Maria* sank, the water 'became greatly agitated', but watching sailors reassured Mr Falck that this was always the case when a ship went down. Patron and financier Mr Blake was rather less optimistic, believing the gurgling eddies had been caused by 'a violent ebullition of air'.

Spectators gathered on the hills around the Sound, attracted by the strange events below them. By two o'clock on 23 June speculation and rumour rippled over the water, as the watching crowd anticipated the appearance of a coloured buoy on the surface to announce the imminent reappearance of Mr Day. But the waters remained unbroken over the spot where the ship had last been seen. It had been calculated that the air in his underwater chamber would last Mr Day three days. As the clock ticked on, the resources of the dockyard were summoned to help bring the sloop to the surface. Two hundred men worked for three days to raise her, but without success.

With all hope abandoned for the safe recovery of the ingenious Mr Day, the salvage man began his search. At low water on Saturday 30 July he swept the area with a spike attached to a rope. Splinters of fresh wood, pitch, tar and red paint were brought to the surface. He had found the wreck of the *Maria* lying in soft, clayey mud, at a depth of 22 fathoms at low water. The site was 150 fathoms from the Plymouth shore due south of Drake's Island, with Firestone Bay north by west. Falck was certain he would be able to raise her, but bad weather intervened. Undaunted he managed to get the *Maria* in tow but the hawser broke with a tidal surge, while the exhausted Falck was taking a nap below decks. He gave up on 21 October.

In his account of the episode published the following year, Falck didn't mince words on the subject of the character of the man behind the disastrous experiment.

His temper was gloomy, reserved and peevish; his disposition penurious, his views pecuniary; and he was remarkably obstinate in his opinion, and jealous of his fame. But withal he was . . . penetrating in his observations; acute in his remarks; faithful to his patron; and unshaken in his resolutions.

There's a hint in Falck's description that Mr Day was financially motivated, but we will never know. Falck evidently felt a certain respect for a man who had all the character traits of an explorer, who could as we would say today, think outside the box. Armed with the knowledge of the twenty-first century, it is easy to scoff at this attempt to expand the boundaries of human experience and endurance. But it is just that approach which put man in space, and led Columbus across the Atlantic at a time when it was believed that the world was flat. Under other circumstances, Mr Day might have been regarded as a pioneer.

His fate is however to be regretted! As his talents appear to have been such, which if they had been properly cultivated by education, would doubtless have rendered him an useful member of society.

CHAPTER 24
THE PIED PIPER
OF PLYMOUTH

On Sunday 21 January 1787, Reverend Robert Hawker went out into the streets of his parish like the Pied Piper, gathering children from their games for their first steps on the road to education. They trotted after him to rooms in Friary Court where many would see books for the very first time. Some nine years later on 7 March 1796, the foundations of the first purpose-built Sunday school in England were laid on the corner of Norley Place and Vennel Street. It was known as The Household of Faith and with its construction the town of Plymouth had made history.

The Reverend Robert Hawker was vicar of Charles Church and was one of an enlightened minority in eighteenth-century England. The unenlightened Establishment was predominantly against the education of the masses. It was commonly believed that a literate population would pose a threat. Mass literacy would be accompanied by the dissemination of ideas. The working classes would no longer know 'their place', but would acquire ideas above their station, and perhaps worst of all, aspirations.

But it was the establishment of the first Sunday school which knocked a hole in the wall of ignorance, establishing a principle which would result in compulsory schooling for children. It had been set up by journalist Robert Raikes, who saw it as a route to dealing with the causes of crime. As a prison visitor he had been shocked by what he saw. But it was his attempt to recruit a gardener's boy for his Gloucester home which gave him his place in history. As he searched for his new employee among the ragged children playing in the streets, he was told that there would be even more playing out on a Sunday. Many children of course were working six days a week in this era, and Sunday was their one day off. He realised that it was the poverty and deprivation which he witnessed on the streets which led people to follow in their parents' footsteps to the city gaol. As a prison visitor he knew intimately the tough regime implemented in the nation's gaols. But he reasoned it was no good for a society to be tough on crime, if they were not tough on the

Robert Hawker, who gathered children from the streets to study at the Household of Faith.

causes of crime. The first tactic in this battle was education, and he set up four small Sunday schools in 1780.

But how did Robert Hawker hear of this innovation? Raikes wrote about the school in the *Gloucester Journal* of which he was editor, and four years later it had received publicity in *The Arminian Magazine* and the *Gentleman's Magazine*, so these were probably Reverend Hawker's sources.

The philosophy behind the Sunday School Movement is outlined in an essay written by a liberal Roman Catholic priest Joseph Berington and published in 1788. In *An Essay on the Depravity of the Nation with a View to the Promotion of Sunday Schools*, he compared the state of late Georgian England to that of Rome before it fell to the barbarians.

> With pain I look to England. Every symptom which the most accurate historian described, as preceding the dissolution of Rome, I see furrowed on her countenance.

Father Berington laid blame for the state of the nation on the industrial revolution. And he viewed the countryside with a romantic idealism so typical of his age, an idealised view of the rural idyll which persists to this day.

> The towns where manufactures are established, are seminaries of vice. The contagion reaches to the peasant, and infects the villages. Before the love of gain had extended commerce, and luxury had quickened the loom and the anvil, England was less rich; but had we fewer honest citizens, and fewer patriots? Indeed were we less populous? The country is drained of its inhabitants to supply the losses, which disease, contracted from a thousand causes, never fails to make in the crowded cities.

He also argued that moral pollution had entered the country through trade with 'other climes'. Father Berington was a great campaigner on behalf of the poor, and in his essay argued that different denominations should bury their differences to set up these new Sunday schools for the poor. Above all he rejoiced that teaching children to read would bring them to God.

> It has been objected, that learning in the lower ranks of life, is seldom of any use, and is sometimes harmful. Is religious instruction then of no avail? Or can instruction be effectually conveyed, where the ordinary talent of being able to read, has not been first acquired?

Campaigners and propagandists from the largely non-conformist Sunday School Movement delighted in the apocryphal story of the little girl reading the Bible to her parents at home. Thus the virtuous child entertained her parents, keeping them at home so that they did not look for solace in the alehouse. If the children were to enter Sunday school early enough, he argued:

They will grow up with the happy bias . . . If their parents, fortunately should be induced to co-operate, then may themselves be in part reformed, and in their houses during the week, will be strengthened by good example and advice, the scheme of instruction which began in the schools. Perverse and obstinate should they continue to neglect their children, still something will have been learned, which may serve to resist the influence of bad example. In our days should the good be but partial, we know that the next generation will experience more happy effects, in a succession of parents, on whose minds had been sown the seeds of early virtue.

By 1800 there were some 200,000 children enrolled in Sunday schools across the country, and by the 1820s historians have calculated that numbers on the roll were so high that almost every working-class child outside London had attended. It was a movement which profoundly changed society, an expression of the religiosity and philanthropy of the end of the eighteenth century. Whether the movement ever had quite the effect that Father Berington foresaw is hard to quantify, thanks to the multitude of other instruments of change thrown into the melting pot of society.

From the passing of the Elizabethan Vagrancy Act in the closing years of the sixteenth century, it was a crime to be a street child. But in the nineteenth century the government found a more 'benevolent' method of dealing with these children. They sent them to industrial schools where they would be taught practical skills to enable them to find work. By the latter end of the century Plymouth had one of only ten industrial schools in the country, and *Mount Edgcumbe* Training Ship was one of only three ships to educate these young vagrants for a life at sea.

The number of Victorian street children was a cause for national concern. At night, children in Britain's cities could be found huddled together for warmth, round the outside of chimneys. But by day lurid newspaper articles told middle-class readers how the nations' streets were swarming with gangs of kids. Charles Dickens immortalised these children in the story of Oliver Twist, who joined the gang of pickpockets led by the Artful Dodger. But these little pickpockets were subject to the same punishment as adults once they were seven years old!

School was not yet compulsory and in fact there was strong resistance to increasing literacy among the masses. Practical skills, however, were regarded somewhat differently, and so in 1857 with the passing of the Industrial Schools Act, parliament sanctioned a new breed of school.

Children under the age of 14, whose parents were deemed to be neglectful, could be sent there. With low levels of life expectancy, often these youngsters had only one parent who was struggling to support a family. The schools were also intended to provide an education for those children who were exposed to crime. Today Social Services might step in and put these children on the 'at risk register'.

The idea for these truant schools appears to have come from Germany,

The first purpose-built Sunday school in England, demolished by planners at the end of the Second World War, despite surviving the Blitz.

where there were 'Strafschule' or punishment schools. The British version took over from workhouse schools, which were often inadequate. The charity schools movement had begun with the idea of educating children unlucky enough to have parents 'on the parish'. But this was not education as we think of it today. These children were educated for industrial occupations so that, unlike their hapless parents, they would not have to resort to the workhouse for support. So in the industrial schools girls were trained in domestic duties, learning how to dust and 'turn out' a room, working in the laundry, sewing and knitting. Boys were trained in gardening, oakum picking and wood chopping. Annual reports show that a large proportion of those who did not abscond, return to live with friends or die, did find employment. Discipline in these places was harsh, although for example the size and length of the cane, and its use according to age was regulated by statute. A child under the age of 14 could be given a maximum of six strokes and over that age a maximum of eight strokes.

Plymouth's Certified Truants Industrial School, under the headmaster Mr Fairbanks, stood on the site of the present primary school at Prince Rock between 1882 and 1906 when it was demolished. It was one of only ten such schools in the country, all of which stood in major industrial cities. A more benign attitude to children was developing, where they were seen as in need of care and help.

CHAPTER 25

POTTERS PAST

In the potters' hall of fame, Josiah Wedgwood is the name on a pedestal, but in the eighteenth century even he was in awe of the achievements of the first creator of English porcelain, Plymouth apothecary William Cookworthy. The Quaker chemist discovered one of the great secrets of his age by unravelling the formula for true china porcelain. The recipe for this fragile, translucent commodity was the industrial secret of the age, and it took William Cookworthy 20 years to unravel it.

Tea was the drink of the fashionable set in the eighteenth century, but most of it came into the country illegally. Tea was in such short supply, and so highly desirable, light and easy to transport, that it was a golden cow for the smugglers. They made more profit from it than they could on other staples of the trade like gin and brandy, and no doubt plenty of tea made its way into Plymouth! The fashion for tea had been set by the Portuguese princess Catherine of Braganza when she married Charles II. Her dowry included a consignment of tea, plus the gift of the Indian port of Bombay, or Mumbai as it is known today. This was given to the East India Company, which became the major importer of tea. Trade with China increased during the eighteenth century, and the ultimate consumer goods in Georgian England were fine Chinese porcelain. In fact porcelain teacups looked so delicate that milk was added before the steaming beverage in the mistaken belief that this would prevent the china cracking with the heat.

Cookworthy was born in Kingsbridge, but after his father died, walked the 200 miles to London where he became an apprentice to a Quaker family of chemists. Soon afterwards he returned to his native Devon, but this time as partner in the firm of Bevan and Cookworthy in Plymouth. During his time in London he had met many of the great names of his day, including Dr Johnson. They had been impressed by the young Quaker who had taught himself Latin, Greek and French in his spare time. In London no doubt there was talk of the secret formula of porcelain, which had already been

223

discovered by the potters of Meissen and Sèvres. The two ingredients, china clay and petuntse or moorstone, were known by this time; that detail had emerged from China in a letter written by a missionary in 1712. What still eluded the English pottery industry was the production method.

It's not known exactly when William became interested in the manufacture of porcelain, but in a letter to a friend in 1745 he mentions examining samples of china clay from Virginia. While there was frequent contact between the colony and Devon, importing such a bulky substance across the Atlantic would not have made economic sense.

Cookworthy's business took him into the neighbouring counties of Somerset and Cornwall, and it was while on a trip to the latter, that he recognised china clay in the waste heap of a bell foundry. Moorstone was easily obtained from Dartmoor, so for two decades Cookworthy worked in his laboratory trying to perfect the process, building a tall kiln six feet in diameter, in which he fired his experiments. Not only did he have to crack the secret of the exact quantities of china clay and petuntse in the mix, but also the best temperature and duration of the firing. Gradually he discovered that it was the kaolin which gave china its distinctive whiteness, and the addition of petuntse which gave the china its transparency. A glaze with these homogenous materials, fired at very high temperatures, resulted in porcelain. But the coal, which was able to heat the kiln to the desired high temperature, was liable to smoke and spoil the product, so he rejected it for wood. Despite the fact that he was not a potter, in 1768 he took out Patent Number 898 for the sole rights to make and sell: 'A kind of Porcellain newly Invented by me, compos'd of Moor Stone or Growan and Grown Clay.'

The glazing process he had developed was far superior to that used in the great pottery towns, and a subject of envy. For a brief two years, Plymouth China was manufactured at a factory by Sutton Pool, on the site of the China House. It was an ideal location close to the quay, where china clay and petuntse were delivered and the finished goods could be exported. His wood-fired kilns turned out mugs, sauceboats, dinner plates and of course 'compleat sets of Tea China'. Cookworthy employed about 50 people, and used his house in nearby Notte Street as a shop and showroom.

Customers raved about the new china, but the venture was short-lived. Skilled labour was hard to come by, the pool of skilled potters was up in Staffordshire and reputedly Cookworthy even had to decorate some of the china himself. His young partner Richard Champion moved the enterprise up to Bristol, where Plymouth China was produced for another eight years. But the Bristol factory closed when Richard Champion was declared bankrupt.

Although Cookworthy goes down in the history books as the great discoverer of the formula for true porcelain, he and his lab were in more general demand. When there was an outbreak of Devonshire colic in 1768, it was only natural that Quaker chemist William Cookworthy should be brought in. The mysterious ailment, which was closely linked to the consumption of cider, was a plague in the rural districts which in those days were entwined around the Three Towns. Cookworthy took some of the suspect cider to the laboratory at his home in Notte Street and duly distilled it, looking for traces of lead from the still. But he was soon able to exonerate the lead in the 'cider making engines', although the cause of the colic remained a mystery.

As a Plymouth-based chemist, the navy was naturally among his

The site of Cookworthy's home where he entertained luminaries such as Captain Cook.

customers. The night before the *Endeavour* departed for Cook's first voyage of discovery to the Pacific, her officers spent their last evening ashore at Cookworthy's home. Captain James Cook was leading an expedition for the Royal Society to observe the transit of Venus across the sun. It was this three-year voyage of discovery which was to establish his reputation as a great navigator. But he also built up a reputation, during his career, for looking after his crew: only one man was lost in three voyages during nine years at sea. They sailed through what are still regarded as some of the most testing waters: round the Cape of Good Hope, into the Antarctic Circle, to the Bering Straits and across the sparsely populated expanse of the Pacific. William Cookworthy must get some of the credit for the stamina and health of Captain Cook's crew. He was the manufacturer of protein rich 'stock cubes', which accompanied Cook on these voyages. Although the recipe for this portable soup had been invented by a Mrs Dubois, it was Cookworthy who held the contract to manufacture it for the naval bases in Plymouth and Portsmouth. It was made from offal, including animal hides, which would have ensured a high gelatine content, making it easy to store and transport.

When William Cookworthy died in 1780, huge crowds lined the street at his funeral. It is a measure of the esteem in which he was held by the towns-people.

CHAPTER 26

THE PLYMOUTH
BANK BUBBLE

November 26 1825 was a black day for Plymouth. The town was in uproar; wages had not been paid; and Whimple Street was so crowded that it was impassable. It was market day but little food was changing hands as *The Morning Chronicle* described:

> The people were almost frantic. Holders of notes are crossing and jostling each other in all directions. At Plymouth the uproar was dreadful. There was literally a whole population, with food in abundance staring them in the face, and yet without the means of obtaining it, for gold alone would the sellers take, and gold was not to be had. By break of day all the banks were surrounded by mobs, and the civil powers were mustered in front of them. To an agitated and tumultuous day, succeeded a night of fearful omen to many an unfortunate family.

The town's most trusted bank had collapsed, bringing down with it the local MP, merchants, farmers, shipbuilders and hundreds of small savers. Today a Plymouth Bank pound note can fetch £2,000 at auction, but that disastrous day in 1825 such banknotes were worthless. The story of that great 1825 banking crash is one of mismanagement, overspending and embezzlement.

The concept of a safe building in which to house valuables goes back nearly 4,000 years to Babylon, where grain was stored in royal palaces and temples. Such institutions were considered to be safer than private houses, and the receipts from these early banks have been unearthed by archaeologists on cuneiform tablets. Recorded deposits in the bank enabled trading expeditions to be financed against the security of that deposit. In England, the Tower of London was used as a place of safety, until the spendthrift King Charles I decide to purloin the deposits of various merchants in 1640. Local banks were established in the seventeenth century; the first was set up in 1658

227

in Nottingham. Usually they consisted of one room, which was the manager's office, with a safe and a bank clerk to record daily business. Before there were banks in every town and city in the country, money was kept in a strong box, under the floorboards or under a mattress. In times of unrest and war, coins were buried, to be discovered hundreds of years later by the 21st-century bleep of a metal detector.

In the mid eighteenth century and over the next 70 years the needs of industry and enterprise led to a mushrooming of provincial banks. By the 1820s Devon had more banks than Scotland. Every small community had a bank, even the tiny North Devon village of Hartland Quay!

These eighteenth century banks were cosy clubs, small groups of businessmen, landed gentry, and their friends and relations. According to contemporary press reports, the Plymouth Bank had been trading for more than 70 years before the great crisis. Its three partners were noted and respected men in the community. Sir William Elford was the senior partner, a pillar of the establishment with friends in the highest places, among them William Pitt the Prime Minister. In 1801 Sir William who was Plymouth Recorder and had been an MP, had the honour of presenting Horatio Nelson, the nation's naval hero, with the Freedom of Plymouth, he was Plymouth Recorder and had been an MP. Four years before the crash which ruined so many pockets and reputations he had married the wealthy widow Mrs Waldron, owner of Manadon Mansion. His banking partners were Jonathan Were Clarke and John Tingcombe, both wealthy members of the local gentry.

When Sir William Elford joined the bank in 1790, he did not ask to see, nor was he shown, a full set of accounts. In fact his investment in the bank was only £700. Four years later, two businessmen brothers, the Herberts, became partners, and when they left in 1813, the Plymouth Bank was £36,000 in the red. The baronet could not understand why the Herberts wished to leave the partnership, but when they insisted, the other partners only asked the brothers for £6,000 towards the deficit rather than their actual share of £12,000. Banking was a very profitable business they reasoned, things would improve and anyway the remaining partners had private fortunes to back them up. But Sir William had a small problem in the form of his profligate son Jonathan. This Regency buck also became a partner in the bank, but on his early death in 1823, his grief-stricken father discovered to his surprise that Jonathan owed the bank £30,000. But it transpired that he had only followed his father's example. At the bankruptcy commission, which convened two

OPPOSITE. *Notes issued by the Plymouth Dock Bank, victim of the great crash of 1826.*

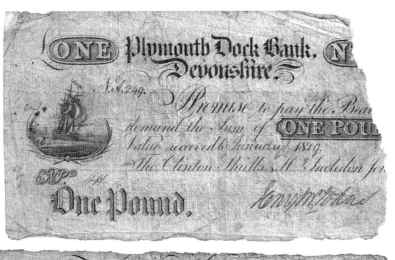

Plymouth Dock Bank, N
Devonshire.
N° 249.
Promise to pay the Bear
demand, the Sum of ONE POU
value received 6 January 1819.
The Clinton Shiells & H^r Incledon Jo^r
One Pound.

PLYMOUTH DOCK BANK,
DEVONSHIRE.
N° 551
Promise to pay the Bearer
on Demand, the Sum of FIVE POUNDS,
here, or at Sir John Perring Bar^t Shaw,
Barber & Co Bankers, London, value received.
January 1819.
FOR THOMAS CLINTON SHIELLS
& HENRY INCLEDON JOHNS.
FIVE POUNDS.

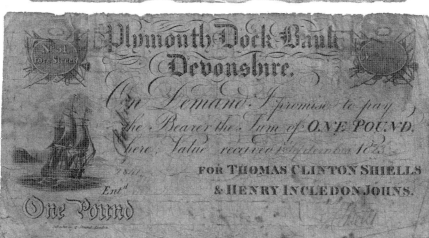

Plymouth Dock Bank
Devonshire.
On Demand I promise to pay
the Bearer the Sum of ONE POUND.
here, value received 18 September 1823.
FOR THOMAS CLINTON SHIELLS
& HENRY INCLEDON JOHNS.
One Pound

days after the bank collapsed, it emerged that Sir William had paid himself an annuity of £800 a year even though the bank was not in profit. He had also borrowed £11,000.

The origins of this great banking crisis lay back in the previous century during the long years of war with revolutionary France. Barter and small coin had been the main currency, and banknotes were rather more like IOUs, which promised to pay the bearer on demand. As these notes proved popular in the burgeoning commercial world of the eighteenth century, parliament tried to restrict their circulation. Beginning in 1773, smaller denominations were banned, but country businesses wanted the free flow of ready cash to circulate in the provinces. In 1797, £1 and £2 notes were allowed for the first time, and as the numbers of small country banks grew so did the number of these notes. In a parliamentary debate following the crisis in February 1826,

Manadon House was the home of Lady Elford, shown here during its wartime incarnation as Manadon College.

the Chancellor of the Exchequer told the House of Commons that in 1820 there were an estimated 3,433,000 country banknotes in circulation. By 1825, the year of the crash, he said, this had risen to 8,755,000, most of which were £1 notes. The national financial crisis that autumn had a huge effect on the poor, and had been exacerbated by a period of intense speculation and share trading with high stock market prices.

A great depression swept the country in the autumn of 1825, and the press was full of reports of 'distress in the manufacturing districts'. Cotton mills in Lancashire and elsewhere lay silent, families were starving, and people were jittery about the security of their money. The great run on the banks started on Tuesday 27 September when queues formed outside a bank in Fore Street, Kingsbridge as people rushed to retrieve their money. By 11 o'clock the next morning the bank had stopped paying out. By Thursday 28 September, news of this run on the bank reached Plymouth and people in the Three Towns were quickly infected by the rumour. The Plymouth Dock Bank in Fore Street, Devonport was the first to crash on 1 October. Four days later one of its partners, Thomas Clinton Shiells who lived at Woodlands, near Ivybridge, collapsed and died just as his bank had done, but it was rumoured that he had taken his own life. In an attempt to control local panic, other Plymouth banks put notices in the local papers, reassuring their customers that all was well and their establishments were solvent. But it was well known that the Plymouth Dock Bank had been well run and managed, and obviously these reassurances were not believed.

The Naval Bank sent to London for gold, which arrived in Plymouth by coach on 15 October. It was able to pay out to its customers, and tension started to ease. Just as local businesses and investors began to feel secure, no one suspected that the esteemed Plymouth Bank would be next. When its customers panicked there was not enough cash in the kitty to pay them; the bank was over £100,000 in debt.

Rumours started at four o'clock that Friday afternoon that something was amiss. But only hours earlier investors were still depositing their cash with the bank. At the subsequent inquiry all the partners admitted filling their pockets with sovereigns from the till, and the three clerks also took some £30–40 each. During the bankruptcy hearing, more nefarious goings-on were revealed. Jonathon Were Clarke had been recruited as a partner by his great friend John Tingcombe, who had failed to reveal the true extent of the bank's debts after young Elford's death. As these revelations piled up, both Clarke and Tingcombe dramatically burst into tears in the hearing at the Royal Hotel. All three partners had run the bank in a slapdash fashion, failing to spot embezzlement and fraud by one of their clerks who had borrowed thousands to fund a lavish lifestyle. As they left the hearing, the bankers ignominiously handed over their watches, removed their wives' jewellery and emptied their pockets of small change to help pay the hordes of creditors.

The three men were forced to sell their houses and land to pay the bank's creditors. Lady Elford tried to hang on to Manadon House, which she had owned prior to her marriage to Sir William, but without success. Under the auctioneer's hammer went Sir William's house, Bickham; John Were Clarke's house at Burrington; and Tingcombe's property Hartley at Compton Gifford. Sir William Elford was a substantial landowner with land at Western Hoe, Prince Rock and Cattedown; wharves on both sides of the new bridge; as well as lime kilns, warehouses and industrial premises. He owned property in New Street, including the building which was built on the site of Palace Yard; Southside Street and Mutton Cove; as well as a swathe of properties in Prospect Place, Millbay including the Prospect Inn. Fields, meadows and strips of land were all advertised as ideal building opportunities. Sir William Elford retired to Totnes where he died in 1837 aged 88.

It was as a direct result of the great banking crisis of 1825 that the Bank

The tomb of Sir William Elford in Totnes.

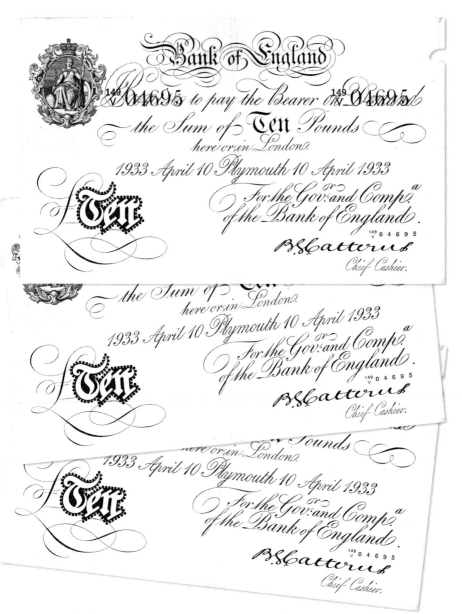

An example of a note issued by the Plymouth branch of the Bank of England.

of England decided to open provincial branches. Initially a branch was opened in Exeter, but the navy complained this was inconvenient and so it was relocated to Plymouth. The bank had a number of addresses, but in 1844 moved into its new Plymouth branch in Bank of England Place. Although the building survived the Blitz, it did not survive the post-war planners.

CHAPTER 27

THE DARK SIDE

William Jenkins was tipsy as he made his way home down Vauxhall Street one dark night in 1811. On his way home from his job at the workhouse in Catherine Street, where he was employed as a clerk, he had stopped off for a few drinks. The night was exceptionally dark and starless, but ahead of him beamed the lamp at the Pier. Befuddled by drink, William Jenkins lost his bearings and thought the lamp ahead was the light at a local pub, and therefore he was almost home. As he made his way a little unsteadily towards the pool of light, first one foot then another launched him into space. William Jenkins had succumbed to one of the hazards of Regency Plymouth and fallen into the dark waters of Sutton Pool. Passers-by appear to have made an attempt to raise the alarm by rousing the Town Sergeants at the Guildhall. But the night watchmen were unavailable, and 'the Town was without light'. The unfortunate, inebriated William Jenkins drowned.

He was not the first. As the jury heard at his inquest, a few nights earlier a stranger was making for another lamp shining in the darkened streets on the other side of Sutton Pool. As he walked down Pike Street towards the light at Coxside, the unnamed man fell over Sutton Wharf. In a letter to the mayor, the coroner made the practical suggestion that walls be built on Foxhole Quay and Sutton Wharf to prevent similar accidents. Certainly by September 1825, when the *Devonshire Freeholder and Plymouth, Devonport and West of England General Advertiser* reported the death of a foreigner and an unnamed local man who drowned near Coal Quay, chains had been installed. But the chains were 'in a defective state' and once again the 'darkness of the night' led to a fatal accident.

While the streets of modern Plymouth blaze with light, street lamps are a relatively new invention. The walls of the crowded courts and tenements of old Plymouth loomed over the narrow streets. Candles in houses would have cast little light on the streets below. Locals navigated in the dark by landmarks such as raised cobblestones and the gradient of the street.

The first gas street lamps in Britain were installed in Pall Mall, London in 1807. Their inventor was a German, Frederick Winsor, a pioneer of gas street lighting who, despite the brilliance of his ideas, died a pauper. Gas street lights arrived in Plymouth 20 years later. In September 1824, pipes to carry coal gas were laid along Union Street between Stonehouse and Devonport, and in 1826 Plymouth's Commissioners for Paving Lighting and Watching signed a contract for gas and oil lamps to be lit every night between 16 September and 16 April. Until well into the twentieth century, lamplighters walked, or later cycled, miles before perching precariously on a ladder beneath each light, with an oil-burning torch, to bring illumination to the streets. The difference street lamps must have made to the quality of life is

Prince Rock Generating Station from the air.

Devonport's Electricity Works sited in Stonehouse.

inestimable. Children could play their games outside on winter nights, rather than sitting indoors. The streets were safer. The last few gas lamps in the Barbican, Stoke and St Budeaux were replaced with electricity in 1973.

The wonders of the new phenomenon, electricity, were revealed to the Three Towns when an arc lamp was demonstrated from the top of the Devonport Column. The public was amazed, but it was not until 35 years later on 29 May 1884 that the first electric lights were installed. Driven by two gas-powered generators they lit up the Pier, and some of the earliest lamp posts were put up in 1898 powered from Prince Rock.

Electricity was not available to the wider Plymouth public until 1899 when the Prince Rock power station came on line in September. The people of Devonport and Stonehouse had to wait another three years and, when the

Newport Street station began to operate in April 1902, the good burghers of Devonport chose the direct current system, which was incompatible with the system chosen by neighbouring Plymouth. In the same way that railway companies had favoured different width gauges, so electrical entrepreneurs embarked on a battle of the systems, arguing the merits of 'direct' versus 'alternating' current.

Although electricity was taken up eagerly by the people of Plymouth, those in Devonport saw little point. Electricity in those days was largely used for lighting, and both the streets and homes of the dockyard town were adequately supplied with gas lights. But the residents of Stonehouse were disgruntled. Although they had supplied the Newport Street site for Devonport's electricity station, *they* had no electric lights and had to put up with pollution from the chimney, which blackened their washing. The great electricity debate was not solved until 1937 when all consumers were converted to the 'alternating' system. Devonport Dockyard's own power station was built in 1906 and demolished in 1961. It was also on 'direct' current to be compatible with naval vessels, but it too was converted in 1926. During the Second World War the Royal Navy reimbursed the community that had fostered it for 250 years. When the Prince Rock station was hit on 13 January 1941, leaving the Three Towns without power, the Dockyard generator stepped in to provide emergency power, while the Prince Rock generating station was repaired.

The advent of street lighting meant that shadowy figures glimpsed in the half-light were now identifiable. As with the more recent arrival of CCTV, it was anticipated, wrongly, that the new gas lamps would wipe out street crime. But they were not bright by modern standards, and criminals still had to be apprehended.

In dark courts and alleys, crime flourished, and miscreants were held in a handful of cells by the old Guildhall in Whimple Street, which was demolished in 1800. These local gaols were used for short sentences or as holding cells for criminals until their transportation or execution. Until the reform of the penal code in the 1820s and 1830s, the death sentence was imposed for offences as varied as impersonating a Chelsea pensioner, forgery, shoplifting and arson. Executions were carried out on the Hoe and there was a gibbet, which stood at the foot of the south wall of the military hospital in Mill Bay, but was blown down in September 1827. For many comparatively minor crimes the sentence was transportation for a minimum of seven years.

CHAPTER 28

PLYMOUTH
FIRST FLEETERS

Transportation overseas was a grim but logical successor to the medieval practice of banishment. Exiles banished from the kingdom were friendless and alone in a foreign country, forced to wander with no visible means of support. Strangers who arrived in close-knit interdependent communities would not be welcomed, unless perhaps they had a trade or skill to offer in return for board and lodging. Britain had been offloading her unwanted citizens in North America since the early colonial days. It was all perfectly legal and enshrined in the Act for the Punishment of Rogues, Vagabonds and Sturdy Beggars passed in 1597 in the reign of Queen Elizabeth I. But with the outbreak of the American War of Independence in 1775, this was no longer an option. Attempts had been made to send criminals to the coast of Africa and to British colonial interests in the West Indies, but in 1785 Britain was keen to establish her claim to the continent on the other side of the world – Australia. Why not kill the proverbial two birds with one stone and transport convicts there to establish a toehold? In this era of land grab, France was also among those turning greedy eyes towards the southern hemisphere. Among those who sailed with the First Fleet of convicts transported to Australia were petty criminals from Plymouth.

On 26 January 1785, Edward Perkins walked through the streets of Plymouth for the last time. Shackled at the ankles with chains, his hands tied, Perkins was destined for the rotting carcass of a hulk moored in the Sound. It was the last time his feet would touch the soil of his native land. What awaited him was a voyage into the unknown, for Edward Perkins was destined to sail on the first convict transport to Botany Bay. It was a destination so alien he might as well have been travelling to Mars.

The 57-year-old labourer must have been hungry when he stole a cockerel in January 1785, but when he appeared in court on 26 January, the prosecution postulated that the squawking creature was worth the sum of one shilling. Theft was a serious charge in eighteenth-century England when people had few material goods, and Edward was sentenced to be transported overseas for seven years. If his friends and family were in court that winter's day, the sentence was tantamount to death. With the breadwinner gone, his family would almost certainly have ended up in the workhouse. And as for Perkins himself, he was being sent to an uninhabited land full of strange and terrifying dangers, from which it was assumed he would never return.

A few months before the First Fleet sailed in May 1787, *The Times* summed up the establishment view of transportation:

> It is said to be the intention of Government, as soon as the settlement in Botany Bay is fully formed, and Commodore Philips has sent home his despatches to send out two ships every year with convicts for the complete peopling of the colony, and getting rid of a set of people whom this overcloyed country vomits forth. In the mean time the convicts will be employed at Woolwich in raising ballast, and on board the prison ships at Portsmouth and Plymouth, in picking oakum and spinning rope-yarn etc.
>
> This transportation to Botany Bay has the advantage of the former mode of transportation to America, in saving the kingdom from the dread of being infected again with these pernicious members of society. – From the mortality which has already taken place on board the transports it is supposed not more than one in five will survive the voyage; should the remainder live to expiration of their sentence, they can never pay the expence [*sic*] of a passage home.

Those smug tones of metaphorical hand washing are deafening.

The First Fleet, as it came to be known, had to be mustered, provisioned and staffed for such a voyage, so the unfortunate men and women about to make the unwilling journey had to be temporarily housed. Eighteenth-century prisons were overflowing, so Edward Perkins and his fellow prisoners were consigned to retired, ancient, leaking warships appropriately called hulks. Sir Francis Drake's *Golden Hind* and Captain Cook's *Discovery* both came to an ignominious end as hulks. Disarmed, derigged and unloved, these grand old ships became even more notorious prisons than those on land. The *Illustrated London News* carried a drawing of a hulk at Woolwich in 1846. The sails and most of the rigging are gone, and from the rope that remains, washing hangs, although it is unlikely that this belonged to any convicts, most would have owned only one suit of clothes.

A sad survivor from the age of Nelson at anchor in the Hamoaze. Hulks such as this housed convicts prior to transportation.

With Edward Perkins on board the *Dunkirk* hulk, were two other Plymouth men, Charles Granger and Edward Petherick; all three had been sentenced to seven years' transportation. Petherick had stolen a shilling's worth of clothes; Granger who was a 28-year-old breeches maker had been sentenced by magistrates for an unspecified 'petit' theft. Moses Tucker, who had been sentenced at Plymouth for fraud was also on board the *Dunkirk*. In 1785 he had been press-ganged into the navy at St Kitts in the Leeward Islands, and had served in the navy for a year before the fraud which led to his sentence of transportation. Described as a 35-year-old carpenter at his trial, his behaviour on board the *Dunkirk* was recorded as 'tolerably decent and orderly'. But those same documents record that Edward Perkins and

Edward Petherick were both 'troublesome at times' during the months spent waiting to leave for Botany Bay. Unsurprising in the light of conditions on board the notorious prison hulks.

Quaker prison reformer John Howard visited the ship in 1783, for his *Report on the State of Prisons* which was published a year later. About 350 convicts were housed there. 'There are among them many fine young fellows who all live in total idleness, although some useful employment might here easily be found.' Eight months later John Howard visited the *Dunkirk* again:

> The prisoners were all in total idleness, except 6 or 7 who were making a boat for the captain. One ingenious man had made a small

inkstand (which I have by me) out of a bone of his meat; but his knife had been taken from him. I saw some with Bibles in their hands; but there is no chaplain, nor any religious service. Here also some of the keepers by their profaneness, set a bad example to the prisoners.

Some four years after Howard's visit, the prisoners were occupied with that good old staple of eighteenth-century naval life, picking oakum. This was a tedious naval punishment, which shredded fingers as old ropes were frayed and picked apart by hand for use as mattress stuffing. But it could be done on board ship, rather than sending the men and women ashore, thus depriving voyeurs of a fashionable form of entertainment. Nothing was more delightful in eighteenth-century society than to view convicts at work, and speculate on the awful crimes which they must have committed. This fashionable predilection even led sightseers out to the muddy banks of the Thames at Woolwich where the first hulks were moored, but this was so disruptive that the authorities had to build a wall round the area where prisoners worked.

Space between decks on the hulks was cramped; few would have been able to walk upright in the confined space. Chained round the ankles to prevent any attempt at escape, conditions on the *Dunkirk* were so bad that the officer in charge complained that many of the prisoners were almost naked, and some women prisoners held on board were abused by men from a detachment of marines who were supposed to be guarding them.

Brutal treatment was common, as was punishment for trivial misdemeanours. Among the convicts John Howard met on his tour of inspection of the *Dunkirk* while it lay at Plymouth were

Three miserable objects, (who) for attempting to break out, were let down into a dreadful dark and deep hole in the bottom of the ship, where they lay almost naked, upon a little straw; but having been thus confined for some weeks, upon their entreaties, I obtained their release.

The *Dunkirk* served as a collection point for prisoners from prisons all over England as they were assembled for the First Fleet. This first voyage to Botany Bay had been viewed as an opportune moment to disgorge hundreds of prisoners from the overflowing prisons in London. Hardened criminals, who were sentenced to transportation for life, and children convicted of petty theft mingled on board. Among the children was James Grace who had been tried at the Old Bailey for stealing clothing worth nine shillings; he was only

11 years old. Age was no protection in the harsh eighteenth-century courts, and he was sentenced to be transported for seven years. But in one respect the *Dunkirk* offered marginally better living conditions by comparison with her sister hulks. Instead of mixing all convicts in together, some sort of division was made, although it's not known exactly how this was done.

Perkins, Tucker, Petherick and Granger were all transferred to the *Friendship* for the historic voyage of endurance to the other side of the world. Although some ships in the First Fleet were ex-slavers, the *Friendship* had been built only three years earlier in Scarborough, and was one of the fastest in the fleet. This would not make the eight-month voyage any easier. There were 76 male convicts and 21 females, plus 44 marines to guard the prisoners and the crew. Conditions in the hulk may have been cramped, but on board the *Friendship* 142 people were confined in a ship only 75 feet long. Convicts slept in cramped conditions little different from those Africans snatched from freedom to slavery. In fact captured slaves and early convicts had something in common: complete ignorance of their destination and fear of their ultimate fate. It's not hard to imagine the convicts trying to catch a last view of their homeland as the ship sailed on 13 May 1787. As the *Friendship* vanished into the Atlantic heading for its first port of call, the sea sickness and misery below decks can only be imagined.

First stop on this historic journey was Tenerife, where captain and officers were entertained on the island, while their human cargo languished in the heat on board – one man made a break for freedom but was recaptured a day later. After a week, reprovisioned, the fleet sailed for Rio de Janeiro. During this two-month voyage across the Atlantic, the fleet of 11 ships was beset by huge storms followed by hot weather. Fever and dysentery added to the convicts' misery, and one of the *Friendship*'s unwilling passengers died. When they reached Rio, an exotic location only viewed by the convicts when they were allowed above deck for exercise, fresh supplies were loaded and a month later the fleet sailed for Cape Town. This was their last landfall. In the sleet and snow of the southern ocean that December, Edward Perkins and his fellow convicts shivered in the damp and foetid atmosphere below decks.

After 251 days and a voyage of 15,000 miles, the *Friendship* arrived and cast anchor in Botany Bay on 19 January 1788. Only a week later two French ships were sighted sailing into the bay; the First Fleet had arrived to garrison and ultimately colonise New South Wales in the nick of time.

It was the height of the Australian summer when they arrived, and the lush and fertile landscape viewed by Captain Cook, and described by his expedition botanist Joseph Banks, was dry and inhospitable to crops. Captain

Arthur Phillip, commander of the First Fleet, decided to move the convict settlement further north where the flag was duly raised in a small bay to be named Port Jackson.

Two years' worth of supplies had also been carried in the holds of the fleet, but these had to be rationed. Edward Perkins was a brickmaker and Moses Tucker a carpenter, so their skills would have been put to good use, although the British government had made no effort to single out convicts with the relevant skills to found a settlement. Nevertheless ten months later there were two 'streets' of wooden huts. All the glass had been used in the windows of the Governor's house, so the windows were covered with lattice screens of twigs. Many of the women had got used to luxuries such as tea, thanks to the seamen on the fleet. But the fleet had returned home, leaving them without tea and many of them with child. Clothes and food were in short supply, but the enterprising turned to the resources of their new country. Kangaroo was said to taste like a leaner version of mutton, and a local weed tasted like spinach.

James Sticke and Dennis Connor were sentenced to transportation for life on 17 March 1788 at Plymouth, and were on board the notorious Second Fleet. While casualties had been low among those on the first transport, the contractor who won the commission for the Second Fleet was careless for the well-being of the convicts on board. Payment was made for each prisoner taken on board the transport, rather than for every person who arrived at their destination. This was changed so that more attention was paid to subsequent convict transports. Ships carried surgeons who kept detailed accounts of the health of the men and women in their care. And as news began to filter back to England, some of those sentenced to transportation began to view it as a potential route to a better life. This may explain the report from a correspondent in Plymouth published in *The Times* on Christmas Day 1791:

On their way to be shipped to Botany Bay, 22 convicts in an open wagon, and two (who are stiled [*sic*] gentlemen convicts) in a tilted cart. They had each of them an iron collar, and an iron chain run through a ring in each collar, which fastened them all together; the next morning, at eight o clock, they set off again in the same manner, and though there was a violent storm of wind hail and rain, they were singing hallooing, as they passed through the streets, with great glee and jollity.

Arrival in the nascent colony of Australia gave many convicts the opportunities which they were deprived of in the motherland. Saturday afternoons were free to enable convicts to grow their own food, but those who transgressed could face re-transportation to Van Diemen's Land. Here conditions were so appalling that men committed murder in order to be hanged, and therefore 'escape'. Transportation to New South Wales was stopped in 1848, and to the rest of the continent in 1868. The Devonport Borough Prison and Plymouth Prison were both built in 1849. As the British government began to build a state-operated system of prisons, they realized that it was cheaper to house those who had broken society's laws in Britain, rather than transport them halfway across the world. The discovery of gold in Victoria and New South Wales in 1850–51 boosted the argument of abolitionists, as the growing number of free-settlers resented the arrival of convicts on the Australian shore.

CHAPTER 29

INNS OF OBLIVION

When Jacobean dramatist Thomas Heywood created his fictitious Plymouth barmaid Bess Bridges, The Fair Maid of The West, in 1631, he put her behind the bar of the Castle Inn. She was a tanner's daughter and 'a girl worth gold': there was nothing tawdry associated with the loyal Bess who followed her man on his adventures to foreign climes. Two centuries later the pubs and beerhouses of Plymouth were considered the root cause of many of the city's problems, and the street which ran up the steep hill to the old Castle was notorious for its drinking holes. Castle Street was a mere 150 yards in length but in 1805 when patriotic Plymothians celebrated Nelson's victory at Cape Trafalgar there were 15 licensed premises in the street, one every ten yards. There is no Castle Inn among the pubs listed in the Guildhall records of the early 1800s, but Thomas Northam was the publican of the Castle Keys.

Lists of licensed premises and the licence holders have survived in the city's archives recorded on scraps of paper by the constables of each division, some of whom were barely literate. In Castle Street they recorded that Catherine Pinnick was landlady of the Lord Cornwallis; almost next door was Hood's Defence run by Morgan Lewis. Then there was The Rising Sun run by Hannah Hill, the only pub in Castle Street not linked to the navy by name. Many of these pubs celebrated great naval commanders and their victories. William Northam was the licensee of Nelson's Victory, while confusingly William Miles ran Lord Nelson's Victory nearby; John Fowler ran Dunken's [sic] Engagement, a salute to Admiral Duncan, commander of the North Sea Squadron from 1795. Richard Feet ran the Anson and Phaeton, the name of an eighteenth-century naval fire ship, which had given a decoy signal to an imaginary fleet over the horizon, allowing Admiral Cornwallis to escape a French attack. Samuel Bowden ran the Strap and Block, a jovial reference to one of the many harsh punishments meted out by the navy. Thomas Ellis's pub was called the Salvadore-Del-Mundo, a ship captured from the Spanish by Admiral Collingwood at the Battle of Cape St Vincent on

St Valentine's Day 1797. There were also The Fountain, Old Somerset, Waterman and Seventeen United Stars. It was no wonder that Castle Street acquired the soubriquet Damnation Alley. Here a man could spend his pay, find female company and wake up in a strange bed with a hangover but without his wallet. Just round the corner in New Street the pub names have a different flavour. The Anchor and Hope, The East and West Country House, Rose and Crown, and Gibraltar.

Licensing of alehouses and 'tippling' houses had been introduced in 1552, and a survey of 1577 revealed there were 24,000 alehouses, one for every 142 inhabitants in England. By 1816 there were 48,000 licensed alehouses in England and Wales. With the Beerhouse Act of 1830 anyone was able to set up a beerhouse for two guineas, resulting in a 50 per cent increase in the number of pubs in the next 50 years. It's no coincidence that the first parliamentary inquiry into drunkenness was in 1834.

One reason for the proliferation of pubs was that the drinking water was unsafe. Drake's Leat, celebrated as a source of drinking water for the city, was an open conduit from its source at the River Meavy to the city itself. Inevitably it attracted both feral and farm animals who used and abused it, plus the inevitable rats, the main purveyors of disease for centuries. Surviving street names record the location of city wells long lost and hidden

A cast iron water fountain in the wall of Morice Yard, donated by an erstwhile Devonport resident who made his fortune in Liverpool.

Buckwell Street, site of one of Plymouth's ancient wells.

beneath the modern street pattern: Westwell, Buckwell and Finewell.

As the city grew, these wells and the springs that fed them were polluted with the effluent which soaked into the water from numerous cesspools. So beer was the drink of the masses from pensioners to children, it was the safest way to take in fluid until the late nineteenth century. And as they drank beer all day, our ancestors' lives must have been passed in a haze of alcohol, which for many was no bad thing.

Pubs made their own beer and ale, the difference being that while beer was made with fermented malt, water and hops, ale contained no hops but instead was flavoured with spices. Beer became more popular by the end of the seventeenth century as it was stronger, and could be kept and transported without affecting its quality – for the same price as ale. These malt beverages were the staple drink of the working classes, but imported wine was also on the menu. Much of the early wealth of Plymouth was built on the wine trade with France. But in the same way that shoppers boycotted South African fruit in the apartheid era of the 1980s, so the choice of tipple in seventeenth-century Plymouth betrayed the drinker's political sympathies.

During the English Civil War the royalist Cavaliers had been depicted as heavy drinkers. With the Restoration of the monarchy in 1660 it was considered patriotic to drink the loyal toast, a custom which was de rigueur for gentry and tavern tipplers alike. Political parties became more defined as the century progressed, and those of the Tory persuasion drank French claret. When James II was elbowed off the throne in the Whig-backed Glorious Revolution of 1688, he made a hasty and undignified retreat through Kent to Catholic France. A year later Parliament slapped an embargo on French imports, thus depriving the Tories of their claret, the parson of his brandy, and opening a new and lucrative market for smugglers.

The embargo on French goods was lifted in 1697, but by then wine imports were coming in to Plymouth from Spain, Portugal, the Canary Islands, Madeira, Italy and Germany. Portuguese wines had seized a major share of the market, and dynastic wars were about to boost their popularity even more. A West Country clothier, John Methuen had lived in Lisbon and negotiated and cemented a treaty that changed the drinking habits of middle England for over a century. In exchange for a market for English cloth, the Portuguese were offered a ready market for their port wine. Port became the drink of the middle classes, in the same way that Australian wine swept into the market in the late twentieth century – both changed the English palate. The Whigs or Liberals, anxious to appear patriotic, became inextricably linked with their drink of choice, port. So by your choice of tipple your political sympathies were revealed.

Throughout the seventeenth century, drink had not been considered a social evil, although drunkards were a source of amusement and were ridiculed. From Samuel Pepys's diary it is clear that he often drank throughout the day. But the eighteenth century saw the first concerns about the evils of drink. In 1726 the Royal College of Physicians was so concerned about binge drinking that they send a letter to the government. Gin was the demon, and the Gin Act of 1736 was passed in an effort to clean up pubs. Drinkers could booze all day and night, until the Public House Closing Act for closing pubs between 1 a.m. and 4 a.m. was adopted in Plymouth and Devonport in March 1865.

It is no coincidence that this is the period of rapid growth in towns and cities. The agricultural revolution and introduction of machinery which in turn led to fewer workers on the land was the catalyst to urban growth. As

Plymouth's population increased 400 per cent from 1801 to 1851, so did a demand for places to eat and drink. A common nineteenth-century assertion was that drink was the only way out of Manchester – the same could be said of nineteenth-century Plymouth. Overcrowded slums pushed people toward the oblivion offered by over indulgence in alcohol. Families with several children lived in one room, without facilities to cook or wash up, and alehouses or beershops offered food as well as drink. With a permanent garrison of marines, and the many regiments which were billeted on the city during the Napoleonic Wars, it was inevitable that a regiment of drinking holes would rise to serve their thirst.

At a time when labourers worked six days a week, illegal Sunday trading was commonplace among pub landlords. As the Breakwater was under construction, dusty workmen fresh from Oreston Quarry piled into the pub at nearby Cattedown, or strolled around Sutton Pool to the many pubs of

The old Passage Inn at Cattedown, favourite haunt of thirsty breakwater labourers, demolished in the early twentieth century.

Castle Street. Labourer John Rogers appeared before magistrate George Bellamy on 23 August 1813 charged with being drunk and disorderly, and profaning the Sabbath. Mr Bellamy issued a general caution.

It having appeared upon the examination of the above offender, that some great number of the labourers employed about the Breakwater under pretence of settling their weekly accounts, resorted to the alehouse particularly at Cat Down and in Castle Street, on Sundays, and spent the greater part of the day in scenes of drunkenness and disorder, wasting the earnings of the preceding week, which ought to have been expended in the support of their families, thereby setting an evil example to the labouring classes in general. The undersigned magistrate being resolved to use his utmost endeavour for the preventing of such highly undesirable and pernicious practices and for putting the laws in place against all such offenders.

Bellamy warned publicans that if they allowed people to 'tipple' on the Sabbath they would lose their licences. The mayor ordered town constables to spot-check local pubs. The only drinkers who were exempt from the Sabbath rule were captains of vessels and travellers, and even they could not be served 'during the hours of Divine Service'. But peruse the pages of the *Devonshire Freeholder* and other local newspapers, and it seems landlords were too tempted by the potential profits. On 4 March 1826 a host of licensed victuallers were summonsed.

For permitting tippling in their houses on the Sunday preceeding, during the hours of divine service; 'mine hosts' were called on respectively to answer the charge preferred, the excuses were as various as the offenders were numerous, and the risibility of the audience, was often risen to hear the shifts these worthy Landlords were put to, to show their conduct in the fairest light. – One was sorry but he was at Church, and his wife let the customers in – Another only had his brother-in-law and his friend from Devonport in his house, and they had only drunk a glass of beer – a third had a sick son-in-law, and two ship mates came to see him- Another's clock was too slow, he thought it was not much after ten o'clock – One thought that Pilots and Sailors might drink at any time, supposing them amphibious, and therefore he let them in – Several had friends and relations come from abroad whom they had not seen for a great while, they were of course thirsty – One had his customers drinking under peculiar circumstances! Such were the excuses they used to get off – one and only one pleaded guilty.

The annual licensing sessions were ripe for satire, and Plymouth's own satirical newspaper, *The Thunderbolt*, was first printed in 1870. In its pages can be read work penned by luminaries such as Mark Twain and poet Algernon Swinburne. It was edited by G.V. Keast, also famed for his pantomimes, and the scenes described would not have been out of place in a Gilbert and Sullivan operetta. On 23 September 1871, the columnist Argus reported on 'the annual tournament between the publicans of Plymouth and the Guardians of Public Virtue upon the Plymouth bench':

It is a pitched battle that is looked forward to with some degree of excitement. The contending hosts assemble, and face each other defiantly and though in point of numbers and physique the publicans appear to have the best chance; in reality the fight is conducted upon principles which give virtue odds equal to about 10 to 1. The publicans are a study, and their prominent characteristic is to fat. Let the Morning Chameleon denunciate as it likes about alcohol – the Plymouth Publicans are evidence that its high priests thrive upon it. The wiles of the Publicans are numerous. One takes to selling cabbages, and though there is no affinity between cabbages and beer, a penny cabbage and a pint of beer are easily commingled on a Sunday morning. Another is the happy possessor of a bakehouse. This appears to be the safer investment. He contrives that people shall pass through the house to get at the bakehouse; and to take the morning nip in passing through is the most natural thing in the world. A third constructs five back doors to his house – This is ingenious and would entail the services of half a dozen policemen to battle. Here and there a 'lorn widder' comes on, (the vending of beer appears to be the favourite consolation of 'lorn widders'), but all these tricks avail not, for the Guardians of Public Virtue are relentless to the female publican, and the majority of them retire discomforted.

A week later it was the turn of Devonport magistrates to come in for a tongue-lashing from *The Thunderbolt*.

A strangely empty photograph of two city centre pubs – Noah's Ark, Saltash Street and Bedford Vaults, Old Town Street.

According to the declaration of the wiseacres (who adorn or otherwise) the Devonport bench, Publicans in that favoured borough may harbour prostitutes, do barefaced Sunday trading (assisted by friendly watermen who tap at the window when danger approaches) have any number of exits, may get as many people drunk as they possibly can in the way of business, but – must not get drunk themselves! Oh, happy town, possessing such virtuous magistrates! After this it is pleasing to note the Bench were determined to weigh the personal character of landlords. We suppose this excellent rule was adhered to in the cases of Susan Gorrald, Dock Gates, Fore Street, whose house was 'crowded with prostitutes every night and was the source of nearly all the disturbances in Fore Street; or William Leader, Cornish Arms, Pembroke Street' who allowed boys to assemble there to drink and play bagatelle, and had a brothel at the back of his house! These are two specimens out of seventeen queer ones, whose licences were granted with a 'caution'. Truly the Devonport magistrates, if not 'wise as serpents', are – to the publicans 'harmless as doves.'

It was in the nineteenth century that sobriety became a virtue. The first Temperance Society was formed in the United States in 1829. Two years later at a meeting to set up the first Temperance Society in London, the American group was credited with what was described as a 'moral revolution' in the United States. The aim of these groups was to 'abolish the use of distilled spirits as a customary beverage', but they did not promote total abstinence. Temperance propaganda claimed Britons 'squandered' £30,000,000 a year 'in enervating their bodies, darkening their minds, enfeebling their faculties, debauching their morals, and destroying their souls'. Temperance campaigners crusaded vigorously in the Three Towns, venturing onto the streets to combat the twin evils of drink and prostitution.

Fore Street, Devonport, which was obliterated by German bombers.

The city slums were recognised as the worst in Britain, and were second only to Warsaw in the European league. At the Rawlinson Inquiry of 1852 prompted by this dubious honour, Plymouth magistrate William Prance revealed that the fishing industry brought its own peculiar problems. Trawler apprentices earned 'squid money' from selling bait to fishermen and then spent the money in beer shops.

> Boys from 10 to 16 years of age make as much as 3, 4, 5 shillings a week, which they expend in beer shops opened to them at most improper hours, and each of these lads has his young prostitute of from 8 to 10 or 12 years of age. He had been told that in many cases these boys remained in the beer shops with these young girls until six or eight o'clock in the morning and were turned out in a state of drunkenness.

Even worse were 'tiddlywinks' or 'bunker shops' where people congregated when they were chucked out of beerhouses and remained there till very late hours. Giving evidence at the same inquiry the Reverend John Hatchard, Vicar of St Andrews drew attention to 'the beerhouses which literally swarm in the town of Plymouth, and constitute the greatest curse with which we are afflicted'. He estimated that there were as many as six beershops for every 20 houses, usually in the poorest part of town. He picked out the beershops of Stonehouse in particular, which were 'open half the night and a nuclei of vice and immorality'.

But some people were dependent on pubs and beershops to make a living. A Methodist missionary, who preached the evils of drink and gave out religious tracts in the city, met the Easterbrook family who made clay pipes in Back Lane, behind King Street. The father told him

> I do not drink much myself, but were it not for beershops and public houses our trade would be worth nothing. Why? Because if men only smoked at home they would not smoke one pipe of tobacco for twenty that they do in the beershop or public house, and they would take down their pipe and put it up carefully when they had done, a pipe would last them ever so long.

CHAPTER 30

AN INSPECTOR CALLS

In the wake of the behemoth of the industrial revolution, public health became a cause célèbre among Victorian philanthropists. Fortunes had been made in the great industrial towns, and it was a badge of kudos for wealthy industrialists to endow institutions for the poor. Britain's vast empire provided a ready market for the industrial goods churned out in hundreds of factories. Ships returning from glamorous and exotic destinations carried new and exciting products for the consumer, all showcased in the Great Exhibition of 1851. Britain's commercial fleet was protected by her navy, which ruled the seas. British hearts swelled with national pride, yet beneath this proud exterior lay a dark underbelly of social deprivation in overcrowded towns, and nowhere more so than in the West Country's premier naval port of Plymouth: in the 1840s housing and public health was condemned as worse than any other European city except Warsaw.

It was a sign of the growing concern about the health of the populace, and the unnecessary death toll, that on 31 August 1848 parliament passed the Public Health Act. Under this legislation, if the average death toll of an area consistently topped 23 people per 1,000 of the population, the government had power to intervene. In January 1852 the British government called a public inquiry into living conditions in Plymouth and Robert Rawlinson was despatched to investigate. He was shocked by what he found.

> Many of the old back streets of Plymouth are narrow, crooked, and steep, with a wide-jointed rough pavement and a dirty surface channel down the centre. Originally many houses, now in ruins, were erected as residences for the nobility and gentry of the town; but from being the abodes of those possessing wealth, they now give partial shelter to the improvident, the vagrant, the vicious and the unfortunate. The quaint carving on the stonework looks out of place; the walls are half in ruins, the gables are shattered, and foul

weather-stains of damp blotch the surface. Within matters are even worse; the rooms are now divided and sub-divided on every floor; the staircase is darkened, its massive hand-rail and carved balusters are crippled and broken; the once firm stairs are now rickety and dangerous; the stucco-finished plastering is blackened and in holes, the dusty and rotten laths being in many places bare; the landing windows, when the space is open, have neither frame nor glass, so that the rain drives in right and left; make-shift doors lead into small places let off as separate tenements. The narrow space of street betwixt the houses is further contracted by rude looking poles rigged out of windows on either side, story [sic] above story [sic], on which clothes are hung to dry. Thus a free flow of air is impeded, and an atmosphere, usually very damp, is made more so. In the same street houses may be found which were erected in Queen Elizabeth's reign, with others of more modern date; the walls are of hewn stone, of granite or limestone rubble, or of brick. Some have been plastered over, and others have been covered with slates; some are plain vertical fronts, and others project at each story. Out of these streets, covered passages, lead into still narrower, dirtier and more crowded courts. In many instances, the ground rises abruptly, and slippery half-worn limestone steps lead to houses more ruinous and more crowded than those fronting the street.

When archaeologists excavated parts of St Andrews Street during the 1970s, their trowels uncovered a hotchpotch of walls in each tenement area, confirming the higgledy-piggledy nature of that part of Plymouth. They also discovered the remains of cesspits, abandoned as they filled up over centuries of occupation.

Rawlinson's Report on the Sewerage, Drainage and Supply of Water, the State of the Burial Grounds, and the Number and Sanitary Condition of the Inhabitants survives in the city archives. He must have toured the slums in person, to have left us such a detailed description of the lack of sanitation – landlords had never been forced to put water supplies inside these buildings; as a result a tenth of the population had no piped water, instead drawing it from pumps and wells.

One privy serves a whole court, and this is usually filthy; the cess pool full, overflowing and the foetid refuse stagnant over the

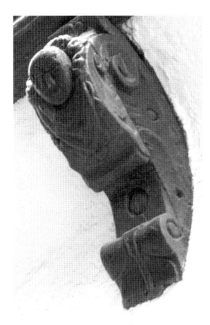

ABOVE. *Carved detail from Plymouth's heyday.*

RIGHT. *Part of the eclectic remains behind the Elizabethan House in New Street, saved from demolition by the Old Plymouth Society.*

surface. An external stand-pipe, the water on only for one hour in twenty-four, supplies water to an entire court with many tenants.

Rawlinson cited the example of Market Alley, a narrow passage with a row of dirty privies and one tap shared between 145 people. Only 300 years earlier the city had been provided with sparkling Dartmoor water by Drake's Leat. The water was still described in 1853 as 'pure and of exquisite brilliancy requiring only to be settled and without the slightest need of filtration', but it was polluted en route: 'The impurities of the water at Plymouth are imparted to it on its way through the open leat. The washings of farm-yards, fields and roads, drain into it, and cattle wade in it.'

As a succession of witnesses took the stand, the thumbnail sketch so ably given by Rawlinson became more detailed. Streets were so narrow that no carriage could pass, and planks had to be thrown across to enable people to extricate others who had, literally, got stuck in the mud. Rotting refuse filled the streets and, as was only natural in a fishing port, this included fish heads and entrails. Lambhay Hill was reported to be 'notorious for filth'. In Quarry Lane 50 or 60 people lived in one house of four rooms. This was an area in which many poor and destitute Irish immigrants, refugees from the potato famine of 1846 had congregated. In nearby Quarry Court the 'houses' had mud floors, and 105 people lived in 16 rooms with one privy. Other streets of shame were picked out by the report: St Andrews Street, Notte Street, Looe Street, Stokes Lane, Wyndham Lane, No Place Lane, Frankfort Street, Market Place, Back of Market, Kinterbury Street, High, Middle and Lower Lanes.

An average of nine people lived in each dwelling in Plymouth as compared with the national average of 5½. The state of the interior was as decrepit as the exterior, as Rawlinson described:

Within, the furniture accords with the premises: it is old, rotten, broken and ruinous. One room serves for a family of father, mother and children, not infrequently grown up sons and daughters. Dogs and fowl inhabit the same apartment, and, in some instances, ten human beings.

Domestic rubbish collection is a modern innovation. Plymothians in the first half of the nineteenth century had no such service, with resultant problems. On Monday 18 January 1802, 50 years before Rawlinson's damning report, the Grand Jury assembled in the Guildhall to review the problem. This account survives:

Having viewed the situation of sundry streets within this borough and found that the inhabitants or tenants of the premises belonging to the undermentioned persons had thrown great quantities of dirt and filth in the streets and gutters before their houses, and suffered the same to remain there to the great annoyance of the neighbouring inhabitants and the public at large, feel it their duty to present to the Court of Quarter Sessions, now sitting, the names of the several persons whose tenants have occasioned and suffered such nuisances to remain.

No record of the sanctions imposed has survived, but it is no wonder that the Rawlinson report found that the city streets were a sea of mud in winter and dusty in summer. He did praise the local authority for its efforts: the streets were swept every night and in summer nine water carts travelled the streets every day sprinkling water on the dusty surface.

The one dumping ground easily available to the people of Plymouth for centuries was the sea. Unfortunate sailors who died on board ship were 'buried' in The Sound, leading to complaints about the number of bodies floating in the harbour. These rotting corpses mingled with raw sewage: 12 public sewers discharged into Sutton Pool as well as numerous private drains, according to the Inspector's 1852 report.

> The quantity of soil and detritus annually discharged is unquestionably injurious to the Harbour Company, and detrimental to the health of the inhabitants. When the tide ebbs there are offensive exhalations from the mud slobs of the Pool, especially in the vicinity of the Parade, where the flood-tide has least scouring action.

A waste leat also regularly overflowed over Union Street. Coupled with the stink of raw sewage were the fumes from the sugar refinery in Mill Lane and the smell of butchered carcasses from the slaughterhouse. Even Plymouth's enviable seaside location and the salt-laden breeze could not compensate for the stinking, stale air trapped in its narrow streets. It is no wonder that the mortality rate was higher than in London. Rawlinson even used a complicated mathematical formula to calculate the average cost of each fatality from preventable sickness at £5 'including attendance relief and funeral'. According to this formula, every year fatalities caused by poor public health were costing the city £23,465.

> In Plymouth the causes of excessive mortality are overcrowding, defective ventilation, human refuse in and near houses, water supply and lack of proper sewers and drains. The causes producing this excess of sickness, misery and death, are structural, and may be lessened if not entirely removed.

The graveyards were overflowing, or as the inspector put it, 'full to an extent dangerous to health, and disgusting to the imagination'.

The forthright Rawlinson was quite happy to apportion the blame to the debt-ridden local authorities. By an extraordinary anomaly, Plymouth in 1853 was run by two entirely separate bodies: the elected Corporation and the

OPPOSITE. *A slum in Old Town Street.*

non-elected, and indeed self-appointed, Commissioners. The Corporation led by the mayor was based at the Guildhall and was £52,000 in debt, while the Commissioners had run up debts of £15,000, largely by widening Treville Street (formerly Butchers Lane).

Witnesses told the public inquiry that £2,000 had also been 'wasted' in buying a house at the corner of Old Town Street and George Street. This was demolished 'there being not room enough for the carriages driving there, when in fact there was room enough for four abreast'. The inspector concluded:

> The Local Commissioners have expended considerable sums of money in widening main streets, in rounding off prominent corners, in paving and flagging front streets, and in constructing isolated sewers, without house drains. There is nothing positively wrong in doing these things; the mischief exists in leaving undone, works of more general utility.

The Rawlinson report would signal the extinction of the Commissioners, but it would take a century for the slums of the Three Towns to disappear.

CHAPTER 31

CASUALTIES OF THE HOUSING CRUSADE

To the modern eye, the warrens of higgledy-piggledy narrow streets and alleys that climbed the hillside above Sutton Harbour, or clustered in the confines of Morice Town, appear quaint and delightful. Historic they certainly were, but for their nineteenth- and twentieth-century inhabitants they were squalid, cramped and unhealthy. For generations landlords neglected these historic streets, which housed the city's poor. Nazi bombs may have given Plymouth the unenviable reputation as the most Blitzed city outside London, but it was slum clearance, not the Nazis, which destroyed the character of much of the Three Towns.

In the heyday of Good Queen Bess, grand timber-framed houses with casement windows rose above the ancient narrow streets of the Barbican. From their windows merchants could see their goods arriving at the quayside. Adventurers like Sir Francis Drake and Hawkins cemented deals and sold their bounty in this town. Exotic imports like spices, sugar and foreign wines were landed here, and duties were paid at the Customs House on what is now the Parade. The wheeler-dealing merchants grew rich on this trade and abandoned the narrow streets for pastures new, outside the confines of the town. Dockworkers, fishermen, watermen and casual labourers took their place. The sixteenth- and seventeenth-century houses were left to decay, and ramshackle extensions were thrown up in the courtyards and erstwhile gardens. Landlords were not forced to make repairs or connect mains water – after all, these quaint relics of Plymouth's past were inhabited by the poor.

The origin of the word 'slum' is unknown but the word dates back to the nineteenth century, a time when the pressure on housing stock was exacerbated by the inevitable march of labour from the agricultural areas. Rural workers forced from homes and jobs by poor harvest, new machinery, or just lured by the attraction and opportunity offered by the city, vied for space with existing inhabitants. Between 1801 and 1831 the population of Plymouth doubled, and some resorted to building on open ground outside the city

A family sun themselves in an old court in Bilbury Street.

walls. On 25 April 1808 John Collier wrote to the mayor with this grievance:

> Sundry huts dwellings and pig styes have been at various times
> erected on a waste or highway near the glacies [*sic*] of the Citadel,
> which are become great nuisances to myself and others having prop-
> erty near the place as is particularly evinced by a recent case which
> has come under your notice. I am the man desirous to draw your
> early attention to these encroachments because the parties already
> seem to consider that they have a freehold property in the premises
> and are in the habit of transferring them one to another. Having
> brought these encroachments under your notice, I write with

confidence that by causing them to be timely removed it will render it unnecessary for me to take any measures against the Corporation for having so long suffered the existence of such nuisances to the public.

His complaint has survived in the city's archives, although the mayor's reaction has not. One example of these squatters was the family of Mrs Woodward. Her letter of 4 October 1814 is in an educated hand.

> The case I have to lay before you Sir is simply this – Being now a poor widow with five children, and being in possession of a hut wherein I now reside with my little family at the foot of the Glacis and near the Jews Burying Ground: which spot of ground was granted by George Mercer about the year 1800 to William Sibley then an invalid, to build a hut on for his residence. . . . And being soon after discharged, sold the said hut to my then husband Joseph Pitcher, for the sum of £20 a receipt for which I have in my possession dated 2nd January 1802. My said husband Joseph Pitcher dying soon after and leaving me with two children I since became married to William Woodward an invalid also, by whom I have three children, and who being sent abroad to Madiera [sic] in the Royal Veteran Battalion there died in the month of July 1813, so that I am now a widow with five children aforesaid. But lately gentlemen from the Board of Ordnance said they will be pulling down this and others adjoining.

Did her appeal tug at the conscience of the men at the Guildhall? One suspects not.

It took another three decades before the eyes of England were opened to the conditions of the poor. Campaigning reports from men like Edwin Chadwick and journalist Frederick Engels revealed the conditions in which the poor lived. The tide of concern for the masses which washed over middle-class Victorian society would eventually engulf the crabby gables of the Sutton quarter.

Cholera was a frequent and unwelcome visitor to the Three Towns, spreading through cramped and overcrowded streets with alarming speed. In 1832 a wooden hospital was built on the site of Five Fields to nurse the sick, but it was the epidemic of 1849 which became legendary.

Discovered on an emigrant ship in February, the disease had migrated

Cholera Humbug;

OR,

NO CHOLERA MORBUS.

ALL you that do in England dwell,
I will endeavour to please you well,
If you will listen I will tell
About the Cholera Morbus.

CHORUS.

They tell me now it's all my eye :
No more you'll hear the people cry,
Have mercy on me, I shall die,
I have got the Cholera Morbus.

They say it's lately come to town,
To affect the people all around,—
But every voice does now abound,
It's gone, the Cholera Morbus.

If the Cholera Morbus should come here,
The best of clothes you then must wear,
Eat and drink the best, then never fear
You will get no Cholera Morbus.

They say the doctors all went round,
Through e—'y part of London town ;
But it was no where to be found,
It was off, the Cholera Morbus.

Some people say it was a puff,
Just done to raise the doctor's stuff,
And there has now been near enough,
About the Cholera Morbus.

This nation long has troubles borne,
The people have been left forlorn,
It was reported that the Reform
Had caught the Cholera Morbus.

Doctors Grey and Brougham, men of wealth,
And Russell purged him well himself,
The Bill is now in perfect health,
It has got no Cholera Morbus.

In Parliament of late did pass
A motion for a general Fast,
And if it very long did last,
It may bring the Cholera Morbus.

I can tell you what we want at least,
Not a Fast, but a general Feast,
That will be a good receipt at least,
To cure the Cholera Morbus.

Them that will not hear the people's groans,
Were compelled to sweat their lazy bones,
On the turnpike roads a breaking stones,
They would feel the Cholera Morbus.

For beef and bread's the only stay,
It will keep disorders all away,
We'll never mind what people say,
About the Cholera Morbus.

The thing we want, as William said,
The rich to take it in their head,
To feed the poor with beef and bread,
To cure the Cholera Morbus.

To report about they did begin,
If you should drink either beer or gin,
Or any liquor, what a sin !
You would have the Cholera Morbus.
It is my opinion as a man,
That trade has long been at a stand ;
There are thousands starving through the land,
And THAT'S the Cholera Morbus.

In many parts, mark what I say,
Men cannot earn a shilling a day,
Which puts their families in the way
To get the Cholera Morbus.

While state peers strive with great delight,
To tax the people day and night,
I'm certain very well they might
Give them the Cholera Morbus.

The farmers cannot sell their wheat,
The poor can scarce get bread to eat ;
The tradesman is ruined now complete,
Aye, and that's the Cholera Morbus.

Some do monopolize the corn,
And drive the people all forlorn ;
If all things don't get great Reform,
They will get the Cholera Morbus.

I'm afraid, as you shall understand,
Unless something is speedily took in hand,
All trade and commerce through the land
Will have the Cholera Morbus.

You must acknowledge what I say,
When thousands go from day to day
With scarcely food or clothing, they
May have the Cholera Morbus.

Some live in luxury,—some deplore,—
And if the rich don't help the poor,
When the d***l gets them to his door,
They will have the Cholera Morbus.

Bates, Printer, Plymouth.—Hawkers supplied.

into the slums by 2 July, making its first appearance in Quarry Court, Stonehouse Lane. On 3 September *The Times* reported uncharitably:

> One remarkable feature in the present visitation of the disorder in Plymouth has prevailed throughout, viz the attacks being confined almost exclusively to the labouring, the pauper, and the itinerant classes, especially the latter. Quarry Court in Stonehouse Lane where the disorder first appeared, was depopulated, and thoroughly cleansed by the local board of health. The structure of the place however, and the mode of its occupation, are circumstances over which the board has no control. This infectious vicinity is being fast occupied again by vagrants, who nightly crowd the small, ill-ventilated rooms, bringing a large revenue to the landlords, and a serious evil to the town, the ratepayers of which have to provide food and medicine for them directly they are overtaken by sickness or want, real or feigned.

Several uninfected families were moved to the *Leda*, a hulk moored off Mutton Cove. At its height in the sultry weather of mid August, 154 deaths were recorded in Devonport, and there were more than 200 dock workers on the sick list. By October, when the disease had run its course, there were over 1500 dead in the Three Towns. In a subsequent cholera epidemic in 1866, *The Times* pinpointed Cooksley Court, off Castle Street, where two brothers had been infected:

> Cooksley's Court consists of six or eight tenement houses with insufficient space behind, if any. The town water supplied to this district comes for several miles, and is exposed to the reception of all kinds of decomposing animal and vegetable matter likely to be injurious to health.

In damp overcrowded rooms whole families saw birth and death, slept and worked, ate and cooked. Such conditions were seen by great social reformers like Edwin Chadwick as encouraging vice. Implicit in the descriptions of Victorian slums, and particularly the 'one room family', is the link to immoral behaviour – incest, promiscuity and vice. Certainly some women were driven to prostitution in these areas; certainly criminality was found there; certainly

OPPOSITE. *Cholera was a constant threat to the poor and ill-housed.*

drink must have been used as a panacea for some.

Plymouth Town Mission was established in 1836 to extend the gospel to the poor and destitute in Plymouth, and to preach the evils of sin and drink. Miss Sarah Venn was one of the missionaries who braved the city slums, and in her diary she recorded regular forays into the homes and lives of inhabitants. On 23 January 1876 she described the poverty she found in one dwelling in Lower Batten Street. The occupant was in bed with a head injury and fractured ribs after falling down the stairs. 'It is a sad sight as you enter the room at the top of the house scarcely any thing in it. She lying on a old bed the only covering a few old things the largest the skirt of a dress.' The anonymous occupant made a tenuous living selling fruit at the market and at the theatre doors in the evening. Sarah Venn who lived at 50 Union Street, Stonehouse, was obviously deeply affected by such encounters. People she visited were so desperate they were driven to sell their clothes for food. On another winter's day that year she visited the Egg family.

When I entred [sic] the room such a sight the poor woman surfing [sic] from Asma [sic] at times hardly able to speak to you. A daughter 19 years old in a decline only able to get up part of the day, one boy a sailor home on his three weeks leave; one at school; also a baby. In the room there was two beds, or rather I should say dirty mattress stuffed with straw, on the girls bed the only covering was some old pieces of Sinsey [type of fabric] on the other there was a blanket made of pieces sewed together which I should think some kind friend had given them, on the table was a broken teapot and some old china, everything in the room was in a dirty untidy state, the poor woman seems quite broken down in sprites [sic], the man gets 14 shillings a week when he can work.

During her conversation with the family, Miss Venn was told that the husband 'a times drinks and is [sic] also a very violent temper'. A week later she returned to find that the sailor son had cleaned the room, but by her subsequent visit on 3 February 1876, the mother had broken her arm 'by a fall', perhaps the result of her husband's violent temper.

Criticism of the landlords and owners of these properties is surprisingly absent from her accounts. They were after all to blame for failing to mend

OPPOSITE. *Cooksley Court behind Castle Street survived the war but not the planners; cholera broke out here in 1866.*

roofs and repair windows, replace rotten floorboards and staircases, and maintain guttering.

At the height of increased agitation for housing improvements 30 years later in September 1906, a leader writer on the *Western Daily Mercury* did lay blame at the landlords' door:

There are no worse landlords than small owners of freehold cottage property. Overcrowding in the Three Towns generally is undoubt- edly due in large measure to the grasping greed of landowners, who by sitting tight and refusing to sell have forced up the price of land in the Three Towns to three times the figure it would fetch in the suburbs of some of our provincial cities, or even of London itself; but they have been able to do this by the natural configuration of the land, which is so water-locked that expansion is only possible in one direction.

Much of the agitation for improved housing conditions arose from the Three Towns Association formed in 1897. For nearly 40 years they were at the fore- front of campaigns for better housing in Plymouth, organising open-air meet- ings as part of their strategy.

Local councils had been 'entitled' to arrange re-housing under the Artisans and Labourers Dwellings Act of 1875, but they were not *obliged* to act. Fifteen years later parliament passed the Housing of the Working Classes Act, which empowered local authorities to build council houses. Plymouth Council's first local authority housing can still be seen on Laira Bridge Road. The red brick terraces were built in 1897, and Plymouth reputedly was the first council to comply with the act. Looe Street and Vauxhall Street followed when the council opened Housing for Working Men in 1898.

During the First World War, campaigners did not stop their agitation for housing improvement. In a series of pamphlets on housing congestion in the Three Towns, there are shocking descriptions of the dilapidated state of the housing stock. In one example, a woman whose husband was away in the trenches lived in a cottage in a lane in Devonport with her eight children. Only three of the rooms were habitable. Her eldest son worked at the dock- yard, but had been forced to take time off because his siblings were suffering from diphtheria, croup and measles.

The back room is almost empty, the windows being broken. Upstairs the eldest daughter's bedroom is quite dark until a carpet

Model homes for working men put up in the 1890s in the first phase of slum clearance.

covering the broken window there is taken down. They say pigeons
are kept opposite behind the house and stones are thrown and the
windows smashed. The girl is washing out a room measuring eleven
feet by eight which gave temporary shelter to a family of ten from a
house a few doors away which was coming down on them! They
hope to let this to some respectable person. The floor in the upper
front room is 'proper rotten', the windows in it too are broken.

The census of 1911 had revealed that Plymouth was one of the seven most
overcrowded towns in England. Only heavily industrialised northern towns,
such as Gateshead, Newcastle and St Helens, were more crowded with a
higher proportion of the population living more than two to a room. Another

house in Devonport visited by campaigners had 30 people living in it with one tap and one toilet. Conditions had improved only slightly since the visit of the Government Inspector, Robert Rawlinson in 1852.

In January 1920 Plymouth Council nominated 19 areas for slum clearance, including the historic area bounded by High Street, Woolster Street, Vauxhall Street and Looe Street. In these 7½ acres, lived 1640 people. The scheme planned to reduce this to 450.

In Stonehouse it was the High Street and Peel Street district which was earmarked, where 1488 people were living on 4 acres of land: 372 people per acre. These statistics shocked town planners, who recommended 60 people per acre. Add to these figures the fact that Peel Street measured 9 feet 4 inches between the windows of houses on opposing sides of the street. In Devonport's North Corner, between the Gun Wharf and South Yard and west of Queen Street, five times the recommended population were squeezed in. The other notorious neighbourhood was Granby Street in Devonport, where 822 people were housed instead of the recommended 150.

An unnamed *Western Morning News* reporter described on 7 January 1920 how:

I tramped through a long succession of back streets and narrow lanes, and looked in at numerous courts all in the condemned areas, which are to be dealt with under the housing scheme . . . and the impression left on me by the confused jumble of buildings, heaped together without consideration of light and space, decency health and comfort, is not only that the Plymouth Corporation have not moved too soon, but that large though their scheme is, it might justifiably be larger.

Earmarked these areas may have been, but during the troubled times of the Great Depression of the 1920s and 1930s, the demolition ball was still on the sidelines. In 1925 the city's Medical Officer of Health, A.T. Nankivell outlined the housing needs of the Three Towns in his annual report. He cited unventilated houses, without proper damp courses, overshadowed by other buildings.

In many cases it is only by living cheaply in one or two rooms and

OPPOSITE. *St Mary Street, Stonehouse looking along Peel Street in 1935, swept away by slum clearances.*

by taking in lodgers that the poorer class of the community is able
to keep alive.

In his report five years later the medical officer was deeply frustrated by
what he described as, 'a vast inertia (which) seems to surround every active
desire which would lead to slum clearance.' According to Mr Nankivell, the
City Council ought to have finished the clearance of three unsanitary areas
three years earlier, but nothing had been accomplished except some patching
and reconditioning. Several acres of the city centre in Stonehouse ought to be
bulldozed, he suggested, and rebuilt to make it a clean and beautiful place of
broad, tree-lined streets. But he picked out five streets for particular condem-
nation: Castle Street, New Street, Batter Street and High Street, plus Peel
Street in Stonehouse.

Into the ring stepped the Old Plymouth Society. In 1930, appalled at
plans to obliterate the old streets of the city, the society published *A Schedule
of Ancient Buildings in Plymouth Nominated for Preservation*. The results of
their efforts are visible in the Barbican area. Behind The Elizabethan House
in New Street, the present gardens were the site of tenement cottages thrown
up by the poor. The mish-mash of walls which survives gives some idea of the
unhealthy, cramped conditions in which the poor were forced to live. In the
1930s, the ancient courts of little houses climbed the hill, 'picturesquely' one
above the other, off Castle Street and Lambhay Hill. It is due to the lobbying
of the Old Plymouth Society that the line of Castle Street remains, a relic of
the medieval city plan.

The Old Elizabethan Customs House on the Parade was saved by the
Society, but the list of losses is far longer. Nichols Court at 48 High Street, the
remnant of a fine Elizabethan mansion including an arcade with mullioned
windows, was demolished on the orders of the Housing Committee. Gone is
the old Emigrant Depot in Commercial Road, with its twin roles in the
town's history first as the eighteenth-century naval Victualling Yard, then in
the nineteenth century as the last resting place of the thousands who abandoned British shores for a new life abroad. When Palace Street Schools were
built in the 1880s, 8 High Street including the fragment of a fifteenth-century
mansion was destroyed. Gone too is the Watch House, a part slate-hung
building with granite columns supporting the upper stories, a relic of the
port.

Destruction was speeded up as central government offered cash incen-
tives for every slum building demolished, a tempting carrot for local authorities in the Depression. The Old Plymouth Society, and national organisations

Plymouth in its infancy showing (16) the old Victualling Office below the Citadel, (17) the cooperage and (18) Lambhay.

such as the Society for the Protection of Ancient Buildings, preferred repair, refurbishment and alteration of the remnants of heritage.

The first major slum clearance of the post-war period was the 20 acres surrounding Foulston's neoclassical centre of Devonport, an area bounded by Duke Street, James Street, Clowance Lane and George Street. In 1959 it was the turn of Castle Street and Lambhay Hill, whose picturesque 'ancient courts of little houses' had been so lauded by the Old Plymouth Society three decades earlier.

CHAPTER 32

THE LAST BATTLE

The battle which swept away the old city of Plymouth was just as one-sided
as the destruction in the Blitz which had been its major catalyst. The forces
were drawn up on both sides, the battleground an area of 140 square miles.
The result was a terrible defeat for the heritage and history of Hawkins and
Drake, but a victory for modern town planning and the health of the city.
While the battle raged, the dead were disinterred, their coffins dug up from
their last resting place, gravestones and monuments removed. The living
watched the destruction of their shops and homes, which had survived the
Blitz, but were in the path of progress. Unlike the bombed towns and cities
of our erstwhile enemy Germany where restoration was the name, in
Plymouth, reconstruction was the game.

Like all generals, Lord Astor was a man with a mission, and that mission
was outlined in a plan of battle, The Plymouth Plan of 1943. In it he wrote:

> The Plymouth Plan if seen as our contribution to a new and better
> world can bring prosperity and happiness. But the plan must be
> fought for. . . . If Plymouth and the adjoining region is to move
> forward into prosperity it must be planned boldly.

In the mode of wealthy Victorian philanthropists, Waldorf Astor and his wife
Nancy had dedicated themselves to improving the squalid conditions in their
adopted city. The city's cramped, damp housing horrified Lord Astor, who
suffered from bronchitis. Model homes at Mount Gould were built under
their auspices, and the Astor name is commemorated in the names of playing
fields, gardens and schools in the city. The American couple were generous
in using their time and connections in the interests of Plymouth. Despite the
respect he commanded within the wartime coalition government under
Churchill, Waldorf Astor relinquished the offer of a ministerial job in order
to dedicate his time to the role of Lord Mayor. Both he and Nancy were

Coffins are moved out of Westwell Street burial ground before the bulldozers move in.

prominent propagandists boosting the morale of the inhabitants during the bleak months in which Plymouth became the most heavily bombed city in Britain. But as part of that propaganda war, Lord Astor saw the opportunity to offer a carrot of hope to the homeless, battered survivors of the Blitz.

The battle for Old Plymouth began on 4 July 1941, when Lord Reith, founder of the BBC but at this point Minister for Works and Buildings, visited Plymouth while on a tour of the nations' bombed cities. He told the Lord Mayor to seize this opportunity to 'plan boldly and comprehensively' for post-war rebuilding. The old boy network swung into action and Lord Astor recruited a visionary town planner. Sir Patrick Abercrombie was an academic with dreams of creating an open, modern city centre, designed, like American towns and cities, for the motor car. Homes would be built in 'neighbourhood units' to foster a sense of community. Broad boulevards of shops would be shaded by forest-sized trees. His concrete ideas were published in the Blitz and Blight Plan of 1943, at a time when the outcome of the war was still uncertain.

At this stage, the Rural District Council of Plympton attacked on the flank. The plan proposed incorporating rural settlements such as Plympton within the city. Plympton was reluctant at this proposed transgression of its boundaries. The town held a proud tradition as the precursor of Plymouth, its pre-eminence swept away by the tide of silt created by tin miners, which filtered down the Plym.

Letters sped from Plympton to every single Member of Parliament prior to a vital debate on 9 October 1944. MPs were discussing the Plymouth Amendment, an addition to the Town and Country Planning Bill, which would allow seven blitzed cities to extend their boundaries into rural areas. Sunderland was another of these bombed cities which needed to enlarge its boundaries in order to rebuild on sound and imaginative lines. Its MP Mr Storey eloquently outlined the case:

Such planning demands that they should reduce their congestion, both industrial and human, by re-housing some of their citizens and re-siting some of their industries, as well as their civic services and amenities, in surrounding areas with due regard to agricultural and rural interests and to maintenance of the amenities of the whole area. Such planning, will result, if the boundaries are not extended, in a loss of population and rateable value which will be crippling to the parent city and will leave it with a burden of debt dispropor-tionate to the remaining population and rateable value. It will leave it also with public services and an administrative organisation on a scale quite unsuited to its reduced status. Furthermore there will follow a loss of civic interest which anyone who has knowledge of Special Areas, when anyone who can, lives outside the area and takes no part in civic affairs, results in a most deplorable state of affairs.

If we refuse an extension of boundaries to these towns they will be faced with an overload of debt and left with a top-heavy administrative unit and with public services designed for a popula-tion which will not again be achievable.

In Plymouth's case, an estimated 40–50,000 people would be moved outside the city boundary into the new neighbourhood units, leaving the council's income with a corresponding shortfall, *unless* the boundary could be enlarged. Wide roads designed to ease the traffic flow would of necessity have to be built over people's homes.

In that same debate in October 1944, Plymouth MP Nancy Astor had a dig at the intransigent people of Plympton:

We have all heard complaints about Plympton. We asked Plympton to co-operate in the planning of Plymouth, and what did Plympton say? They said no. They did not want to. We told them about the devastated area where we have a chance to rebuild under one of the world's best planners, and we asked them to come in. What was their answer? They said they did not want to; their charter was twenty years older than Plymouth's and they were going to have the Borough Surveyor.

We cannot afford in these blitzed areas to listen to local prejudices.

Some honourable members have said they don't want to see the towns spreading out into the counties, and that is exactly Plympton's attitude. In Plymouth's plan there is no reckless sprawl. We want to preserve what is best in the country and what is best in the town.

In fact, Plympton's reluctance to be included in the wider Abercrombie plan was partly thanks to its lack of bomb damage. But it was the great open spaces surrounding Plympton which made its territory so desirable to the plan's proponents.

Lord Astor and Sir Patrick Abercrombie both had a pedigree in campaigns for rural preservation: The Council for the Preservation of Rural England was set up in 1926 with Sir Patrick as a founder member. So they can not be viewed as rural vandals. Lord Astor was critical too of the desecration which the lack of proper planning had caused already. He said in 1944:

Already some of the finest bits of the coast (beach, cliff, valley etc) have been vandalised and spoiled. Had they been properly developed, they would have been profitable assets not only to Plymouth but to the whole neighbourhood. The whole district would benefit by a large influx of visitors and holiday makers.

Today holiday makers have difficulty in discovering any easy ways to beaches, to the coves, to the cliffs, to the places also where people (inhabitants and visitors) might wish to have summer villas. Beautiful scenery has been irretrievably spoiled or neglected by the smaller councils. Tin shacks and ugly bungalows without drainage desecrate places which would have been gold mines to the neighbourhood.

Although Lord Reith, long since out of the battle, had encouraged Plymouth's

Weston Mill. With the post-war expansion of the dockyard, 7,000 homes were built here.

city fathers not to worry about the financial implications of bold planning, parliament still had to stump up the cash. On 19 November 1945, Lord Astor put the case for financial aid:

> If the bombs had all dropped on the dockyard and on the ships therein the whole cost of repair and replacement would have been borne by the state. Because the Germans made bad shots and hit shops and houses instead of lock gates and warehouses is no reason why the ratepayers, the business community, the consumers, house occupiers, and population generally of Plymouth (or any of the other blitzed towns) should be expected to shoulder a burden ruinously greater than the people lucky enough to live in areas safe from large scale destruction.

It was the commercial heart of the city which had been so maimed by the Nazi bombs. But there were many traders on the periphery of this devastation whose businesses had kept going through the war, and were undamaged. In August 1946 they received Compulsory Purchase Orders to enable planners to bulldoze their buildings in order to rebuild. The purchase was to be made at pre-war prices! Their objections survive in the numerous reconstruction files deposited at Plymouth and West Devon Record Office. Quite naturally traders worried about the loss of goodwill and clientele built up over decades of trading at their existing addresses. But what some saw as 'wholesale robbery' by the council was the loss of their freehold shops in exchange for leases offered in the new development. The anger felt by traders was expressed by Mr J. Lloyd, a chemist at 3 King Street. He wrote on 7 August 1946:

> When we were blitzed by the Nazis in 1941 we little thought that the job would be finished by a final treacherous stab in the back from our own countrymen. That is what the compulsory purchase of our homes and business premises amounts to. Offering us places at high rents in return just adds insults to injury. It takes a mean advantage of the plight we Plymothians are in, and instead of helping us on to our feet again, seeks to trample us into the dust and make us perma- nent rent slaves to Plymouth Corporation. Many of us have put our life savings into our property. . . . .large numbers of us feel like that and will resist any tyrant – Nazi or otherwise – who tries to rob us of our independence. The fine city you plan, founded on injustice to the small tradesman and property owner, is doomed from the start, as anything must be which is built on sand.
>
> Plymouth City Council do not need this block of very solidly built houses in order to get on with war damage repairs. The blitzed centre of our city is still awaiting their efforts.

There was no provision for workshops in the new commercial heart planned for the city. Tradesmen like the Swain brothers, whose family carpentry business at Willow Plot off Russell Street, had served shops and offices nearby for two generations, would be forced to find a workshop far from their customers. Doctors would be divorced from the patients who lived in the areas around their surgery, and Buckland Terrace the Harley Street of Plymouth would be demolished. One poignant letter on behalf of a blind man at 40 Cambridge Street, who had coped with the piles of rubble altering familiar streets throughout the war, objected that he did not 'wish to purchase property in a new and strange area'.

But they would all become the casualties of Abercrombie's bold plan. More than two-thirds of the families in the area bounded by Palace Street, Stillman Street, Southside Street, Friary Lane, Vauxhall Street and the water's edge did not want to move. Some former residents had no choice. Human remains, tombstones and monuments had to be removed from

George Street Baptist Church Burial Ground, Charles Church, Westwell Gardens Burial Ground and Treville Street Unitarian Burial Ground to Efford Cemetery.

Charles Church, the symbolic survivor whose hallowed precincts commemorate the civilians who died, was rescued from certain death. The Church of England, faced with the restoration costs of numerous other bombed churches, demanded it be pulled down. Thanks to the efforts of the Old Plymouth Society and Lord Astor himself, it survived. In a letter in Plymouth Archives, Lord Astor suggested the solution we know today:

As you know there is a roundabout, the exact location of which has yet been fully settled, but my impression is that it should be possible to preserve the church on an island – I am afraid a small one – in the middle of the road. Perhaps public opinion may make this felt and save this structure, which is quite interesting.

The Old Vicarage, home of Sunday school founder Reverend Hawker, would be a casualty, despite still standing two years after the end of the war. Secretary of the Old Plymouth Society, G.W. Copeland wrote in its defence:

It has been given first aid but the workmen carelessly knocked off the face of one of the carved corbels supporting the oriel. Structurally it still seems sound, with its thick end-walls and massive limestone chimney-stack.

But the vicarage was judged to be in the path of the automobile, and the death sentence passed.

The Old Plymouth Society had been formed in the inter-war years in a bid to retain buildings that reflected the rich heritage and history of Plymouth. In deference to the city's history, parts of the Barbican area were to be retained. The Society's secretary, Mr Copeland was unimpressed.

It seems to me that, in spite of a so-called 'Old Plymouth Precinct' in the new Plan, everything worth saving in that area is gradually being removed, or threatened with removal. There will soon be too little of which to make a 'precinct'.

OPPOSITE. *Inside Charles Church, showing the theatrical pulpit.*

Why all these structures should go in favour of extravagantly wide thoroughfares to cater for the assumed exigencies of modern transport, I can not imagine.

But the demolition to make way for these thoroughfares continued despite protests. In January 1957, the *Western Morning News* reported the demolition

A forgotton and unloved remnant of Plymouth's past, symbolically defaced by the twentieth-century sign.

of The Ring of Bells, which had stood on Woolster Street for 400 years. The paper reported that the bulldozers had moved in the day after the council had taken the decision, suggesting 'a strange state of military-like preparedness and pre-knowledge of the council's decision'.

It is a matter of civic pride that the slums of Plymouth were swept away and homes rebuilt surrounded by grass and trees. Modern Plymothians have the benefits of fresh air and sanitation which their ancestors did not, and they no longer sleep ten to a room. But when heritage is no longer visible because buildings have been bulldozed or stand rotten through neglect, it is collective identity which suffers. Despite the best efforts of conservationists, generations of city fathers have squandered the most valuable asset of The Three Towns: their history. It is harder to celebrate the past if there is little physical evidence of it. History is about the lives of people like us; it gives us a connection with the past which helps us to understand the present; and shows that the past is not 'another country'. The past is the collective memory of the community, and memory gives identity: it is not too late to reclaim the city's history, restore and revere what is left and by doing so celebrate the history of Plymouth and its place in the history of the world.

BIBLIOGRAPHY

Arnold, S.A. *The Merchant and Seaman's Guardian in the British Channel*, T. Carnan 1778

Beddoes, Thomas *A Collection of Testimonies Respecting the Treatment of Venereal Disease with Nitrous Acid*, J. Johnson 1799

Binns, J. Were *Journal 1840*, privately published, 1964

Blane, G. *Observations on the Diseases Incident to Seamen*, Joseph Cooper, 1785

Bligh's Sydney Rebellion, Historic Houses Trust and State Library of New South Wales, 2008

Blight, F.S. 'Captain Tobias Furneaux RN' in *Transactions, Plymouth Institution* 22, 1952

Blight, W. *A Voyage to the South Seas for the Conveying of the Breadfruit Tree to the West Indies Including the Narrative of the Mutiny*, 1792

Branch Johnson, W. *The English Prison Hulks* London, 1957

Brayshay, M. *Post War Plymouth: Planning and reconstruction: essays marking the fortieth anniversary of the 1943 Plymouth Plan*, South West Papers in Geography, 1983

Brooke, A. and Brandon, D. *Bound for Botany Bay: British Convict Voyages to Australia*, National Archives 2005

Clark, Peter *The English Alehouse 1200–1830*, Longman, 1983

Clarke, E.D. *A Tour Through the South of England and Wales and part of Ireland during the summer of 1791*

Clarkson, T. *The History of the Rise, Progress and Accomplishment of the Abolition of the African Slave Trade by the British Parliament*, J.W. Parker, London, 1938

Coad, J. *The Royal Dockyards 1690–1850*, Aldershot: Scholar Press 1989

Cook, J. and Furneaux T.T. *A Voyage to the South Pole and Round the World Performed in His Majesty's Ships the Resolution and The Adventure in 1771, 1773, 1774 and 1775*

Corvisier, A.; Childs, J.; Charles, J.; Childs, R. and Turner, C. *A Dictionary of Military History and the Art of War*, Blackwell 1994

Crowther, M.A. *The Workhouse System 1834–1929. The History of an English Institution* London, Methuen, 1983

Deere, Noel *The History of Sugar,* London: Chapman and Hall, 1949

Drake's Drum, A History of the Devonport Naval Base and Dockyard, HM Naval Base and Dockyard, 1998

Ellis, A. *Educating our masters: influences on the growth of literacy in Victorian working class children,* Aldershot: Gower, 1985

Falck N.D. *A Philosophical Dissertation on the diving vessel projected by Mr Day and sunk in Plymouth Sound,* London 1775

Fiennes, C. *Through England on a side saddle in the times of William and Mary, Field and Tuer 1888*

Gill, C. *Plymouth – A New History* Devon Books, 1993

Greenwood, J. *The Wilds of London* Chatto and Windus, 1874

Hibbert, C. *The Roots of Evil: A Social History of Crime and Punishment,* Boston: Little, Brown and Company, 1963

Howard, J. *The State of Prisons in England and Wales with preliminary observations and an Account of Some Foreign Prisons,* Warrington, 1787

Hutchinson, J.R. *The Press Gang Ashore and Afloat,* Eveleigh Nash, 1913

Ignatieff, Michael *A Just Measure of Pain: the Penitentiary in the Industrial Revolution 1750–1850,* New York: Pantheon, 1978

Kinross, J. *The Palmerston Forts in the South West: Why Were They Built,* Bce Books New & Old, 1999

Lind, J. *A Treatise on the Scurvy,* 1753

Mackanness, G. *The Life of Vice-Admiral William Bligh,* Angus and Robertson, Sydney and London, 1931

Marcus, G.J. *A Naval History of England: The Formative Centuries* (vol. 1); *The Age of Nelson* (vol. 2), 1961

Mercer, John 'Commercial places, public spaces: suffragette shops and the public sphere', *University of Sussex Journal of Contemporary History 7,* 2004

Pye, A. and Woodward, F. *The Historic Defences of Plymouth* Exeter Archaeology Fortress Study Group South West, 1996

Report on the Health of the Royal Navy 1860, PRO

Risdon's Survey of Devon, Rees and Curtis, Plymouth, 1811

Shiman, Lillian Lewis *Crusade Against Drink in Victorian England,* New York: St. Martin's Press, 1988

Smollett, T. *The Adventures of Roderick Random* Oxford, Blackwell, 1925

Smyth, A. (ed.) *A Pleasing Sinne: Drink and Conviviality in Seventeenth Century England,* Boydell and Brewer, 2004

Sponza, L. *Italian Immigrants in Nineteenth Century Britain: Realities and Images* Leicester University Press 1988

Stuart, E. (compiler) *Lost Landscapes of Plymouth: Maps Charts and Plans to 1800* Alan Sutton Publishing, 1991

The Report of the Committee to Inquire into the Prevalance of Venereal Disease in the Army and Navy in 1862 – Parliamentary Papers, PRO

Thompson, W. *An Appeal to the Public,* 1761

Thompson, W. *Royal Navy Mans Advocate,* H. Slater 1757

Walkowitz, J.R. *Prostitution and Victorian Society, Women, Class and the State* Cambridge University Press, 1980

Walter, Thomas L. *Religion and Respectability: Sunday Schools and Working Class Culture 1780–1850* New Haven, 1976

Watt, J.; Freeman, E.J. and Bynum, W.F. *Starving Sailors: the Influence of Nutrition Upon Naval and Maritime History* National Maritime Museum 1981

Weekes, H. *The New Plymouth Settlement,* 1843

Weiler, J. Royal Engineer Architects, PhD thesis, University of York 1987

Whitfield, H. *The Curse of Devonport* Devon and Cornwall Newspaper Co.,1898

Whitfield, Henry, *Plymouth and Devonport In Times of War and Peace,* E. Chapple, 1900

Williamson, James, *Hawkins of Plymouth,* A & C Black, 1969

Woodward, F. *Forts or Follies,* Devon Books, 1998

INDEX